Trade, Growth and Inequality in the Era of Globalization

Globalization has been the major phenomenon of recent years, open to a variety of interpretations and the subject of considerable research and comment. In particular, the debate over trade liberalization, growth and inequality has come under close scrutiny as demonstrations against globalization gather pace.

This volume provides a much needed comparative study of the link between globalization, growth and inequality, and assesses how it affects growth, inequality and poverty in developing and transition countries. Looking at 11 low and middle income countries, the authors argue that globalization can actually help reduce poverty and inequity when institutions and physical infrastructures are efficient. Divided into four parts, the book documents the lessons drawn from case studies on Africa, Latin America and Central Asia.

Trade, Growth and Inequality in the Era of Globalization will be of interest to students and researchers of development economics, globalization and international trade.

Kishor Sharma is Associate Professor of Economics and Sub-Dean (International Research) at Charles Sturt University, Australia. **Oliver Morrissey** is Professor in Development Economics and Director of Centre for Research in Economic Development and International Trade (CREDIT) at the University of Nottingham, UK.

south essex college

FURTHER & HIGHER EDUCATION
SOUTHEND CAMPUS

Routledge studies in development economics

Trade, Growth and Inequality in the Era of Globalization

Edited by Kishor Sharma and Oliver Morrissey

 Routledge
Taylor & Francis Group

LONDON AND NEW YORK

30130504083812

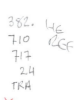
382. 4E
710 RGF
717
24
TRA
X

First published 2006
by Routledge
2 Park Square, Milton Park, Abingdon, Oxon OX14 4RN

Simultaneously published in the USA and Canada
by Routledge
270 Madison Ave, New York, NY 10016

Routledge is an imprint of the Taylor & Francis Group, an informa business

Transferred to Digital Printing 2009

© 2006 Kishor Sharma and Oliver Morrissey for selection and
editorial matter; individual contributors their contributions

Typeset in Baskerville by Wearset Ltd, Boldon, Tyne and Wear

All rights reserved. No part of this book may be reprinted or
reproduced or utilized in any form or by any electronic, mechanical,
or other means, now known or hereafter invented, including
photocopying and recording, or in any information storage or
retrieval system, without permission in writing from the publishers.

British Library Cataloguing in Publication Data
A catalogue record for this book is available from the British Library

Library of Congress Cataloging in Publication Data
A catalog record for this book has been requested

ISBN10: 0-415-35265-7 (hbk)
ISBN10: 0-415-49405-2 (pbk)
ISBN10: 0-203-17967-6 (ebk)

ISBN13: 978-0-415-35265-9 (hbk)
ISBN13: 978-0-415-49405-2 (pbk)
ISBN13: 978-0-203-17967-3 (ebk)

Contents

400904990010

Figures

Tables

Contributors

Antonio Aguirre is Associate Professor of Economics, Center for Research in International Economics (CEPE), Department of Economics, Universidade Federal Minas Gerais (UFMG), Belo Horizonte, Brazil.

Lykke E. Andersen is Chief Economist, Grupo Integral, La Paz, Bolivia.

Prema-chandra Athukorala is Professor of Economics, Department of Economics, Research School of Pacific and Asian Studies, Australian National University, Australia.

Afonso Ferreira is Professor of Economics, Center for Research in International Economics (CEPE), Department of Economics, Universidade Federal Minas Gerais (UFMG). Currently on leave as Director, Escola de Governo, Fundação João Pinheiro, Belo Horizonte, Brazil.

Worku Gebeyehu is Research Fellow, Ethiopian Economic Association, Addis Ababa, Ethiopia.

Pushkar Maitra is Senior Lecturer in Economics, Economics Department, Monash University, Australia.

Andrew Mold is Senior Economist, Trade and Regional Integration Division (TRID), United Nations Economic Commission for Africa (UNECA), Addis Ababa, Ethiopia.

Lars Moller is Young Professional at the World Bank, Washington DC.

Oliver Morrissey is Professor in Development Economics and Director of Centre for Research in Economic Development and International Trade (CREDIT), School of Economics, University of Nottingham, UK.

Osvaldo Nina is Director, Grupo Integral, La Paz, Bolivia.

Richard Pomfret is Professor of Economics and Associate Dean Research, University of Adelaide, Australia.

Ranjan Ray is Professor of Economics, School of Economics, University of Tasmania, Australia.

Carlos A. Roza is Associate Professor, Universidad Autónoma Metropolitana-Xochimilco, México D.F., Mexico.

Nichodemus Rudaheranwa is Research Fellow, Economic Policy Research Centre (EPRC), Makerere University, Kampala, Uganda.

Kunal Sen is Senior Lecturer in Economics, School of Development Studies, University of East Anglia, UK.

Kishor Sharma is Associate Professor of Economics and Sub-Dean (International Research), Faculty of Commerce, Charles Sturt University, Wagga Wagga, Australia.

Dirk Willem te Velde is Research Fellow, Overseas Development Institute (ODI), London, UK.

Peter Warr is John Crawford Professor of Agricultural Economics, Research School of Pacific and Asian Studies, Australian National University, Australia.

Preface

Despite growing debate about the effects of liberalization on growth and equity, studies examining the experience of individual countries in comparative perspective remain sparse. While Sharma (2003) provides evidence on the link between, trade, growth and equity by bring together 11 case studies from Asian developing countries, there has not been any comparative study for African, Latin American and Central Asian countries – which emerged after the collapse of the former Soviet Union. Hence, the idea for this volume emerged in 2003 to fill this gap in the literature and contribute to the ongoing debate about the effects of trade liberalization on growth and equity. Given the time and resource constraints, however, the case studies presented in this volume are limited to 11 developing countries from Africa, Latin America and Central Asia.

All papers included in this volume are commissioned by leading academics from Australia, Europe, Latin America and Africa. This volume would not have seen the light of the day with out their commitment and cooperation. We are indebted to them. We also take this opportunity to thank Routledge's reviewers for very constructive suggestions, as well as Prema-chandra Athukorala, Chris Manning and Edward Oczkowski for reviewing some of the papers included in the volume. Last, but not least, we express our thanks to Hal Hill, the Convenor of the Economics Division, Research School of Pacific and Asian Studies at the Australian National University (ANU), for inviting one of us (Kishor) to be a visiting scholar while working on this volume. This provided an excellent opportunity to interact with leading trade and development economists at the ANU and significantly improved the quality of the volume. We hope this volume will provide some useful development lessons to students of development economics and policy makers in Africa, Latin America and formerly central planned countries of Asia.

Kishor Sharma, Australia
Oliver Morrissey, United Kingdom

Part I

Introduction

1 Trade, growth and inequality in the era of globalization

Kishor Sharma and Oliver Morrissey

The second half of the twentieth century witnessed major developments in international politics and economics. The creation of international institutions (such as the United Nations (UN) system, World Bank and more recently World Trade Organizations (WTO)), the fall of the Berlin wall and collapse of the former Soviet Union (FSU), and widespread removal of barriers to trade and investment by the majority of countries are diverse examples. These developments have promoted greater integration of the global economy, reflected in increased mobility of goods, people and capital between countries. Together with developments in transport and especially communications, this has significantly increased economic interdependence among countries, leading to an unprecedented growth in world output and international trade. For example, from 1947–97, world output grew sixfold whilst international trade increased 16-fold. In common parlance the term 'globalization' encompasses all of these developments, and the beneficial and adverse effects associated with them. Globalization is a major phenomenon, open to a variety of interpretations and the subject of considerable research and comment. This volume concentrates on one element of globalization, trade between nations, and uses case studies to attempt to assess how increased trade affects growth, inequality and poverty in developing countries (although some of the countries included may be called transition countries, we adopt the more general term developing).

Something of a consensus has emerged that to address deep poverty in developing countries, achieving sustained higher economic growth is essential (but perhaps not sufficient). A key question is then how to accelerate and sustain higher economic growth. The experience of many countries suggests that achieving higher economic growth through an inward-oriented development strategy is unsuccessful, either because the country has a small domestic market or because inward-orientation promotes inefficiency, or both. It has been argued that creating an incentive for efficient utilization of resources is a key to sustainable growth and an outward-oriented development strategy is conducive for creating such an environment (Easterly, 2001; Srinivasan, 2001). When there is an incentive for efficient utilization of resources, resources are deployed in line with a nation's comparative advantage, leading to efficiency gains. This can help to sustain higher economic growth and lift millions of people out of poverty, as suggested by comparing the experience of growth and poverty reduction in East Asia to the stagnation and increasing poverty in Africa since 1970 (Sala-i-Martin, 2002).

Trade liberalization can contribute to this process, increasing efficiency both by reducing price distortions and by increasing incentives for competitive producers. The economic benefits may be limited in the short run, as domestic producers face increased competition from imports and exporters need time to respond to new market opportunities. The econometric evidence linking trade liberalization to growth must be interpreted with caution (Rodrik, 1999), although the evidence linking exports and growth is strong (Greenaway *et al.*, 1998). Furthermore, there is very little evidence that trade reduces growth, although liberalization can create balance of payments problems in poor developing countries (Thirlwall, 2003). Trade liberalization is generally a desirable economic policy reform, but it does not guarantee growth and any impact on an economy is conditional on the initial economic structure and the prevailing policy and institutional environment.

Mainstream economists argue that developing countries have a comparative advantage in unskilled labour-intensive products and an outward-oriented development strategy creates an environment for increasing the production of such products, leading to an increase in demand for unskilled labour. This in turn will alleviate poverty by increasing the real income of the poor and increasing the growth rate (Sharma, 2003). More rapid growth means more revenue, which will enable the government to spend more on social welfare programmes, increasing the access of the poor to basic services. However, the ability of second generation (post-1980s) liberalizers to increase their exports of labour-intensive products is limited, mainly due to low supply-side elasticities and restricted access to the rich countries' markets, particularly for textile, clothing and agricultural products in which they have a comparative advantage. The supply-side elasticity is low due to fragmentation of the local product and factor markets, as well as low levels of physical infrastructure and human capital. To address the lower levels of human and physical capital, poor countries need investment in these areas but they lack financial resources to do so. Ironically, international assistance is on the decline. In real per capita terms, net official development assistance (aid) disbursements to poor countries fell by 46 per cent between 1990 and 2000 (UNCTAD, 2002). This drop in aid may have reduced gross domestic investment in poor developing countries (see Table 1.3 below), making poverty alleviation a more challenging task.

Even if developed countries continue to maintain protection, it does not mean that developing countries should follow the same path. Development experience has shown that barriers to trade and investment retard growth through inefficiency and rent-seeking behaviour and result in a large welfare loss (it may be that rich countries are better able to absorb this cost of protection). Developing countries should not postpone liberalization reforms just because they lack efficient institutions or infrastructure or because developed countries continue to maintain protection in sensitive sectors. Globalization, however defined, is an actual phenomenon – it is happening and individual countries must react to this changing environment (Basu, 2003).

Few countries engage in trade reform in isolation, and typically they undertake a variety of macroeconomic, trade, exchange rate, price and fiscal reforms together (see Greenaway and Morrissey, 1993). Consequently, it is very difficult to disentangle the effects of a particular policy on growth or poverty, or on other performance measures. For example, devaluation and removal of subsidies could worsen welfare and increase poverty in the short run, by increasing the prices of goods and services that the poor consume, even if associated trade reforms aim to increase returns to productive activity. In principle, a coordinated structural adjustment programme (SAP) can mitigate these adverse effects, although the success of SAPs is debatable to say the least (e.g. McGillivray and Morrissey, 1999). The idea is that domestic economic adjustment, following the policies that rich countries have long had (Bhagwati, 2004: 223), facilitates the efficient response of the economy to the improved incentives associated with trade reform. Aid donors like the World Bank provide resources to support adjustment, but SAPs have paid insufficient attention to mitigating the social problems arising in the process (Stiglitz, 2002; Nayyar, 2002). 'Regrettably, the World Bank, which is crippled now by overreach into everything under its so called comprehensive development strategy, appears to suffer from a lack of appropriate prioritization' (Bhagwati, 2004: 236).

The experience of the East and South Asian countries over the past few decades suggests that countries that engage with global integration grow fast and thereby reduce poverty. For example, in the last four decades Asia as a whole has doubled its share in world income – from 12.1 per cent in 1960 to 25.9 per cent by 2000 – mainly through a superior growth performance in East Asia initially and China and India more recently (Table 1.1). As income grew, at least in part owing to economic liberalization, poverty fell. In Africa and Latin America, however, poverty rose because growth rates were not fast enough to increase savings and investment. As a result, their shares in the world income either fell, in the case of Sub-Saharan Africa (the one region of the world where living standards are probably lower now than they were 30 years ago), or rose marginally in the case of Latin America (Table 1.1).

The East and South Asian experience also suggests that efficient institutions, infrastructure and good governance are crucial to benefit from

Table 1.1 Regions' shares of world income and population (per cent).

Region	Share of world population				Share of world income			
	1950	1960	1980	2000	1950	1960	1980	2000
Asia	53.0	49.7	52.5	53.5	12.6	12.1	12.2	25.9
China and India	41.1	36.5	37.7	37.6	8.4	7.9	6.5	16.8
Sub-Saharan Africa	6.6	7.4	8.6	10.9	3.2	3.2	3.0	2.5
Middle East and North Africa	3.8	4.4	5.1	6.2	3.0	3.5	5.1	4.7
Latin America	6.2	7.2	8.2	8.5	7.7	7.9	9.9	8.4
Developing world[a]	72.0	71.4	76.9	81.3	28.8	29.3	32.5	42.4
Developing world, excluding China and India	31.0	35.0	39.2	43.7	20.4	21.4	26.0	25.6
Eastern Europe	10.2	10.4	8.7	6.8	11.2	11.3	12.6	6.1
Non-industrialized world[b]	79.7	79.2	83.0	86.0	37.5	38.1	42.8	47.6
Industrialized world	20.2	20.8	17.0	14.0	62.5	61.9	57.2	52.4
World	100.0	100.0	100.0	100.0	100.0	100.0	100.0	100.0
World, actual*	2,696.0	3,022.0	4,432.0	6,071.0	6.2	9.7	23.1	39.2

Sources: Bhalla (2002) which takes from World Bank, *World Development Indicators*, CD-ROMs, 1998, 2001; Heston and Summers (1991).

Notes
Nominal purchasing power parity (PPP) data, 1993 base, have been converted into constant PPP data, 1993 base, using the US GDP deflator, a practice followed in World Bank, *World Development Indicators*, 1998. World population figures are in millions; world income is in trillions of 1993 PPP dollars.
* World population is in millions.
a The developing world is the world excluding the industrialized world and Eastern Europe.
b The non-industrialized world is the world excluding the industrialized world.

global integration. The high performing East Asian countries have been committed to develop these essential ingredients of the market economy. Effective institutions provide support services to the losers to move from one economic activity to another by way of training and market information, and facilitate increases in economic efficiency (World Bank, 2003). Good governance is associated with sound macroeconomic policies and a sound legal system. These are essential ingredients for the operation of a market economy, but market failure is widespread in poor countries. For example, market failure can occur when people do not have the basic skills that are acquired through education and training, or where there are inefficient infrastructure and institutions (Stiglitz, 2002; Nayyar, 2002). Weak institutions are not only a cause of market failure, they also undermine the ability of government to address such failures. Consequently, weak institutions undermine the ability of governments to implement reform and to support sectors of the economy in responding to reform. Institutions also mediate how the effects of reforms on the economy are distributed, and especially whether any benefits accrue to the poor.

The possible linkages between trade liberalization, growth and poverty are many and complex. International trade provides access and exposure to a global market that is very competitive, so success in exporting or competing with imports requires increased efficiency in producing high quality, niche or price competitive goods. The major share of the benefits from trade for any economy will accrue to those households owning the factors that are most in demand, and these are not necessarily the factors in which the economy is best endowed. In principle, increased global trade should benefit unskilled labour in developing countries as that is the factor they have most of. In practice, however, the need to be competitive often means that it is relatively skilled labour that is most in demand. In general, poor households do not own factors that are in demand (and that is one reason why they are poor), their labour is the most unskilled and they rarely own land or capital. This does not mean that trade cannot benefit the poor, but suggests that benefits will tend to be indirect (perhaps via growth) and that the poor will derive the least direct benefit from trade. Insofar as trade expansion fuels economic growth, aggregate demand in the economy increases and this benefits all.

In the short run, and in general, there will be winners and losers from trade liberalization. Producers and those earning their incomes in expanding sectors (typically exporting) will gain, whereas those earning incomes in contracting sectors (typically import-competing) will lose. From the perspective of households as consumers, however, trade is generally beneficial as it should mean that a greater variety of products are available at lower prices and/or higher quality. Trade therefore has interacting effects on households, some good and some bad, depending on their consumption pattern and the sector in which they are employed.

It is not therefore so surprising that evidence on the effects of trade on incomes and the poor is quite mixed (see Cornia, 2004; Shorrocks and van der Hoeven, 2004; van der Hoeven and Shorrocks, 2003).

Trade liberalization should not be confused with trade performance. Trade performance is an outcome; policy is only one factor affecting the outcome, and it is the outcomes that in turn affect growth and poverty. Trade liberalization is a policy input that influences the outcome by altering relative incentives. The performance outcome depends on the ability of agents and sectors to respond to these altered incentives, and this in turn depends on characteristics of the economy. Although countries' characteristics and conditions are varied, it seems obvious that globalization works better in countries with efficient institutions, infrastructure and good governance. In determining the speed of reform these country-specific characteristics have to be recognized. 'While globalization can bring economic and social benefits once the transition to it is made, this leaves open the question of how rapidly the transition to globalization should be made. Indeed, some of the hostility to globalization stems not from globalization *per se* but from the speed with which it is pushed as policy makers liberalize trade, capital flows, and so on, and to the occasional lack of institutional mechanisms to make such a transition smooth' (Bhagwati, 2004: 898).

In this context, this volume aims to improve our understanding about the links between trade, growth, inequality and poverty in developing countries using a case study framework. An increasing number of studies have examined the links between growth, inequality and poverty – some cross-country, some country specific, some including trade and some not – although the findings are often contradictory or weak (see Cornia, 2004; Shorrocks and van der Hoeven, 2004; van der Hoeven and Shorrocks, 2003). To the extent that trade liberalization is an indicator of economic policy reform in which distortions are reduced and market incentives increased, it should be growth promoting. In general, one expects poverty to be higher if growth is lower. However, there is only very weak cross-country evidence that trade liberalization is associated with poverty reduction (Mbabazi *et al.*, 2003).

Even if the findings of cross-country studies about the links between trade, growth and poverty are not contradictory, they have limited use for policy formulation in individual countries. This is because such studies ignore the country-specific features and assume that structural parameters are constant across the countries in the sample (Srinivasan and Bhagwati, 1999). Cross-country studies provide only a partial picture of the effects of market-oriented policy on the poor because the same reform may have different effects in different countries, hence 'average' results can provide only a rough guide to the impact of reform on the poor. Although the East Asia experience suggests that trade liberalization is conducive to growth and poverty alleviation (Sharma, 2003), the findings can't be generalized to other regions. Case studies of a large number of countries from different backgrounds may provide a better insight into the complex links between trade, growth and poverty, taking into account each country's structural and institutional features. This volume does so by bringing together case studies from Africa, Latin America and formerly central planned Asian countries. We limit our case studies to 11 countries, all of which have gone through market-oriented reforms to different degrees and at different points in time, but these can be seen as complementing the 11 Asian countries covered in Sharma (2003).

Characteristics of the sample countries

For the world overall, indicators of living standards have improved significantly over the past few decades. For instance, using world averages, life expectancy improved from 58 years during 1970–75 to about 67 years during 2000–05, infant mortality per 1,000 live births fell from 96 in 1970 to 56 in 2002 and adult illiteracy rates halved, from 45 per cent in 1970 to 22 per cent by 2002 (Table 1.2). While these overall achievements are pleasing, they are not evenly distributed across countries and achievements in the area of poverty reduction is far from satisfactory, particularly in developing countries. For example, almost one third of the people in developing countries live in poverty and cannot meet their basic needs. About 840 million people suffer from malnutrition and about 230 million children have no access to schooling.

Table 1.2 gives an overview of the diverse experiences of the countries included in our sample. Some such as South Africa and the Latin American countries are near or above the world average on most indicators in the 2000s. Others, such as Ethiopia, Myanmar and Uganda are below the world average on most indicators. Most have shown significant improvements in all indicators since the 1970s, the exception being life expectancy, which deteriorated in Kenya and South Africa. Most countries experienced a large fall in gross domestic investment as a percentage of GDP during 1990 to 2000, except for Ethiopia and Myanmar (Table 1.3). When investment is falling it is difficult to develop and maintain the institutions and infrastructure crucial for growth. This is a matter for concern as trade liberalization typically required efficient institutions and infrastructure to accelerate growth. Growth performance has generally been poor, especially in the 1990s (Table 1.4). The Central Asian countries experienced negative growth in the 1990s, and for Kenya per capita income declined. However, others such as Uganda and Myanmar appear to have done quite well in the 1990s.

There are considerable inter-regional and inter-country differences in the incidence of poverty among our sample (Table 1.5). Poverty is extremely high in Africa, with the exception of South Africa, but relatively low in Sri Lanka, Central Asia and Latin America (excluding Bolivia). This

Table 1.2 Indicators of some non-monetary measures of living standards in the sample countries

Country	Life expectancy at birth (years)		Infant mortality rate (per 1,000 live births)		Adult illiteracy rate (% of people age 15+)		Access to improved water source (% of population with access)		Access to sanitation (% of population with access)	
	1970–75	2000–05	1970	2002	1970	2002	1982–85	2000	1982–85	2000
Myanmar	49.3	57.3	122	77	30.1	14.7	27	72	24	64
Kazakhstan	64.4	66.3	–	61	–	0.5	–	91	–	99
Kyrgyzstan	63.1	68.6	111	52	–	–	–	77	–	100
Tajikistan	63.4	68.8	78	53	9.3	0.7	–	60	–	90
Ethiopia	41.8	45.5	160	116	87.4	58.4	–	24	–	12
Kenya	50.9	44.6	96	78	59.2	15.7	27	57	44	87
South Africa	53.7	47.7	80	56	30.2	14.0	–	86	–	87
Uganda	46.3	46.2	110	79	63.9	31.1	16	52	13	79
Bolivia	46.7	63.9	144	60	42.2	13.4	53	83	36	70
Brazil	59.5	68.1	95	31	31.8	12.3	75	87	24	76
Mexico	62.4	73.4	79	24	25.1	8.2	82	88	57	74
World	58.4	66.6	96	56	45.1	22.42	–	82	–	61

Source: World Bank (2003).

Table 1.3 Gross domestic investment in the sample countries (% of GDP)

Economy and region	1970–79	1980–89	1990–2000	1970–2000
Myanmar	13.3	16.1	14.7	14.6
Kazakhstan	–	–	−11.9	−11.9
Kyrgyzstan	–	32.9	12.6	22.75
Tajikistan	–	29.5	–	29.5
Ethiopia	–	14.2	13.4	13.8
Kenya	23.2	20.3	4.9	16.1
South Africa	20.7	18.8	3.0	14.1
Uganda	9.7	8.5	9.9	9.3
Bolivia	30.1	15.3	10.1	18.5
Brazil	22.9	20.8	3.1	15.6
Mexico	22.6	22.2	3.9	16.2
World	*25.31*	*23.2*	*22.25*	*23.58*

Source: World Bank (2003).

Table 1.4 Growth in population and GDP, and agricultural productivity in sample countries

Economy	Population growth		GDP growth		Agricultural productivity (1995 dollars)	
	1980–90	1991–2002	1980–90	1991–2002	1979–81	1996–98
Myanmar	1.8	1.17	2.0	7.3	–	–
Kazakhstan	0.9	−0.69	−0.8	−1.2	–	1,450
Kyrgyzstan	1.9	0.87	6.5	−2.6	–	–
Tajikistan	2.9	1.57	0.7	−1.4	–	396
Ethiopia	3.1	2.27	1.7	4.3	–	–
Kenya	3.5	2.5	6.2	1.6	262	228
South Africa	2.4	1.68	2.0	1.9	2,899	3,958
Uganda	2.4	2.9	3.4	6.3	–	345
Bolivia	2.0	2.3	0.0	3.3	–	–
Brazil	2.0	1.37	2.3	2.5	2,047	4,081
Mexico	2.1	1.67	2.5	2.9	1,882	2,164
World	*1.7*	*1.1*	*3.2*	*1.2*	–	–

Source: World Bank (2003).

confirms the pattern for non-monetary indicators in Table 1.2. Levels of per capita income and its distribution vary significantly between the countries (Table 1.6). Income inequality (as shown by the Gini coefficient) tends to be highest in Latin America (a well-known phenomenon), and a feature of our sample for other regions is that countries with lower per capita income have lower income inequality. The association between the high per capita income and high inequality suggests that growth may only benefit a minority of the population. However, empirical evidence suggests no systematic relationship between economic growth and inequality within countries (e.g. Ravallian, 2004), although inequality may help to

Table 1.5 Income poverty in sample countries

Country	% of population below international poverty line	% of population below the national poverty line	
	1996	*1996*	*2000*
Myanmar	–	–	–
Kazakhstan	1.5	34.6	–
Kyrgyzstan	2.0	64.1	–
Tajikistan	10.3	–	–
Ethiopia	81.9*	45.5	44.2
Kenya	23	–	–
South Africa	7.1	–	–
Uganda	82.2	55	–
Bolivia	14.4*	–	62.7
Brazil	9.9*	–	–
Mexico	<8*	10.1	8.0**

Source: World Bank (2003).

Notes
* indicates 2000 not 1996.
** indicates 1998 not 2000.

explain growth across countries (higher inequality being associated with lower growth). Insofar as trade and trade reform alter the relative returns to owners of factors of production, such as skilled versus unskilled workers, it may affect inequality (at least wage inequality). This is one way in which trade may affect poverty, by increasing the incomes and income-earning opportunities of the poor (at least, the relatively poor). Other effects may be indirect, through growth.

Overview of the volume

This volume is organized into four parts, this introduction being the first. Part II documents the lessons from four African countries, while the experience of formerly central planned Asian countries, most of whom became independent after the collapse of the FSU in the early 1990s, are presented in Part III. Part IV documents the experience of three Latin American countries. In the remainder of this chapter we provide a brief overview of the main lessons from these case studies.

   In Chapter 2, Prema-chandra Athukorala and Worku Gebeyehu examine the growth and equity implications of Ethiopian reforms with special emphasis on the manufacturing sector. While manufacturing output grew in the post-liberalization period, achievements in terms of employment creation and productivity improvement remained far from satisfactory. Employment growth in manufacturing lagged behind output growth throughout the post-liberalization period. The average annual

Table 1.6 Income consumption and distribution in sample countries, 1960–2000

	Per capita income			Per capita consumption			Share of 1st quintile			Share of 5th quintile			Gini			Survey type Survey
	1960	1980	2000	1960	1980	2000	1960	1980	2000	1960	198	2000	1960	1980	2000	
Ethiopia	586	734	692	523	586	560	8.6	8.6	7.2	41.2	41.2	47.7	32.2	32.2	39.9	Exp.
Kenya	878	1,219	1,081	632	814	818	3.4	3.4	5.0	62.2	62.2	50.2	57.7	57.7	44.6	Exp.
South Africa	7,838	12,627	9,977	5,502	6,857	6,243	2.9	2.9	2.9	64.7	64.7	64.7	60.7	60.7	60.7	Exp.
Uganda	699	624	1,299	522	596	1,107	4.9	4.9	7.1	49.9	49.9	44.9	44.6	44.6	37.5	Inc.
Kazakhstan	–	–	5,521	–	–	3,950	9.5	9.5	6.1	35.2	35.2	43.1	–	–	36.9	Exp.
Kyrgyzstan	–	–	2,822	–	–	2,191	4.3	4.3	10.7	48.7	48.7	34.3	–	–	23.6	Inc.
Myanmar	483	771	1,577	394	521	1,205	10.0	10.0	10.0	48.5	48.5	48.5	37.8	37.8	37.8	Exp.
Tajikistan	2,052	3,493	–	1,119	1,904	–	–	–	–	–	–	–	–	–	–	–
Bolivia	1,720	2,814	2,588	1,378	1,883	1,971	3.5	3.5	1.9	61.0	61.0	61.8	56.1	56.1	59.0	Inc.
Brazil	3,257	7,861	7,562	2,158	5,479	4,584	3.8	2.9	3.5	54.0	61.6	56.2	49.7	57.9	52.0	Inc.
Mexico	4,169	8,838	9,532	3,300	5,751	6,486	4.4	3.1	4.0	61.4	60.2	56.6	56.0	56.2	51.8	Inc.

Source: Balla (2002).

Notes
i Annual per capita income and consumption data are in purchasing power parity dollars at 2000 prices (1993 base year).
ii The shares of 1st and 5th quintile represent the quintile shares on income or consumption depending on the type of survey.
Exp. = Based on expenditure data.
Inc. = Based on income data.

employment growth during 1992/93–2000/01 was 1.6 per cent compared to 7.1 per cent growth in real output, indicating the widespread use of capital-intensive sectors particularly in public enterprises. During 1993/94–2000/01 labour productivity in domestic medium and large scale manufacturing grew at an average annual rate of 5.5 per cent. This was however the outcome of capital deepening rather than 'true' productivity improvement.

Athukorala and Gebeyehu put forward two possible explanations for the lacklustre performance during the post-reform period. First, it may reflect invariable adjustment lags, which can be rather long in an economy like Ethiopia where reforms were undertaken following a long period of central planning, which had virtually decimated the private sector in the economy. It would naturally take a long time for the private sector to come to terms with the new economic setting. Second, and perhaps more importantly, the liberalization process has not yet been deep enough to generate the anticipated improvement in manufacturing performance. In particular, the privatization process has proceeded much slower than planned. The authors argue that policy makers seem to place great emphasis on domestic input linkages and value added in formulating industrial development policy. Of course, the greater the linkages between the export sectors and the rest of the economy the greater would be the benefits to the economy, provided such linkages are the natural outcome of industrial deepening. However, attempts to create linkages through direct policy intervention can be counter productive.

Kunal Sen examines the link between trade, growth and poverty in Kenya in Chapter 3. While Kenya has opened up its economy in recent years, the author finds no significant positive impact on economic growth, employment creation or poverty alleviation. The one exception is that the growth of horticultural exports appears to have increased employment and incomes among poor workers. He puts forward two possible explanations for the limited aggregate effects of liberalization. First, the reforms in Kenya were 'stop–go' in nature; this may have undermined the credibility of the reforms and discouraged private agents from responding (e.g. by altering investment decisions). Second, the reforms were implemented in the presence of significant macroeconomic uncertainty and in a political environment where the relationship between the government and major bilateral and multilateral donors has not been the most conducive. This would also have undermined confidence in the reform process. Sen concludes that it is natural that when reforms are not seen to be credible and accompanying conditions of macroeconomic stability and political commitment are not met, they fail to achieve the expected gains.

The reform process in Uganda has been much more comprehensive than in Kenya, and is examined by Oliver Morrissey, Nichodemus Rudaheranwa and Lars Moller in Chapter 4. The authors found evidence that trade policy reform contributed to growth, and through growth to poverty reduction, in Uganda. The headcount poverty index fell from 56 per cent in 1992 to 46 per cent in 1996, due largely to growth in coffee production, and to 35 per cent by 2000, with the most recent reduction reflecting growth in food crop production. While the gains from trade and growth are widely distributed, with average incomes in most regions and types of households increasing, they are not evenly distributed, and there are currently concerns regarding the sustainability of poverty reduction. Some households have been unaffected, and some may even have suffered a loss of income, including some urban wage labour and especially households with a non-working head (AIDS is an important factor here). The incidence of poverty is greater in more remote, and less secure, regions, which are the ones least likely to be directly involved in trade.

The authors argue that while trade has benefited the Ugandan economy on aggregate, and increased average incomes, almost a fifth of the population remains rooted in poverty. This is to be expected: trade and growth can reduce poverty, but trade alone will not eradicate poverty. This is not surprising as the vast majority of poor households are not engaged in activities directly related to international trade, and where they are they are the lowest paid workers. Furthermore, the poor tend not to consume goods that are traded internationally (or, at least, such goods are not a large share of their consumption). The evidence from Uganda suggests that trade can benefit the economy (and note that, unlike Kenya, the reforms were credible), but the poor are only likely to benefit if the resulting economic growth increases demand for their services, mostly unskilled labour in the informal or agriculture sector.

Pushkar Maitra and Ranjan Ray examine the effects of political reforms on black households in South Africa in Chapter 5. The authors argue that in South Africa many of the differences in living standards between different segments of the population are the direct result of apartheid policies that denied equal access to education, employment, services and resources to the non-White population. Maitra and Ray conclude by arguing that while much has been achieved in the five years following the dismantling of apartheid a good deal more needs to be done to achieve social and economic equality between the different segments of the South African population. Their analysis is not directly related to trade, but demonstrates how institutions determine redistribution, and thereby mediate any effect of growth on poverty reduction.

In Chapter 6, Richard Pomfret investigates the links between global integration, growth and equity in Kazakhstan, which became independent after the collapse of the FSU in the early 1990s. Pomfret argues that the 1990s decade was characterized by dismal economic performance, including negative economic growth and increased inequality, largely because of the difficulty of managing the transition from central planning. Since 2000, the country has enjoyed rapid economic growth, the main source of which was increased oil production. The author argues that economic growth since 2000 is clearly associated with the global integration of Kaza-khstan's economy, but the unresolved question is whether this will produce long-term growth with equity given evidence of growing corruption. This highlights another feature of institutions: the widespread nature of corruption that tends to sustain inequality and prevent sustained poverty reduction.

The experience of Kyrgyzstan is examined in Chapter 7 by Kishor Sharma. The author argues that while Kyrgyz is one of the most open countries in Central Asia, its achievement in sustaining growth and alleviating poverty has been far from satisfactory, mainly due to internal and regional rather than external factors. These include cumbersome and time-consuming customs formalities, transit problems in neighbouring countries, inefficient transport networks and poor governance – again, highlighting institutional and infrastructure constraints. It is obvious that liberalization *per se*, in the absence of a comprehensive reform package, has failed to generate the desired benefits in Kyrgyzstan. As all Central Asian countries are land-locked economies, Sharma argues that regional cooperation can significantly facilitate the global integration of not only Kyrgyzstan but all countries in the region.

Peter Warr considers the case of Myanmar in Chapter 8. The author notes that by pursuing a close-door policy, Myanmar's government has denied its citizens the achievement of better growth and equity outcomes.

The growth and equity implications of reform in Tajikistan are analysed by Kishor Sharma in Chapter 9. While there has been significant reform since Tajikistan became an independent nation in the early 1990s, it has failed to accelerate growth and reduce poverty. This is partly due to civil war and partly due to a poor business climate (caused by transit problems in neighbouring countries, and lack of efficient institutions and infrastructure). The enforcement of rules of law, protection of private property and political stability also seem to a problem in developing the private sector's confidence. The author notes that regional cooperation in trade and transit, together with efficient institutions, infrastructure and good governance, can significantly enhance Tajikistan's economic future.

The Brazilian experience is documented by Afonso Ferreira and Antonio Aguirre in Chapter 10. The authors argue that aggregate impacts of the Brazilian trade reform have been minimal: GDP growth has not increased, overall productivity has not increased, average wages have declined and indices measuring inequality have remained unchanged. Although poverty has decreased, and part of this is due to the effect of trade on real incomes, this is largely explained by the minimum wage, higher growth and lower inflation. The Brazilian case is quite interesting, as the manufacturing responded quite well, after an initial adjustment period, to increased competition from imports following liberalization. However, the response was to increase competitiveness by increasing productivity, typically by reducing employment due to skill-biased technical change. As a consequence, average manufacturing wages fell as did the return to education. Wages only increased for those at the highest skill level but, as these are a small proportion of the total, this was insufficient to alter wage inequality. Employment tended to increase in the non-traded sector (mostly services) where productivity is lower but wages are higher, implying that the sector contributing most to gains in the economy was that least affected by trade liberalization. Average wages were almost constant between 1980 and 2000, disguising a decline in traded sectors and an increase in non-traded sectors. The case highlights the importance of the ability of an economy to respond to the competitive pressures associated with liberalization: the exposed (traded) sectors increased productivity and reduced wages, but the sheltered (non-traded) sectors increased wages despite low productivity. For the economy overall, neither productivity nor average wages really changed.

In Chapter 11, the Bolivian experience is presented by Lykke E. Andersen, Osvaldo Nina and Dirk Willem te Velde. The authors argue that despite two decades of reform, there has been little progress in expanding exports and reducing poverty, although poverty did decline in the 1990s. Inequality appears to have increased dramatically. One explanation is that the most dynamic export sectors, which are also the sectors that have attracted FDI, are biased towards skilled workers. As a result, the skilled/unskilled wage differential has increased, and the return to education has increased, but the position of unskilled workers has deteriorated. This implies that the way in which the economy has grown, with the composition of exports shifting in favour of relatively skill-intensive activities, has tended to exclude the poor (the most unskilled). Trade reform in Bolivia, and the associated inflows of FDI, has not benefited labour-intensive export sectors or modern agriculture, the two sectors that can significantly contribute to reducing poverty because they employ the least skilled workers.

The Mexican experience is addressed in Chapter 12, by Andrew Mold and Carlos A. Roza. Mexico has implemented significant trade liberalization since the 1980s, most importantly after joining NAFTA. On the face of it, this has led to a significant increase in exports, and Mexico has become one of the largest suppliers to the US market. Mexico has also experienced a significant increase in FDI inflows. However, despite the evident growth in exports, there has been no positive impact on growth and no evidence of a reduction in poverty. The authors suggest three inter-related reasons. First, the export sector is highly import intensive and has few linkages to the local economy, and even domestic firms have become more import intensive. Thus, although exports have grown the trade balance has not improved. Second, the exports are primarily to the US, and in a limited number of sectors (that are facing increased global competition), which forces wages down to be competitive. Thus, the export growth has not tended to increase real wages. Third, inequality remains very high and the economy is susceptible to debt and currency crises. To the extent that the economy does grow, the benefits accrue to a small group while the majority of the population, and especially the poor, are excluded. Mexico has adopted an export-oriented strategy that has undermined domestic productive capacity and increased dependence (perhaps in a *dependencia* sense) on the US, with the results that it has weakened the ability of Mexico to achieved sustained growth and poverty reduction.

Taken together, the case studies provide few examples of countries where trade liberalization has had a direct beneficial impact on reducing poverty. Uganda may be one of the most positive examples, and a notable feature there is that the reform process was credible and export growth has not been biased towards relatively skill-intensive activities. Even in this case, it was not a direct effect of trade on the poor, rather trade expansion was associated with economic growth that in turn was poverty-reducing. It is equally true that none of the studies show that trade liberalization is associated with increased poverty; where there are adverse effects on specific sectors, these are usually offset elsewhere in the economy. However, trade liberalization does appear to be associated with increased inequality, at least in terms of wages, largely because dynamic export sectors are skill intensive. Thus, contrary to the predictions of standard theory, export growth in unskilled labour abundant economies appears to offer the greatest benefits to relatively skilled labour.

For most of the cases, trade liberalization appeared to have a weak positive impact on growth but no discernible impact on the poor. This is to be expected, as trade liberalization provides opportunities to some sectors while other sectors are exposed to increased competition, while the poor are rarely directly involved in the production (and perhaps not even the consumption) of goods that are traded internationally. There are sectors that are exceptions, such as mining in Bolivia and some export crops in Kenya and Uganda, but even where these sectors do benefit from trade any effects on the poor are often insufficient to affect aggregate poverty. Clearly what is important is not the effect of trade on growth *per se*, but the effect of reform on the composition of trade, and especially whether there is an increase in demand for relatively unskilled labour. How any benefits, or costs, of increased openness to trade are spread or shared through the economy also depends on institutions and, where these are weak, distorted (in the sense of maintaining inequality) or corrupt, the poor get few of the benefits but bear many of the costs. This is evident in almost all of the case studies.

Acknowledgement

We thank Prema-chandra Athukorala for providing very useful comments on an earlier draft of this chapter.

Part II
African experience

2 Trade policy reforms and manufacturing performance in Ethiopia

Prema-chandra Athukorala and Worku Gebeyehu

Following the change in political leadership in 1991, the economic policy scene in Ethiopia has undergone fundamental changes. During the military rule (the Derg regime) from 1974 to mid-1991, the Ethiopian economy rapidly developed into one of the most inward-oriented and regulated in the developing world. In 1975, "Economic Policy of Socialist Ethiopia" was declared and subsequently the commanding heights of the economy such as banks, insurance companies, medium and large-scale industrial and commercial firms were nationalized. Economic restructuring based on central planning effectively marginalized the private sector virtually to micro- and small-scale activities. The new EPRDF (Ethiopian People's Revolutionary Democratic Front) regime responded to the dismal economic outcome of the Derg era by embarking on an extensive economic liberalization process in 1992/93 with the support of the international financial institutions, promising a new era of market-driven development. The key elements of the reform program included liberalization of foreign trade and exchange regimes, decontrol of domestic input and output prices, public sector reform to guarantee autonomy of the state owned enterprises (SOEs) and privatize other enterprises, financial market reform and opening the door to foreign investors.

Many of the promised economic reforms are yet to transpire. The eruption of the border conflict with Eritrea in May 1998 delayed the reform process and resulted in erosion of business confidence, leading many to question whether the country is really on the right path. On 18 June 2000, the two countries entered into a ceasefire agreement followed by the signing of a peace agreement on 12 December 2000. Developments in the economic and political scene since then have renewed hope that Ethiopia will regain the growth momentum that it experienced in the post-1992 liberalization period. While the drought and the decline of coffee prices have reduced GDP growth significantly, the reform path has continued albeit at a slow pace.

The purpose of this chapter is to examine structural adjustment and performance of domestic manufacturing in Ethiopia in the context of the trade liberalization and other market-oriented reforms initiated in the early 1990s. Ethiopia is predominantly an agricultural country. Manufacturing accounts for less than 7 percent of GDP and 3 percent of total employment in the economy. For this reason, agricultural development is the prime focus of development strategy of the Ethiopian government. However, the government places due emphasis on industrialization as an integral part of the agriculture-led national development strategy in creating demand for agricultural products and provide growing employment opportunities for the growing urban labor force.

The reform process

Trade policy reform

During the Derg era import trade of Ethiopia remained severely restricted through a combination of high tariffs and a plethora of quantitative restrictions. The tariffs were as high as 230 percent on certain luxury consumer goods and many intermediate and investment goods imports to public sector enterprises were allowed at zero or low duties. The quantitative import restrictions on imports by the private sector included direct import prohibition (a long "negative list"), quotas, strict licensing and foreign exchange rationing.

In August 1993, the new government embarked on a comprehensive tariff reform program aimed at dismantling quantitative restrictions and gradually reducing the level and dispersion of tariff rates. The negative list used to determine eligibility for imports through the foreign exchange access has been reduced significantly. Currently quantitative import restrictions are applied only to used clothes, harmful drugs and armaments for security reasons. Both tariff levels and dispersion have been reduced significantly under tariff reforms. Specific tariffs have been converted into *ad valorem* rates. By 2002, only 2.7 percent of total tariff lines had specific rates. The range of tariff rates narrowed down from pre-reform 0–240 percent to 0–80 percent in 1995 and then to 0–35 in 2002.[1] The average (unweighted) tariff rate declined from 28.9 percent in 1995 to 17.5 percent in 2002. The degree of dispersion of tariff rates measured by the coefficient of variation declined from 82.4 percent to 69.7 percent between these two years. The implicit import duty rate (import duties collected as a percentage of total CIF imports) declined from over 23 percent in the mid-1990s to 12 percent by 2001/02 (Table 2.1).

On the export side, duties on all exports other than coffee (the main export product) were removed. On coffee exports until 2002, there were three different taxes on coffee exports – customs duty of Birr 15 per 100 kg; 2 percent transaction tax and *a cess* of Birr 5 per 100 kg. In 2002, these three taxes were consolidated into a single rate of 6.5 percent, resulting in a significant reduction in the overall tax burden on coffee exporters.

Table 2.1 Implicit import duty rate[1] (%)

1990–91	21.8
1991–92	15.3
1992–93	20.4
1993–94	11.2
1994–95	12.9
1995–96	11.8
1996–97	12.6
1997–98	14.4
1998–99	11.7
1999–2000	11.2
2000–01	10.8

Source: Ethiopian Customs Authority.

Note
1 Total import duty collection as a percentage
  of total import value (c.i.f.).

The impact of the tariff structure on profitability of domestic production operates through both tariff on final goods imports and exports, and tariffs on intermediate goods used in domestic production. The analytical tool used to measure the combined effect of both the end product and input tariff is the effective rate of protection (ERP). The ERP aims to capture the proportionate increase in per unit value added of a sector in the presence of these two types of tariffs. More specifically, it takes into account the protection on output and the cost-raising effects of protection on inputs.[2]

ERP estimates prepared by the World Bank staff for the Ethiopian economy together with the related nominal tariff rates are reported in Table 2.2. It is important to note an important caveat of these estimates. Since Ethiopia currently does not have an input–output table, the input coefficients used in these estimates have been derived from the regional input–output tables for Sub-Sahara Africa used in the Global Trade Analysis Project (GTAP) database. The use of a regional average input–output structure for policy analysis in an individual country is of course rather problematic and can only be used as a rough guide. This is more so given that the economy under consideration has undergone substantial economic restructuring over the whole of 1990s decade whereas the regional input–output table is based on the early 1990s. The estimates need to be qualified for three other limitations. First, despite significant trade liberalization over the past eight years, the government still exercises considerable administrative discretion in influencing import flows. In the presence of such non-tariff barriers, the rate of protection enjoyed by some industries (presumably those dominated by SOEs) could be much higher than is suggested by these estimates. Second, most light manufacturing industries (textiles and garments in particular) are believed to face considerable competition from illegal cross-border imports (Fikry 2003). Illegal

Table 2.2 Ethiopia: nominal and effective rates of protection by input–output classification, 1995 and 2001[1]

Input– Output Industry Code[3]	Input–Output (I–O) Sector	Nominal tariff rate (%)		Effective rate of protection (ERP)[2]	
		1995	2001	1995	2001
	(A) Agriculture, forestry and fishing[3]	29.0	9.3	36.6	8.5
1	Paddy rice	30.0	5.0	35.4	3.4
2	Wheat	30.0	5.0	38.2	1.7
3	Cereal grains	25.8	5.0	31.4	3.7
4	Vegetables, fruit, nuts	35.4	19.7	42.6	23.2
5	Oil seeds	30.0	5.0	38.4	3.9
6	Sugar cane, sugar beet	0.0	0.0	−4.4	−2.5
7	Plant-based fibers	6.3	6.3	2.9	5.5
8	Crops	35.2	25.9	46.5	34.9
9	Bovine cattle, sheep and goats, horses	17.5	7.5	15.4	6.7
10	Animal products	24.6	17.2	26.2	22.2
11	Raw milk	0.0	0.0	−17.7	−7.4
12	Wool, silk-worm cocoons	5.0	5.0	−11.1	0.8
13	Forestry	24.1	13.8	26.9	15.0
14	Fishing	38.1	29.4	51.8	40.8
	(B) Mining[3]	5.1	6.7	0.8	−2.6
15	Coal	5.0	5.0	−13.2	−5.6
16	Oil	5.0	5.0	0.9	2.8
17	Gas	5.0	5.0	4.0	4.7
18	Minerals, other	10.3	6.7	−4.8	−2.6
	(C) Manufacturing[3]	22.7	14.9	39.1	26.6
19	Bovine cattle, sheep and goat, horse meat products	57.5	20.0	124.4	34.9
20	Meat products, other	62.5	29.5	160.0	63.6
21	Vegetable oils and fats	31.7	27.7	87.7	117.8
22	Dairy products	37.6	26.8	90.2	71.4
23	Processed rice	30.0	5.0	39.5	−8.4
24	Sugar	50.0	5.0	218.2	−1.3
25	Food products, other	52.3	28.9	118.3	66.3
26	Beverages and tobacco products	44.6	32.7	85.4	72.8
27	Textiles	47.5	30.1	98.5	63.0
28	Wearing apparel	77.7	39.9	180.2	83.4
29	Leather products	50.8	35.5	95.9	71.9
30	Wood products	32.5	20.4	47.7	29.6
31	Annex products, publishing	26.4	12.1	38.5	11.1
32	Petroleum, coal products	7.7	5.7	21.4	9.6
33	Chemical, rubber, plastic products	17.9	11.9	23.6	16.0
34	Mineral products, other	30.0	21.6	55.5	41.4
35	Ferrous metals	6.7	6.4	−10.0	−2.3
36	Metals, other	11.5	10.0	−2.4	6.6
37	Metal products	22.6	19.8	46.8	44.7
38	Motor vehicles and parts	30.8	19.2	61.4	35.3
39	Transport equipment	9.4	8.9	5.3	7.6
40	Electronic equipment	23.0	21.1	33.6	35.1

Table 2.2 Continued

Input– Output Industry Code[3]	Input–Output (I–O) Sector	Nominal tariff rate (%)		Effective rate of protection (ERP)[2]	
		1995	2001	1995	2001
41	Machinery and equipment	17.0	14.0	22.9	20.5
42	Manufactures	48.3	32.1	93.4	61.6
	Memorandum Items[4]				
	Weighted average	22.2	14.7	36.2	26.0
	Simple average	27.5	15.5	48.7	26.3
	CV	67.1	71.2	110.0	114.9

Source: World Bank estimates. Nominal tariff rates are from official Ethiopian sources. Input–output coefficients are from the Sub-Saharan Africa regional input–output table (based on data for the early 1990s) in the Global Trade Analysis Project (GTAP) database.

Notes
1 Industry classification is based on the Global Trade Analysis Project (GTAP) database.
2 Estimated using the formula,

$$ERP_j = [t_j - \Sigma(a_{ij} {}^* t_i)) / (1 - \Sigma a_{ij})]$$

Where, t_j and t_i are the nominal (scheduled) tariff rates on given industry and input-supply industry respectively, and a_{ij} is the input coefficient indicating the share of industry *i*'s production used as inputs in industry *j*'s output.
3 Global Trade Analysis Project (GTAP) classification.
4 Import-weighted average of the product sectors listed below.

trade normally results in "water in tariff" (that is, in the presence of illegal imports the actual price-raising impact of existing tariff structure could be much lower than is interpreted from the official tariff rates and ERP estimated based on these rates). Third, given Ethiopia's geography, "natural" protection to domestic industry (and negative protection to export-oriented production) arising from transport cost could be substantial. The *ad valorem* tariff equivalents of transport cost tend to be lower for more highly fabricated goods. Therefore, in contrast to the typical tariff structure, for a given industry, the effective rates of natural protection tend to be lower than nominal rates. Moreover, in an inter-industry comparison, light manufactured goods producing industry (e.g. garments, footwear, toys) naturally tends to experience a lower degree of effective natural protection compared to heavy industries (Conlon 1979, Yeats 1981).

Notwithstanding these limitations, a comparison of NRP and ERP estimates reported in Table 2.2 does serve to drive home the point that the use of the latter (as is commonly done in the current Ethiopian policy debate) tends to give a misleading picture of the net resource allocation effects of the existing tariff regime. In both years for which estimates are reported, ERP estimates for most industries/product sectors are much larger than NRP estimates, reflecting the cascading nature of the tariff structures (that is, the tendency to tax intermediate imports at lower rates compared to the end products.) An economy-wide weighted-average rate of protection of 22.2 percent in 1995 was associated with an effective protection level of 36.2 percent. The comparable figures for 2001 were 14.7 percent and 26.0 percent respectively.

The estimates also point to a clear incentive bias in the protection structure in favor of manufacturing compared to agriculture. The level of protection for agriculture has come down at a faster rate compared to that for domestic manufacturing. The weighted-average ERP for agriculture declined from 36.6 percent in 1995 to 8.5 percent in 2001. By contrast, ERP for manufacturing declined from 39.1 to 26.6 between these two years. Given the limitations already noted of the data used in these estimates, the actual degree of anti-agricultural bias embodied in the tariff structure could well be much larger than is suggested by these estimates. The massive anti-agricultural bias in effective protection has largely been the outcome of high protection enjoyed by input-supplying manufacturing industries. Ethiopia does not yet have an effective, duty rebate scheme (or bonded warehouse arrangements) for compensating export producers for duties paid on imported inputs or any other significant export incentive scheme. This means that the measured degree of ERP for domestic manufacturing essentially imply an "anti-export bias" of the same magnitude.

Decontrol of domestic prices

Price controls have been removed on domestic trade in all products except petroleum, fertilizer and pharmaceuticals. This has been accompanied by the dismantling of government monopoly in trade in key products, including freeing of grain and coffee trades. Under the Derg regime, purchase and distribution of grain was the monopoly of the Agricultural Marketing Corporation (AMC). Private firms were allowed to operate only under the condition that the quota of grain imposed on that specific region had been delivered to the corporation. Both domestic trade and export of coffee was under the monopoly of the Ethiopian Coffee Marketing Board. Both these parastatals were dismantled as an important part of market-oriented reforms.

Public enterprises involved in retail trade and services sectors have been privatized. However, public sector manufacturing enterprises are still involved in retail trade in their own products. Thus the government influences market prices through the large number of state-owned enterprises in such areas as "consumer materials, metal and chemical products, and basic consumer goods such as food, beverages, clothing and textiles".[3]

Domestic tax reform

During the Derg era, direct taxes (taxes on personal income and business profits) were highly progressive, ranging from 10 percent to 59 percent in the case of business tax and from 10 to 85 percent in the case of personal tax. Under tax reforms initiated in 1995, the maximum rates were reduced to low unified levels of 35 percent. Tax exemption thresholds of income and profit were also significantly increased, coupled with reduction in the number of taxable income brackets with a view to facilitating tax administration.

These moves to reduce burden have been accompanied by significant reforms in indirect taxation. A new 5 percent sales tax was imposed on selected agricultural and essential consumer goods and a uniform 15 percent sales tax on other goods except electricity, health and education services. At the beginning of 2003, a 15 percent value-added tax was introduced in place of sales and turnover taxes on enterprises generating an annual income of more than Birr 500,000. A smaller value tax was introduced for enterprises whose annual income was below Birr 500,000. Table 2.5 presents effective tax rates on medium- and large-scale enterprises. The average tax rate on total manufacturing has declined from 18 percent in 1996/97 to about 13 percent in 2000/01.

Export promotion

As part of the market-oriented reforms, initiatives have been taken to facilitate private sector participation in export trade. Perhaps the two major reform measures implemented to achieve this objective was the dismantling of the government monopoly in coffee trade and abolishing the mandatory approval requirement for export contracts by the National Bank of Ethiopia. Under the latter policy, exporters were required to obtain approval from the bank for the invoicing price before any shipment could be made. This approval requirement, which constituted an important element of the foreign exchange control regime, hampered exporting by limiting the flexibility of deciding prices in line with market conditions. A foreign exchange retention scheme was also introduced to allow exporters to retain part of their foreign exchange proceeds. The scheme went through a series of amendments and currently exporters are allowed to retain 10 percent of their proceeds for an indefinite period and of course sell the remainder within 28 days.

There is a bonded manufacturing warehouse scheme and an import duty rebate scheme aimed at providing exporters of manufactured goods with world market prices.[4] These schemes however remain virtually inactive because of administrative bottlenecks and some opaque operational rules. Exporters of manufactured goods currently rely solely on an import voucher scheme to obtain duty exemption on imported input. Under this scheme the Ministry of Finance and Economic Development issues vouchers to be used as deposit for duties payable (World Bank 2002b).

An Export Promotion Council (EPC) consisting of high level government officials, exporters and service providers led by the Prime Minister was set up in 1992 to design, implement and monitor export development policies. The EPC was reconstituted as the Ethiopian Export Promotion Agency (EEP) in 1999 to implement a wide-ranging export development agenda encompassing: conducting market research; facilitating participation of exporters in trade fairs, exhibitions and trade missions; and disseminating market information. However, the only export support service EEP has so far managed to provide is the publication of a bi-monthly newsletter "Trade Point", which lists a few addresses of importers and exporters and itemizes certain tradable products. The performance report presented last year to the parliament by the General Director of EEP indicated that the Agency had so far been preoccupied with its own capacity building: designing regulations, organizational restructuring, establishing information system and training its personnel (Abebe 2002). The Agency also suffers from financial constraints, lack of skilled and experienced personnel and inadequate facilities, and demanded the formation of an "Export Development Fund" to provide the intended service at least in a cost-sharing basis.

Privatization

Privatization of public enterprises with the aim of promoting greater participation of the private sector in the economy is a key element of the declared reform program of the EPRDF government. The Ethiopian Privatization Agency was set up in 1994 and became operational in 1996. However, so far, the implementation process has not gone beyond the sale or liquidation of a number of small retail shops, hotels and medium-scale manufacturing establishments. The only notable public enterprises to be privatized so far are the state-owned gold mines and two tea plantations. Four integrated textile mills were placed under the management of foreign companies. One of them was subsequently returned back to the government (by the Italian management partner).

The usual explanation given by the government for the slow progress in the privatization program is the lack of private sector interest (domestic or foreign) in taking over public enterprises. However, the economic press in Addis Ababa often complain about the government's half-heartedness commitment to privatization owing to pressure exerted by interest groups within the ruling party who benefit from the current dominant position of these enterprises. Direct revenue implications may have been yet another deterrent; SOEs generate around 90 percent of federally collected revenue and the government seems to be contemplating widening the revenue base before embarking on privatization (Berhanu 2003).

Private sector perception of the government's commitment to market-oriented reforms has been adversely affected by growing concerns about the ruling party's attempt to use privatization as a means of promoting a "hybrid model" of business ownership whereby most large "private" companies are owned by party affiliates. It is alleged that the Tgray People's

Liberalization Front (TPLF), the dominant partner of the ruling EPRDF, has secretly established a substantial number of large "private" companies in the name of the party cadres using party-affiliated endowment funds (Economist Intelligence Unit (EIU) 2002b, Aynekulu 1996, Vestal 1999: pp. 173–5).

Labor legislation

A new labor law was enacted by Proclamation No. 42/1985, which vested the autonomy to the management of each enterprise to make independent decisions. According to this law, the worker–employer relationship should be governed by the basic principles of right and the obligations of each party to maintain industrial peace and development of the economy. The law permits labor proclamation and allows labor shedding by companies subject to advance notice and redundancy payments.

Foreign exchange market reforms and macroeconomic management

Trade liberalization was accompanied by a significant exchange rate reform backed by a firm commitment to fiscal and monetary frugality. From the late 1940s through to the early 1990s the Ethiopian currency, Birr, remained rigidly pegged to the US dollar. From 1945–71 Birr/$ rate remained unchanged at 2.5. This was revalued to 2.3 in December 1971 and then to 2.07 in February 1973 and remained at that level until October 1992. The natural outcome of this passive exchange rate policy was the development of an illicit parallel market for foreign exchange, where at times the spread between the two rates reached as high as 230 percent. The overvalued official exchange rate coupled with stringent foreign exchange rationing provided fertile ground for illicit cross-border trade, particularly in coffee and live animals.

As part of the overall reform program of the new government, the exchange rate was adjusted from Birr/$2.07 to 5.00 on 1 October 1992 (a 142 percent devaluation in nominal terms). Following the devaluation, the exchange rate was allowed to be determined according to demand and supply conditions in the foreign exchange market, with the National Bank of Ethiopia (NBE, The Central Bank) intervening only to smooth out erratic fluctuations in the rate. By the end of 2002, the rate was around Birr/$8.75.

The NBE has taken a number of initiatives to improve the functioning of the foreign exchange market with a view to help keeping the exchange rate at realistic levels and to harmonize the official and parallel foreign exchange markets. These included eliminating foreign exchange rationing, inaugurating a foreign exchange auction in May 1993 (on a fortnightly basis to begin with and on a weekly basis since September 1998),[5] permitting commercial banks to open foreign exchange bureaus to engage in retail foreign exchange trading (October 1996), and permitting inter-bank foreign exchange trading (September 1998). Currently, the NEB is using the US dollar as the sole intervention currency, but there is a possibility of pegging the Birr to other specially tailored basket of currencies. At present, there are 17 foreign exchange bureaus in the country.

Following these reforms, the gap between marginal and parallel exchange rates (the black market exchange rate premium) has declined sharply. By the end of 2003, the black market premium was a mere 0.5 percent compared to over 270 percent in the mid-1990s.

The floating exchange rate has been appropriately backed by a firm commitment to maintaining macroeconomic stability. The fiscal deficit has kept well within the limits (below 4 percent of GDP) agreed under structural adjustment programs except during 1999–2001 when it increased to 11.2 percent of GDP because of war expenditure. In terms of mode of deficit financing, the Government has used non-inflationary sources, mainly external sources and to some extent non-inflationary domestic sources like public borrowing. Monetization of budget deficit has been largely eschewed while relying predominantly on borrowing from non-bank sources, mainly through the sale of bonds and treasury bills of 28, 91 and 182 days (World Bank 2002b). The Central Bank has kept growth of broad money (M2) in line with growth of nominal GDP.

Despite massive currency depreciation domestic inflation measures by the Addis Ababa CPI has continued to remain low. In fact, during the immediate aftermaths of the introduction of the new exchange rate system, the exceptionally good harvest resulted in a decline in food prices. However, even when corrected for this effect, inflation remained very low. The average rate of CPI inflation during 1992/93–2001/02 was a mere 1.4 percent, compared to over 15 percent in the first half of the 1990s.

Manufacturing performance

Manufacturing began to gain some economic significance in Ethiopia only from about the mid-1950s with the backing of the modernization drive of the imperial government. During the ensuing two decades, manufacturing remained by and large a private sector activity, heavily reliant on foreign direct investment (Hess 1970: Chapter 4). Following the regime change in 1974, all medium- and large-scale manufacturing firms were nationalized and restrictions were imposed on the expansion of private sector small-scale manufacturing. New public-sector plants were set in upstream heavy manufacturing in pursuance of Soviet-style broad-based industrialization. By the late 1980s, public enterprises accounted for over 95 percent of output (value added) and 92 percent of employment in medium- and large-scale manufacturing.

Table 2.3 summarizes data on growth and sectoral composition of gross domestic product in Ethiopia during the period 1980–2001.[6] Data for the

Table 2.3 Ethiopia: composition and growth of gross domestic product (GDP), 1980–2001

	1980–88	1990–91	1991–92	1992–93	1993–94	1994–95	1995–96	1996–97	1997–98	1998–99	1999–2000	2000–01	2001–02
COMPOSITION[1] (%)													
Agriculture	43.1	46.1	55.6	60.2	55.6	48.6	48.6	48.4	48.1	48.3	48.2	47.9	47.5
Other primary sector	6.4	6.4	5.9	4.3	5.5	7.2	7.1	7.5	8.2	7.8	8.0	8.5	9.2
Industry	11.0	11.9	9.5	7.9	9.5	10.3	10.3	10.3	10.2	10.3	10.2	10.2	10.1
Manufacturing	6.6	7.3	5.1	4.6	6.0	6.5	6.5	6.5	6.5	6.5	6.5	6.4	6.4
Construction and utilities	4.4	4.6	4.4	3.3	3.5	3.8	3.8	3.8	3.8	3.8	3.8	3.7	3.7
Services	28.3	35.5	29.0	27.7	29.4	33.9	33.9	33.8	33.6	33.7	33.6	33.4	33.2
GDP	100.0	100.0	100.0	100.0	100.0	100.0	100.0	100.0	100.0	100.0	100.0	100.0	100.0
GROWTH[2] (%)													
Agriculture	1.5	5.3	5.2	–2.7	6.1	–3.7	3.4	14.7	3.4	–10.8	3.8	2.2	13.2
Other primary sector	0.8	–8.7	–11.4	–28.9	43.7	35.5	5.6	10.6	5.2	–1.2	6.3	5.4	7.9
Industry	4.5	–6.8	–19.1	–7.1	28.4	7.0	8.1	5.4	7.0	2.3	11.3	3.0	5.1
Manufacturing	2.3	0.4	–32.0	–5.5	36.1	8.9	9.0	7.6	6.3	–1.0	14.8	4.2	6.4
Construction and utilities	1.5	–16.7	2.4	–8.8	19.7	4.5	6.9	2.4	8.1	7.1	6.8	1.4	3.2
Services	4.5	3.9	–12.7	–4.2	17.4	7.9	9.3	7.0	7.1	10.5	7.6	9.5	3.4
GDP	2.8	2.5	–4.7	–5.1	13.4	3.5	6.1	10.6	5.2	–1.2	6.3	5.4	7.9

Source: World Bank, World Development Indicators database (based on Ethiopian Central Statistical Organization data).

Notes
1 At current prices.
2 At constant prices.

manufacturing sector are plotted in Figure 2.1. The period 1980–88,[7] growth of manufacturing averaged to 2.3 percent, with significant erratic annual changes. The modest 2.8 percent average GDP growths during the period came largely from the services sectors. Following the reforms initiated in 1992 there has been a notable improvement in performance across all sectors, yielding an average annual GDP growth rate of 8.9 percent for the nine years from 1993 to 2001. The average growth rate of manufacturing during this period was 10.2 percent (11.4 percent if 1998/99 when there was a mild contraction in output owing to the Eritrea war is excluded), slightly above the average growth rate of agriculture (9.7 percent). It is important to note that every impressive growth figure during the early post-reform years (1993 and 1994 in particular) partly reflect "natural" recovery of a war-devastated economy. However even after allowing for this, on average the post-reform growth record remains impressive compared to the 1980–88 period. Despite rapid manufacturing growth following reforms, the share of that sector in total GDP remained remarkably stable around an average level of 6.5 percent. This was because of faster growth in services and construction activities.[8]

The reforms initiated in 1992 have set the stage for the re-entry of the private sector into manufacturing. For instance, the number of private

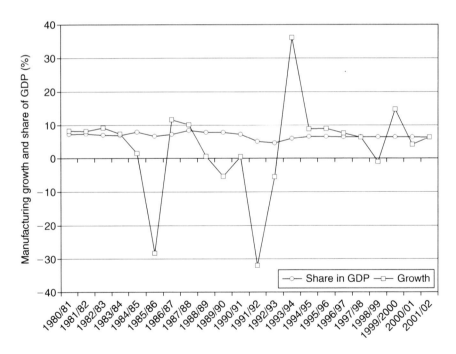

Figure 2.1 Growth rate and share in GDP of manufacturing production (source: Based on data compiled from, World Bank, *World Development Indicators database*).

sector firms in medium and large-scale manufacturing increased from 607 to 657 between 1996/97 and 2000/01. However, in terms of the relative contribution to output (value added) SOEs still occupy the dominant position. Their output share declined marginally from 79 percent to 76 percent between these two years (Table 2.4)

Production structure

Like in least developed countries (LDCs), Ethiopian manufacturing has historically been dominated by food production. By the early 1990s, this sector accounted for 37 percent of total manufacturing value added (Table 2.4). The second largest sector, textiles accounted for 17 percent. Despite emphasis placed under central planning on the promotion of heavy industries, industries such as machinery and transport equipment, iron and steel together accounted for less than 20 percent of total output.

Following liberalization reforms in 1992/93, the food and beverages sector recorded the sharpest increase in output share, from 49 percent in 1991/92 to 50 percent in 2000/01. Public sector dominated capital-intensive industries also recorded output share gains. The greater availability of imported input and investment goods seems to have played a key role. Given heavy transport costs, import competition was also presumably not a major threat to these industries. By contrast, industries such as garments, footwear and other manufacturing which are relatively more labor intensive and have greater private sector participation have recorded contraction in output share. Following trade liberalization, these industries had to face stringent competition from foreign firms. At the same time because of various reasons, there has not been noticeable export expansion to counterbalance output losses due to import competition.

Export orientation

The Ethiopian manufacturing sector is predominantly domestic market oriented. There is no evidence to suggest that recent policy reforms have at least begun to change the long-standing domestic market dependence. According to the Survey of Medium and Large Scale Manufacturing conducted by the Central Statistical Authority, in 2000/01 total exports (Birr 77 million ($9.3 million)) accounted for only 9 percent of total sales turnover (Table 2.5). Processed and semi-processed leather accounted for almost two thirds of total manufacturing exports, with textiles, wearing apparel and other light manufacturing accounting for the balance. Almost 55 percent of total manufacturing exports are accounted for by SOEs.

According to official statistics, from 1996/97–2000/01 textile and garment exports grew at an average annual rate of 19 percent in value terms and at 6.1 percent volume terms. However, given the low starting base, their share in total exports remained around 0.5 percent during this

Table 2.4 Organized manufacturing in Ethiopia: sectoral composition of output (value added) and employment, and ownership structure, 1997/98 and 2000/01

Industry (SITC code)	Output (%)		Employment (%)		Public sector share in output		Public sector share in employment	
	1997	2000	1997	2000	1997	2000	1997	2000
Food and beverages (311–12)	27.6	29.2	35.6	49.6	90.6	83	69.9	56.7
Tobacco products (313)	1.0	0.9	5.4	2.4	100.0	100.0	100.0	100.0
Textiles (321)	26.9	26.0	7.9	6.4	98.3	67.4	97.9	69.0
Wearing apparel (321)	4.5	4.0	0.7	0.7	56.0	41.5	53.3	49.3
Footwear, luggage and handbags (323–4)	8.1	7.5	7.4	5.3	56.4	60.5	58.4	54.6
Wood and products of wood and cork except furniture (331)	1.4	1.1	1.1	0.7	95.3	94.4	88.4	88.8
Annex, Annex products and printing (341)	6.0	5.9	6.5	5.4	79.4	72.8	73.1	67.3
Chemicals and chemical products (351–2)	4.4	4.4	9.8	4.8	34.6	64.4	59.9	59.3
Rubber and plastic products (355–6)	3.3	3.6	5.0	5.5	76.8	68.8	48.7	41.3
Other non-metallic mineral products (361–9)	7.8	7.8	11.9	9.1	87.0	92.1	73.0	72.0
Basic iron and steel(371–2)	1.2	1.2	2.6	1.9	105.2	51.2	91.6	20.7
Fabricated metal products except machinery and equipment (381)	2.0	2.6	1.6	1.7	72.2	50.7	63.8	42.8
Machinery and equipment (382–3)	0.4	0.2	0.2	0.1	2.6	0.0	24.3	0.0
Motor vehicles (384)	1.0	1.1	1.5	4.7	7.6	47.2	34.9	19.1
Furniture and other (unclassified) manufacturing (332 + 390)	4.4	4.5	2.8	1.6	16.9	9.8	18.6	12.3
Total	100.0	100.0	100.0	100.0	78.9	75.9	72.9	57.4

Source: Compiled from Central Statistical Authority, Ethiopia, *Report on Large and Medium Scale Manufacturing* (various issues), Addis Ababa.

Table 2.5 Export performance of Ethiopian manufacturing, 2000/01

	Total sales, Birr '000	Exports, Birr '000	Export/sales ratio (%)	Export composition (%)	SOE share (%)
Food and beverages	3,271,440	206,018	6.3	26.4	98.83
Textiles	665,912	76,603	11.5	9.8	98.76
Wearing apparel	45,881	1,013	2.2	0.1	0.00
Leather and leather products	842,931	494,630	58.7	63.5	30.43
Other non-metallic mineral products	598,095	835	0.1	0.1	15.81
Total	8,017,446	779,099	9.7	100.0	55.18

Source: Compiled from Central Statistical Authority, Ethiopia, *Report on Large and Medium Scale Manufacturing*, Addis Ababa.

period. Exports of textiles were limited, by and large, to semi-processed gray fabrics and garment exports comprising predominantly of low-end outer garments. Ethiopia has a long way to go in benefiting from market opportunities available under the Lome Convention and the US African Growth Opportunity Act (AGOA).

Import intensity and linkages

As in many other developing countries, in Ethiopia the debate on national industrial policy has repeatedly emphasized high import dependence and the resultant low domestic linkages as a major weakness of domestic man-ufacturing. This has been a major consideration behind selectivity in tax concession and other incentives offered to different industries.

Of course, the greater the linkages between the export sectors and the rest of the economy, the greater would be the benefits to the economy from manufacturing expansion (provided such linkages are the natural outcome of industrial deepening). However, attempts to create linkages through direct policy intervention in the context of a labor abundant economy whose initial comparative advantage essentially lies in standard light manufactured goods and simple assembly activities can stifle the evo-lution of domestic manufacturing in line with changing patterns of inter-nationalization of production. This in turn will frustrate the achievement of employment and income growth objectives (Riedel 1974, 1976, Athuko-rala and Santosa 1999). There are two key considerations here.

First, intermediate goods industries are generally more capital intensive than are final goods industries. The importation of intermediate inputs for domestic production, therefore, involves an implicit substitution of labor for relatively capital-intensive intermediate products in the overall domestic production process. This would enhance the labor intensity, and hence employment potential, of domestic manufacturing. In an influential Annex on the Korean and Taiwanese industrialization success, Little (1981) put this point forcefully in the following words:

> Some critics have used the pejorative term "shallow" to describe the development [in the 1960s and 1970s] of Korea and Taiwan, by which is meant that there is relatively little backward linkages. In that case, development in depth must be declared the enemy of employment and equity. All labor-intensive sectors have their K/L ratios raised by backward linkages, because all the intermediaries – petrochemical, artificial fiber, steel, non-ferrous metals, etc. – are highly capital intensive. *These intermediaries are the curse of developing countries.*

Second, emphasis on achieving greater domestic content can run counter to the objective of increase in income levels through rapid market penetration in world trade. In contrast with the closed-economy approach of import-substitution industrialization, the key to success under export-oriented industrialization lies in a country's ability to produce what is demanded in international markets. Using imported input is essential in order to maintain high quality standards (and thus international competitiveness) in the end products.

Table 2.6 presents estimates of import intensity of input structure of Ethiopian medium and large-scale manufacturing. The share of intermediate inputs in total manufacturing has varied in the rage of 51 to 54 percent during this period. The concern that this ratio is "too high" is often made without any discussion on how it can be lowered, let alone discussing the likely economic implications of forced import substitution. The estimates relating to the two-digit industries warrant two important inferences. First, high (above-average) import ratios are for highly capital intensive (and state-dominated) industries such as iron and steel, metal products, machinery and transport equipment. Domestic production of intermediate inputs for these industries cannot be encouraged unless the government is prepared to give excessively high tariff protection or direct production subsidies. A part from the well-known efficiency implications involved, such policy is not consistent with the process of outward-oriented policy reforms. Second, and more important, the industries that have low import ratios are the relatively labor-intensive sectors, in particular textiles, clothing, leather goods, footwear and other manufactured goods. Low import dependence of these industries is simply a reflection of the lingering effects of forced industrialization in the communist era. Under an increasingly liberal trade regime, these industries cannot survive (that is, they cannot face import competition and/or expand exports) without increasing the use of high quality imported inputs. This point receives added force when we compare the Ethiopian import intensity figures for these industries with those for some Asian countries (Table 2.7).

Table 2.6 Share of imported inputs in total inputs used in domestic manufacturing

	1994/95	1995/96	1996/97	1997/98	1998/99
Food and beverages	12.1	20.7	17.4	18.4	29.5
Tobacco products	82.2	94.4	84.4	72.7	85.9
Textiles	56.4	38.3	36.7	35.7	34.9
Wearing apparel	39.0	40.0	30.9	44.0	29.8
Footwear, luggage and handbags	15.1	21.1	22.6	19.5	33.6
Wood and products of wood and cork except furniture	44.3	42.9	45.4	53.7	51.1
Annex, Annex products and printing	67.9	70.9	70.4	68.7	72.7
Chemicals and chemical products	75.5	77.4	75.1	73.5	78.5
Rubber and plastic products	93.8	95.0	94.7	93.4	92.6
Other non-metallic mineral products	53.8	41.8	30.7	36.1	22.1
Basic iron and steel	97.4	99.3	99.4	99.0	98.7
Fabricated metal products except machinery and equipment	84.3	90.1	93.0	90.7	90.8
Machinery and equipment	90.2	68.6	90.0	76.9	66.8
Motor vehicles	91.0	91.5	85.1	92.3	93.1
Furniture and manufacturing	30.1	21.2	22.4	32.5	32.6
Total	45.9	47.6	44.2	43.4	53.6

Source: Data obtained from Central Statistics Authority.

Table 2.7 Share of imported inputs in total material inputs in labor intensive industries: Malaysia, Indonesia, Sri Lanka, Thailand, Taiwan and Ethiopia

		Textiles	Wearing apparel	Footwear	Other light mfg
Malaysia	1991	56.9	63.6	58.2	68.7
Indonesia	1990	54.5	54.3	63.2	45.1
Sri Lanka	1991	70.4	87.2	78.2	52.3
Thailand	1985	51.5	65.2	74.2	49.3
Taiwan	1975	72.0	62.3	84.2	67.3
Ethiopia	1985	63.2	52.2	68.5	53.4
Ethiopia	1995	47.3	41.2	60.2	41.2

Source: Computed from input–output tables for each country for the given years.

Productivity performance

This section examines productivity performance of Ethiopian manufacturing during the post-reform period focusing on both labor productivity and total factor productivity. The analysis also explores the relative importance of total factor productivity and factor accumulation in output growth, and the role played by capital deepening compared to total factor productivity growth (TFPG) in determining labor productivity growth (LPG). The methodology of measuring productivity growth, data sources and the method of data compilation are discussed in Appendix 2.1. Table 2.8

Table 2.8 Ethiopia: decomposition of output growth in large- and medium-scale manufacturing, 1993–2001

	Output growth (Y)	Growth of labor (L)	Growth of capital (K)	L's share in output	K's share in output	Contribution of L to output growth	Contribution of K to output growth	TFPG
	1	2	3	4	5	6 = 2 * 4	7 = 3 * 5	7 = 1 − 6 − 7
Food and Beverages	11.4	2.4	23.7	0.20	0.80	0.48	19.02	−7.8
Tobacco products	−3.5	−2.2	29.5	0.12	0.88	−0.28	25.88	−29.2
Textiles	−2.4	−2.5	4.3	0.63	0.37	−1.58	1.57	−2.1
Wearing apparel	−8.0	−0.4	10.5	0.69	0.31	−0.27	3.24	−10.8
Footwear, luggage and handbags	−3.5	1.5	29.3	0.30	0.70	0.43	20.64	−23.9
Wood and products of wood and cork except furniture	−3.1	−12.6	−2.0	0.35	0.65	−4.48	−1.30	3.1
Annex, Annex products and printing	5.2	2.8	19.1	0.32	0.68	0.87	13.03	−8.5
Chemicals and chemical products	7.5	10.1	37.8	0.19	0.81	1.89	30.72	−24.5
Rubber and plastic products	10.8	8.0	2.0	0.20	0.80	1.62	1.57	7.5
Non-metallic mineral products	15.7	10.2	−0.6	0.19	0.81	1.99	−0.49	14.1
Basic iron and steel	8.0	−0.4	33.8	0.21	0.79	−0.09	26.84	−17.1
Fabricated metal products	8.7	5.7	1.5	0.38	0.62	2.21	0.91	5.4
Machinery and equipment	−2.5	−6.3	−6.8	0.53	0.47	−3.36	−3.18	4.0
Motor vehicles	13.6	13.3	15.7	0.13	0.87	1.76	13.63	−1.7
Furniture and other (unclassified) manufacturing	11.9	13.5	30.9	0.43	0.57	5.79	17.69	−11.4
Total	7.0	1.6	13.2	0.25	0.75	0.42	9.7	−2.9

Source: As Table 2.6.

provides a decomposition of output growth into the respective contributions of input (capital and labor) growth and TFPG. Table 2.9 decomposes LPG into TFPG and the contribution of capital deepening.

Average annual total factor productivity growth (TFPG) in total manufacturing during this period is estimated at −2.9 percent and annual
figures show wide fluctuations with only three of the seven years recording
positive growth (Table 2.8). The average annual growth rate of 7.1
percent has come from growth in factor inputs (labor and capital) which
more than compensated for negative TFPG. More importantly, it was
capital accumulation that accounted for 9.42 percent of the 7.2 percent
growth rate in output. The contribution of labor was a mere 0.42 percent.
Among the 15 two-digit ISIS industries, only four industries exhibited
positive average TFPG. These are rubber and plastic, non-metallic minerals, fabricated metal products, and machinery and equipment.

There are two possible explanations for the poor TFPG performance.
First, it may reflect invariable adjustment lags. These lags can be fairly
long in an economy like Ethiopia's where reforms were undertaken
following a long period of central planning, which had virtually decimated
the private sector in the economy. It would naturally take a long time for
the private sector to come to terms with the new economic setting.

Table 2.9 Decomposition of labor productivity growth, 1993/94–2000/01

Industry	TFPG	Capital deepening	LPG
	1	*2*	*3 = 1 + 2*
Food and beverages	−7.8	16.8	9.0
Tobacco products	−29.2	28.0	−1.2
Textiles	−2.1	2.2	0.1
Wearing apparel	−10.8	3.2	−7.6
Footwear, luggage and handbags	−23.9	18.9	−5.0
Wood and products of wood and cork except furniture	3.1	6.4	9.5
Annex, Annex products and printing	−8.5	10.9	2.5
Chemicals and chemical products	−24.5	21.8	−2.6
Rubber and plastic products	7.5	−4.7	2.8
Non-metallic mineral products	14.1	−8.6	5.5
Basic iron and steel	−17.1	25.4	8.4
Fabricated metal products except machinery and equipment	5.4	−2.4	3.0
Machinery and equipment	4.0	−0.2	3.8
Motor vehicles	−1.7	2.0	0.3
Furniture and other (unclassified) manufacturing	−11.4	9.8	−1.6
Total	−2.9	8.4	5.5

Source: As Table 2.6.

Second, and perhaps more importantly, the liberalization process has not yet been deep enough to generate the anticipated improvement in manu-facturing performance, particularly through private sector participation. Significant trade opening, exchange rate reforms and sound macroeco-nomic management since 1992 have not been matched by adequate reforms to rejuvenate the role of the private sector in the economy. From 1993/94–2000/01 labor productivity in domestic medium- and large-scale manufacturing grew at an average annual rate of 5.5 percent compared to 7.1 percent rate of output (value added) growth (Table 2.9).

At two-digit International Standard Industry Classification (ISIC) level, food and beverages, non-metallic mineral products, basic iron and steel products, and fabricated metal products indicated above-average labor productivity growth. Wearing apparel, textile, leather product and footwear recorded low labor productivity growth. Most of the sectors with negative or low labor productivity growth are sectors whose production process is more labor intensive. As discussed below, the apparent positive relationship between capital-intensity of production and labor productiv-ity growth simply reflect the fact that labor productivity growth in Ethiopian manufacturing during the post-reform period has largely emanated from capital deepening (increase in capital per worker) rather than genuine productivity growth.

The estimates reported in Table 2.9 clearly demonstrate the rather deceptive nature of labor productivity growth as an indicator of productiv-ity performance. In a context where trade liberalization reforms open up opportunities to invest in plant and machinery, labor productivity growth can emanate from capital deepening even if total factor productivity growth is negative. From 1993/94–2000/01, 5.5 percent growth of labor productivity in Ethiopian manufacturing emanated from 8.4 percent annual rate of capital deepening which overwhelmed *contraction* in TFPG by −2.9 percent (Table 2.10). This pattern is observable across all two-digit industries.

The degree of private sector participation in the four industries with positive TFPG (rubber and plastic, non-metallic minerals, fabricated metal products, and machinery and equipment) are generally higher than that of total manufacturing. It is also evident that SOE-dominated sectors have generally experienced negative TFPG of greater magnitudes. There are however two notable exceptions to this overall pattern. These are the garment and leather product industries. The garment industry faced stiff import competition during the post-reform era. At the same time, there was no significant export orientation of the industry to compensate for output contraction caused by import competition. The leather product sector is heavily reliant on primary processing of hide and skins, world demand for which has been deteriorating persistently in recent years. Moreover, because of stiff import competition, a large number of firms in the footwear and leather goods subsectors (mostly domestic market ori-

Table 2.10 Manufacturing employment and related data

	1991–92	1992–93	1993–94	1994–95	1995–96	1996–97	1997–98	1998–99	1999–2000	2000–2001	1993–2001
Employment (no. of workers)	82,644	82,082	88,242	90,213	90,039	92,365	93,216	93,678	95,007	93,515	92,034
Employment growth (%)	–	-0.7	7.2	2.2	-0.2	2.6	0.9	0.5	1.4	-1.6	1.6
Growth of real output (value added)[1] (%)	–	44.0	11.9	6.1	5.7	5.0	-9.3	15.7	20.7	1.1	7.1
Fixed capital per worker (Birr at 1991/92 price)	12,040	14,521	16,158	15,193	17,183	20,028	21,842	26,807	31,912	36,578	–
Nominal wage per worker (Birr per year)	3,379	4,113	4,516	4,726	5,076	5,301	5,474	5,892	6,336	7,028	5,544
Nominal wage index (1991/92 = 100)	100.0	121.7	133.6	139.8	150.2	156.9	162.0	174.4	187.5	208.0	164.0
CPI (1991/92 = 100)	100.0	110.5	114.5	123.1	135.5	128.6	131.7	135.1	145.7	146.7	132.6
Real wage index (1991/92 = 100)	100.0	110.1	116.8	113.6	110.9	122.0	123.0	129.1	128.7	141.8	123.2
Labor share in value added[2] (%)	42.7	32.9	28.0	26.5	24.4	24.0	26.9	22.7	21.3	22.5	24.5
Operating surplus (%)	3.3	14.0	19.7	18.6	19.6	19.9	16.0	18.9	20.6	20.3	19.2

Source: Compiled from Central Statistical Authority, Ethiopia, *Report on Large and Medium Scale Manufacturing*, Addis Ababa.

Notes
1 At factor cost.
2 Wage bill as a percentage of value added at factor cost.

ented) have downscaled their operation or closed down. Ethiopia is yet to exploit fully its comparative advantage in the production of leather goods for the export market.

Employment

Total employment in organized manufacturing grew from 82,600 workers in 1991/92 to 93,500 in 2000/01 (Table 2.10). Employment growth has however lagged behind output growth throughout. Annual average employment growth during the period 1992/93–2000/01 was 1.6 percent compared to 7.1 percent growth in real output. This comparison clearly suggests that the Ethiopian manufacturing sector is still locked in capital-intensive sectors (mostly dominated by public enterprises). An already noted output expansion in the post-reform years has occurred mostly in capital-intensive sectors. Capital per worker (at constant 1991/92 price) recorded a threefold increase between 1991/92 and 2000/01 (from Birr 12,000 to Birr 26,500). Labor intensive sectors grew slowly or even recorded output contraction. Of particular importance is the massive contraction in the employment share of the SOE-dominated textile industry.

The post-reform period has been characterized by modest wage growth. Between 1992/93 and 2000/01 nominal wages increased by about 6.1 percent and real wages (nominal wages deflated by CPI) by 2.3 percent. Given massive unemployment in the urban economy, these wage increases seem to suggest significant "administered" wage increases (discretionary wage adjustment) in the manufacturing sector. However, given the low initial wages, these wage increases have not resulted in erosion in manufacturing profitability. The labor share in value added in fact declined persistently from 43 percent in 1991/92 to 21 percent in 2000/01. The operation surplus in manufacturing (value added at factor cost less wages as a percentage of gross value of production at market price) has also increased throughout, though with mild year to year fluctuations, from 3.3 percent to 20.3 percent between these two years. These points together provide some support for the view that reform has not benefited the poor in Ethiopia.

The share of private sector firms in total employment has increased at a much faster rate than their share in total output (see Table 2.4). SOE share in total employment declined from 72.9 percent in 1996/97 to 57.4 percent in 2000/1. At the two-digit level industry classification, this decline is SOE share in employment is observable in all sectors except wood and wood products, with metal products, motor vehicles, furniture, textiles, Annex and Annex products, rubber and plastic products indicating notable rates of decline. The relatively higher employment share gain of private sector firms (at a faster rate compared to output shares) seems to suggest that production processes of the emerging private sector firms are relatively more labor intensive compared to their SOE counterparts.

A definitive analysis of this important development is not possible using the available secondary data. However, the available data on size distribution of farms do suggest that across all industrial sectors private sector firms are generally at the lower end of the size distribution (more conducive for labor intensive activities).

Conclusion

Following the reforms initiated in 1992 there has been a notable improvement in manufacturing output growth in the Ethiopian economy. High growth during early post-reform years (1993 and 1994 in particular) partly reflected "natural" recovery of a war-devastated economy, but even after allowing for this, on average the post-reform growth record remains impressive compared to the 1980–88 period. However, these growth figures mask poor performance of the manufacturing sectors in terms of other key indicators, in particular employment and productivity performance. Employment growth in manufacturing has lagged behind output growth throughout. Annual average employment growth during the period 1992/93–2000/01 was 1.6 percent compared to 7.1 percent growth in real output. This comparison clearly suggests that the Ethiopian manufacturing sector is still locked in capital-intensive sectors (mostly dominated by public enterprises). The post-reform period has also seen rapid growth in real wages. Given massive unemployment in the urban economy, these wage increases seem to suggest significant "administered" wage increases (discretionary wage adjustment) in the manufacturing sector. From 1993/94–2000/01, labor productivity in domestic medium- and large-scale manufacturing grew at an average annual rate of 5.5 percent. This was however the outcome of capital deepening rather than "true" productivity improvement.

There are two possible explanations for the lackluster performance during the post-reform period. First, it may reflect invariable adjustment lags. These lags can be long in an economy like Ethiopia's where reforms were undertaken following a long period of central planning, which had virtually decimated the private sector in the economy. It would naturally take a long time for the private sector to come to terms with the new economic setting. Second, and perhaps more importantly, the liberalization process has not yet been deep enough to generate the anticipated improvement in manufacturing performance. In particular, the privatization scheme has lagged far behind its performance target and the private sector is in a very rudimentary stage to respond to this measure. As has been demonstrated by the experiences of successful reforming countries in the region (such as Mali, Mozambique and Uganda), a firm commitment to the implementation of a privatization program can play a pivotal role in building up private sector confidence and making the reform process credible.

Ethiopian policy makers, like their counterparts in many other developing countries, seem to place a big emphasis on domestic input linkages/value added in formulating industrial development policy. Of course the greater, the linkages between the export sectors and the rest of the economy the greater would be the benefits to the economy from export expansion (provided such linkages are the natural outcome of industrial deepening). However, attempts to create linkages through direct policy intervention can stifle the evolution of domestic manufacturing in line with changing patterns of internationalization of production. This in turn will frustrate the achievement of employment and income growth objectives. With the gradual depletion of the excess supply of labor and adjustment of the domestic cost structure as a result of greater international specialization, the industrial structure will gradually shift over to more capital and skill-intensive industries. This will lead to strong inter-industry linkages, provided of course that the general business climate of the economy continues to remain conducive for such specialization.

Appendix 2.1

Productivity performance: concepts and measurement

The most widely used (and the oldest) indicator of factor productivity is *labor productivity*, measured as production (normally value added) per unit of labor input:

$$LP = \frac{Y}{L} \tag{1}$$

where
LP = labor productivity
Y = output
L = labor inputs

The rate of growth of labor productivity between two points in time (LPG) can be approximated as the deference between the rate of growth of value added (V) and the rate of growth of number of workers (L):

$$LPG = \hat{V} - \hat{L} \tag{2}$$

where $\hat{V}$ and $\hat{L}$ are the corresponding growth rates.

It is evident from equation (2) that, by definition, labor productivity growth is simply *the residual growth in value added after accounting for growth of labor inputs (employment)*. In other words, when we talk about growth of labor productivity, we implicitly focus on output growth due to an increase in the value of goods produced by the average worker (or, the increased efficiency of the average worker). However, in reality, workers may produce more, not because of their increased efficiency but simply because they have better machinery (more capital) to work with. Put simply, the problem with labor productivity as a measure of efficiency of workers is that it spuriously captures change in capital per worker as part of the measured productivity.

The concept of total factor productivity growth (TFPG) avoids this limitation. TFPG is the residual growth in output after accounting for growth of both labor and capital inputs. TFPG can be estimated in a number of ways. Perhaps the most widely used and also intuitively appealing technique is the Tornquist-Theil formulation which measures TFPG as the difference between the rate of growth of output and the rate of growth of labor (L) and capital (K), the latter being weighted by their respective share in the value of production.[9]

$$TFPG_t = \hat{Y} - \alpha\hat{K}_t - \beta\hat{L}_u \tag{3}$$

where, α and β are average input shares. Note that $\beta = 1 - \alpha$.

The relationship between LPG and TFPG can be clarified by rearranging Equation (3) in the following form:

$$LPG = TFPG + \beta(\hat{K} - \hat{L}) \tag{4}$$

Equation (3) says that the rate of growth of labor productivity (*LPG*) is determined by two factors: total factor productivity growth (*TFPG*) (the first term on the right-hand side) and the change in the mix of labor and capital used in the production process weighted by the capital share in output (the second term). The latter term tells that labor productivity (or output per worker) tends to increase when capital inputs increase at a faster rate than labor inputs (that is when $\hat{K}$ is larger in magnitude relative to $\hat{L}$, or when the production process tends to become more capital intensive). Conversely, an increase in labor inputs at a higher rate than capital inputs (that is when $\hat{L}$ is larger in magnitude relative to $\hat{K}$, or when the production process tends to become more labor intensive) is reflected in a decline in labor productivity growth.

Thus, Equation (4) clearly points to the limitation involved in the use of LPG as the sole indicator of productivity. A decrease in measured labor productivity could well be a reflection of a *decrease* in capital input per employee (or *increase* in labor absorption per given unit of capital) rather than a decrease in "true" productivity as measured by TFPG. For instance, as part of structural adjustment in domestic manufacturing in response to trade liberalization, measured labor productivity (output per worker) could well decline as labor is substituted for capital in existing enterprises, or employment growth takes place in labor intensive industries and new enterprises in response to change in relative factor prices. Such an increase in the degree of labor intensity of production and the consequent decline in labor productivity are simply "positive" (rather than a "negative") effects of market-oriented reforms (as it implies increase in employment potential of domestic manufacturing).

LPG and TFPG are estimated using data compiled from the Annual Survey of Large and Medium Scale Manufacturing conducted by the Ethiopian Central Statistical Authority. The surveys seem to cover over 95 percent of total output in the organized (medium- and large-scale) manufacturing in the country. The output measure used is value added at factor cost. Capital is measured in terms of book value of net fixed assets at the end of each year. Labor input is measured as the number of persons employed. The Survey reports the number of workers after appropriately converting part-time workers into full-time equivalence. A more meaningful measure of labor input is of course hours worked; the number of employees can be a misleading indicator if average hours worked change over time. We do not consider this a serious limitation as there have not been significant changes relating to standard working hours or relative importance of part-time employment in total employment during the period under study. Nominal capital stock and output data are deflated using GDP deflators for manufacturing value added and gross domestic fixed capital formation derived from the Ethiopian national accounts (available online from the World Bank *World Development Indicator Database*). The time period covered is from 1992/93 to 2001/01.

Notes

1 Computed from World Bank Trade and Production database.
2 Of course there are other factors, such as changes in technology and in world prices, which can affect gross output, independently of the impact of the domestic trade regime.
3 US Department of State, *Country Briefing on Ethiopia.*
4 The schemes were announced in 1993 but the Ministry of Finance issued implementing directives only three years later.
5 Only banks and investors with a foreign exchange demand of above USD 500,000 are allowed to participate in weekly auctions conducted by the Central Bank. All other importers are allowed to purchase from commercial banks.
6 Throughout this chapter, the "year" is the Ethiopian fiscal year based on the Gregorian calendar, that is July 1 of the *stated year* to June 30 the next year.
7 For the purpose of growth rate comparison in this paragraph, the turbulent years from 1989 to 1992 (inclusive) are excluded for obvious reasons. The war between the EPRDF and the military government reached a climax during 1989–91, resulting in severe disruption of domestic economic activity. The economic scene regained normalcy under the new regime only from late 1992.
8 A comparison of the post-reform manufacturing performance with that in the pre-reform years however needs to be qualified for the fact that the share of manufacturing in GDP in the latter period may have reflected the distorted domestic prices arising from the protectionist regime.

9 The only assumption required to justify the use of the Tornquist-Theil is that firms pursue profit maximization and/or cost minimization, and hence market return is a good approximation to the marginal product of a factor. No assumption about the properties of the underlying production function is required: production parameters are taken to be subsumed in expenditure (input) and revenue (output).

3 Trade, growth, poverty and equity in Kenya

Kunal Sen

Since gaining independence from Great Britain in 1963, Kenya followed an import-substituting industrialization strategy for the next two decades. Since the early 1980s, Kenya has liberalized its trade regime, though progress on opening up the economy has been uneven, with rapid liberalization often followed by some reversal of reforms. However, by the end of the 1990s, Kenya had witnessed among the largest absolute reductions in tariff rates among developing countries, and had a considerably more liberal trade regime than it had in the early 1980s.

What has been the impact of Kenya's increased integration with the world economy on its economic performance? Has the trade reform process observed in Kenya for two decades led to a reduction in poverty and inequality? This chapter examines the impact of Kenya's increased trade-openness on economic performance, inequality and poverty.

An overview of trade policies

The Kenyan economy performed well in the period 1964–80 with the GDP growth rate averaging around 5.5 per cent per annum during this period. The manufacturing sector grew at a rapid pace, at 10 per cent per annum, fuelled by growth in domestic rural incomes and the expansion of exports to Tanzanian and Uganda under the common market created by the East African Community (EAC).

In the late 1970s, the Kenyan economy was hit by several shocks one after another. First, there was the boom and bust cycle in coffee and tea prices in 1976–79. Second, the EAC broke up in 1977, denying Kenyan exporters preferential access to Ugandan and Tanzanian markets. Third was the oil price shock of 1979. These shocks contributed to a widening of the current account deficit from 3 per cent of GDP in 1975–77 to 10–11 per cent in 1978–82.

A structural adjustment programme was introduced in 1979 that, among other measures, called for eliminating barriers to foreign trade and foreign investment. Furthermore, steps would be taken to promote export-led growth instead of import substitution by reducing protection and controls on access to foreign exchange, adopting a flexible exchange rate policy and providing additional incentives to exporters. In June 1982, one fifth of restricted items were freed from import licensing (World Bank, 1987). Subsequently, there was limited progress with respect to the liberalization of the trade regime with many of the strict controls on the importation of goods remaining in place. On the exchange rate front, there was a series of devaluations in 1982, with the exchange rate at the end of 1982 being 14.06 Ksh to 1 US dollar, as compared to 9.66 Ksh to 1 US dollar in 1981.[1] Trade reforms started picking up pace in the late 1980s with the conversion of quantitative restrictions to tariff equivalents, starting in 1987. In 1990, the government embarked on a phased tariff reduction (particularly in the high-rate bands) and a rationalization of tariff bands (Glenday and Ryan, 2000). Perhaps the most significant policy change in the 1990s was the revocation of import licensing schedules (other than for health, safety and security reasons) in May 1993. However, the trade liberalization process was interrupted by an economic crisis in 1997, following the collapse of an IMF programme, election spending-related budgetary crisis and exchange rate instability (Glenday and Ndii, 1999).

The possible beneficial effects that trade reforms might have had on economic performance in Kenya has been considerably lessened by major slippages in macroeconomic policy in the early 1980s and then again in the early 1990s, leading to high inflation and an appreciation of the real exchange rate during these two periods. At the same time, the trade reforms have proceeded at an uneven pace, with periods of rapid opening up followed by periods of stagnancy or reversal in trade liberalization.[2] The trade volume openness measure (exports + imports as a per cent of GDP) for Kenya also shows no clear trend, with an increase in the late 1980s followed by a sharp decline since 1993 (Figure 3.1). The decline in the openness measure in the late 1990s seems to be driven both by a fall in exports and imports as percentages of GDP.

It should be noted that while the (exports + imports)/GDP measure seems to indicate a decline in openness, recent studies that attempt to classify countries according to the degree of openness of the economy rank Kenya as among the fastest globalizing countries in the developing world. Dollar and Kraay (2002) place Kenya among the top globalizers among developing countries in the post-1985 period based on absolute declines in average tariff rates.[3] Similarly, Rodrik (2000) finds that Kenya is among the ten countries with the largest proportionate cuts in tariff since the early 1980s. This suggests that while Kenya has followed a path of rapid integration with the world economy in terms of deep trade reforms over the 1980s and 1990s, this has not been reflected in terms of outcomes, at least with respect to greater openness of the economy according to the trade volume measure.

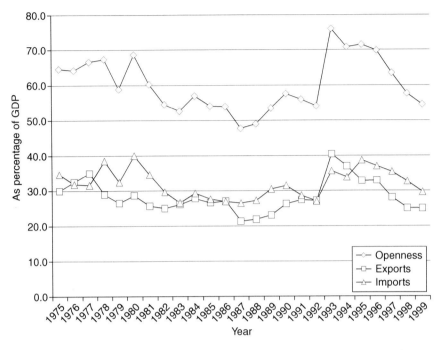

Figure 3.1 Exports and imports as per cent of GDP and openness, Kenya, 1975–98
(source: International Monetary Fund, *International Financial Statistics*,
various years).

Trade and economic performance

Economic growth in Kenya in the 1980s and 1990s has been relatively
weak compared to the 1970s (Table 3.1). In particular, economic growth
in the 1990s has been fairly dismal, with an average rate of growth of 1.9
per cent per annum. Slow growth of output can also be observed both in
the agricultural and industrial sectors in the same period. Thus, the *prima
facie* case seems to be that trade openness has not had the desirable positive effect on economic growth that has been found in cross-country
studies (Dollar and Kraay, 2002). To investigate the trade–growth relationship more systematically, we estimate a simple equation using Ordinary
Least Squares, regressing changes in the GDP growth on changes in trade
volumes as a ratio of GDP (as a measure of changes in trade policy), along
with two variables commonly used in the literature on the empirics of economic growth – changes in the ratio of government consumption to GDP
and the inflation rate (taken as log(1 + inflation rate)), see Dollar and
Kraay (2002).[4] The results are summarized in Table 3.2. We find that the
coefficient on trade-openness is statistically insignificant, suggesting that
there is no clear relationship between openness (trade volume) and eco-

Table 3.1 Growth rates of output (annual, per cent)

	1970–75	1975–80	1980–85	1985–90	1990–95	1995–2000
GDP growth	8.9	5.4	2.8	5.7	1.6	2.2
Manufacturing value added growth	15.4	7.1	4.0	5.6	2.8	1.7
Agriculture value added growth	4.0	5.1	2.5	4.4	−0.2	1.8

Source: World Bank (1993, 2002a).

Table 3.2 Regression results – trade and growth

Variable	Coefficient value	t-ratio
Trade openness	0.063	0.77
Inflation rate	−3.48	−4.04
Government consumption	−1.25	−1.57
R-square	0.31	–
Durbin Watson statistic	2.18	–

Note
Dependent variable is change in the growth rate of GDP; all independent variables entered in first-differenced form.

nomic growth in the Kenyan context.[5] The other variables included in the regression are of the right sign – increases in government consumption and inflation have a negative effect on economic growth, but only the inflation rate is statistically significant.

Another indicator of economic performance is the change in the structure of exports – ideally, trade reforms should bring about changes in the latter towards high growth commodities, and a more diversified export basket. We note that there has been a significant increase in the share of horticultural exports in total exports, while the share of coffee in total exports has fallen over time (Table 3.3). However, there has been little diversification in the export basket towards manufacturing exports, as the share of other exports (including manufacturing exports) in total exports has remained relatively stable over time.

Table 3.3 Structure of exports (per cent share)

Commodity	1980–85	1985–90	1990–94	1994–98
Coffee	24	29	15	14
Tea	17	22	26	22
Horticulture	–	2	12	11
Others	59	47	48	53

Source: Republic of Kenya, *Statistical Abstracts*, various issues, Kenya.

Employment trends for the period 1988–98 for the entire economy indicate a large increase in overall employment, but much of this increase is in the informal sectors of rural and urban areas (Figure 3.2). There has been very little increase in employment in the modern sector. Given that wages in the informal sector tend to be lower than those observed in the modern sector, and that working conditions are inferior in the informal sector, most of the job creation in the Kenyan economy in the 1990s could be said to be of low quality and would not necessarily improve the living standards of households in rural and urban areas. The dismal record of the modern sector in Kenya with respect to employment generation in the 1990s provides further confirmation that the trade reforms of the 1980s and 1990s have not had any appreciable positive impact on economic performance in Kenya, both with respect to growth in output and employment.

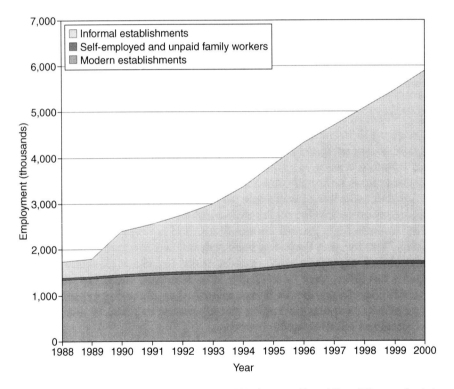

Figure 3.2 Trends in employment, 1988–2000 (source: Republic of Kenya, *Statistical Abstracts*, various issues).

Note: Employment in informal and modern establishments is for both rural and urban areas combined.

Trade and income inequality

An increase in openness can impact on income inequality in two ways. First, the net effect of international trade on living standards may not be the same across different regions of the country. Some regions may benefit from the country's increasing integration with the world economy more than others; if these regions possess better trade-related infrastructure or have inherent advantages in the location of the exporting sectors. This may imply that with greater openness, inequality in living standards across regions may increase, with the more favourably endowed regions seeing greater improvements in living standards than the poorly endowed regions. Second, trade reforms may impact on income inequality between individuals. Trade reforms can bring about a shift in the structure of production towards more unskilled labour intensive sectors in countries which have plentiful endowments of unskilled labour, and so lead to a fall in wage inequality. However, it is also possible that trade reforms may induce the shift in production techniques towards the greater use of skilled labour relative to unskilled labour, thereby worsening wage inequality in the country in question (Wood, 1994).

Regional inequality in Kenya does not show a clear pattern over the period 1980–98 (Table 3.4). While there is increasing divergence in wages in the Central, Nyanza and Eastern regions from wage earnings in the Coastal region, there has been some convergence in wages of the Western and North East regions to that of the Central region. Wages in Rift Valley – the richest of the seven regions – have moved closer to the national average.

There is also no clear evidence on increasing rural–urban disparities in living standards in Kenya in the 1980s and 1990s. Sahn and Stifel (2003) find that Kenya's rural–urban disparities in indicators of living standards is below the average for Sub-Saharan African countries – for example, with respect to asset poverty, rural–urban disparities is the lowest in Kenya in a sample of 24 African countries studied by the two authors. Moreover,

Table 3.4 Trends in regional inequality

Region	1985	1998
Central	80	71
Nyanza	58	51
Western	39	49
Rift Valley	118	110
Eastern	52	49
North Eastern	6	7

Source: Republic of Kenya, *Statistical Abstracts*, various issues, Kenya.

Note
Wage earnings of each region as a ratio of wage earnings of Coastal region.

Sahn and Stifel (2003) find that over the period 1983–98, welfare has not improved more in urban areas compared to rural areas in Kenya in indicators of living standards and well-being such as asset poverty, school enrolments, mortality rates and child stunting.

Trends in wage inequality do, however, suggest a different pattern. First, real wages in Kenya have declined from the late 1970s up to the mid-1990s when it started to increase again (Table 3.5). In the year 2000 real wages were lower than the levels for 1986, but higher than for 1995. However, real wages for individuals with no education continued to decline after 1986. In contrast, real wages of the most educated workers increased at the fastest rate between 1995 and 2000 (the ratio of real earnings of university-educated workers to that of uneducated workers increased from 5.8 in 1995 to 11.5 in 2000). This indicates that there has been a sharp increase in inequality of earnings in the Kenyan manufacturing labour force, particularly since 1995, along with a loss in the real earnings of uneducated workers since 1986. Define individuals with university education as highly skilled employees, individuals with secondary education as semi-skilled and those with primary education and without education as being unskilled. Then, we can conclude that highly skilled employees gained significantly more than the less skilled and unskilled workers during the period of increased openness, and unskilled workers in fact have experienced a decline in their real earnings in the post-trade reform period. However, it is not clear to what extent trade openness can be taken as a causal factor in the increase in wage inequality observed in

Table 3.5 Trends in real earnings in the manufacturing sector[a]

Variables	1978	1986	1995	2000
All	3,453	3,021	2,027	2,802
Uneducated	1,602	1,987	1,418	1,205
Standard 1–4	2,041	2,300	1,576	1,618
Standard 5–8	2,275	2,048	1,456	1,639
Form 1–2	3,194	2,658	2,038	1,973
Form 3–4	5,260	3,133	2,038	2,533
Form 5–6	7,694	7,012	2,061	4,699
University	15,722	14,965	8,279	13,880
Ratio, earnings of university educated to uneducated	9.8	7.5	5.8	11.5
No. of observations	186	312	1,123	1,016

Sources: Appleton *et al.* (1999) and Manda and Sen (2004).

Note

a The observations are from matched worker–firm surveys. The results from the surveys of 1976 and 1978 are reported in Appleton *et al.* (1999); the estimates for 1995 are from the Regional Programme on Enterprise Development (RPED) survey for 1993–95, and the 2000 estimates are from the Kenyan Manufacturing Enterprise Survey (KMES) carried out in the same year. All variables in real Kenyan shillings (the base year of the Consumer Price Index is 1990).

the 1990s as there was also significant deregulation of the labour market in the same period. The relaxation of the wage guidelines made it possible for employees and firms to negotiate and change the level of wages on the basis of productivity and performance, rather than on the basis of cost of living indices as was hitherto the case (Ikiara and Ndung'u, 1997). Furthermore, the amendment of redundancy laws allowed firms to fire redundant workers when necessary without having to seek the approval of the Ministry of Labour. The increased flexibility in labour practices may also have a contributing role in the increase in wage inequality observed in the Kenyan manufacturing sector in the 1990s.

Trade and poverty

Poverty in Kenya has been increasing over time, particularly between the years 1994 and 1997 (Table 3.6). This phenomenon has occurred in almost all regions and in both rural and urban areas (except the rural Central region). The overall poverty rate stands at 52.3 per cent in 1997. What is remarkable has been the increase in urban poverty from 28.9 per cent in 1994 to 52.3 per cent in 1997 – a close to doubling in the proportion of households below the poverty line in a period of merely three years. It is difficult to state to what extent trade reform has been responsible for the increase in poverty in the late 1990s. It is quite possible to

Table 3.6 Headcount poverty rates by region and over time

	1992	*1994*	*1997*
Rural			
Central	35.9	31.9	31.4
Coastal	43.5	55.6	62.1
Eastern	42.2	57.8	58.6
Nyanza	47.4	42.2	63.1
Rift Valley	51.5	42.9	50.1
Western	54.8	53.8	58.8
North Eastern	–	58.0	–
Total rural	47.9	46.8	52.9
Urban			
Nairobi	26.5	25.9	50.2
Mombassa	39.2	33.1	38.3
Kisumu	–	47.8	63.7
Nakuru	–	30.0	40.6
Other Towns	–	28.7	43.5
Total urban	29.3	28.9	49.2
Total Kenya	44.8	40.3	52.3

Source: *Poverty in Kenya: Incidence and Depth of Poverty*, Ministry of Finance and Planning, 2000.

argue that the sharp increase in the urban poverty rate is due to heightened macroeconomic and political instability in the 1990s, which may have negatively affected the growth of manufacturing output (and consequently, employment) in urban areas.

To assess the impact of international trade on poverty in a more systematic manner, we bring together available quantitative evidence on whether trade liberalization in Kenya has led to a net creation of jobs, in both the manufacturing and agricultural sectors.

Has trade openness led to an increase in manufacturing employment?

We first address the relationship between international trade and manufacturing employment in Kenya. In analysing this relationship, we employ three approaches. These are the factor content approach, the growth accounting approach and a regression-based approach. Factor content studies have been widely used, both in order to test theories of international trade and to estimate the employment effects of trade, particularly between developed and developing countries, and provide a useful way of analysing the overall effects of trade changes on the utilization of labour (Lawrence, 1996). The growth accounting approach decomposes changes in employment into the parts accounted for by changes in domestic demand, changes in exports, changes in imports and productivity growth (further details of this approach are provided in Jenkins, 2004). The third approach that has been used in studies of the impact of trade on employment is to regress employment at the industry level on a number of explanatory variables, derived from an econometric model (Greenaway *et al.*, 1999). This approach can take account of the indirect impact of trade on employment via endogenous changes in technology linked to international trade and/or changes in the efficiency of labour use.

The factor content approach

To examine the changing factor content of exports and imports in Kenya, we apply the Krause (1988) classification of manufacturing industries according to their dominant factor input. This classification distinguishes between natural resource intensive, labour intensive, technology intensive and human capital intensive industries. The natural resource intensive industries are further subdivided into agricultural and mineral-based industries.

As noted earlier, Kenya has been a reluctant liberalizer, with slow and uneven progress in trade reforms. This is also evident in the factor content of exports, which does not display great change over 1976–98 (Table 3.7). Agricultural resource intensive exports remain the most important category of exports, with a share of 64.7 per cent in total

Table 3.7 Factor-intensity of exports and imports, 1975–98

Percentage share (except total exports/imports)	1976–80	1981–85	1986–90	1991–95	1996–98
The structure of exports					
Agricultural resource intensive	65.8	64.8	73.9	63.4	64.7
Mineral resource intensive	16.8	15.6	2.5	3.2	4.2
Unskilled labour intensive	4.1	5.0	7.6	15.9	15.8
Technology intensive	8.5	10.0	11.7	13.1	8.6
Human capital intensive	4.9	4.6	4.4	4.4	6.8
Total exports (in US$ million)	286	284	320	385	403
The structure of imports					
Agricultural resource intensive	8.7	10.7	8.2	10.9	9.1
Mineral resource intensive	6.2	9.0	7.3	7.3	6.5
Unskilled labour intensive	13.2	12.7	11.3	15.8	16.6
Technology intensive	35.2	34.5	39.6	33.3	35.7
Human capital intensive	36.7	33.0	33.5	32.6	32.1
Total imports (in US$ million)	1,001	859	1,418	1,402	1,580

Source: Manda and Sen (2004).

manufacturing exports in 1996–98. While there has been an increase in unskilled labour intensive exports from 4.8 per cent in 1976–80 to 15.9 per cent in 1991–95, the share of unskilled labour intensive exports in total manufacturing exports has remained stagnant at around 15 per cent for much of the 1990s. Total manufacturing exports also do not show signs of growth – the growth rate was 1.9 per cent per annum in 1991–98 as compared to 7.6 per cent per annum in 1976–90. The factor content of imports also does not show significant change in the period under consideration, with technology and human capital intensive imports remaining the dominant two components of total manufacturing imports.

To examine the impact of exports and imports on employment, we derive employment coefficients at the industry level which is then weighted by the share of each industry in exports and imports. We calculate employment coefficients separately for female and male labour, as there is evidence that labour intensity of production differs by gender in Kenya's key export industry, the horticultural sector (Dolan and Sutherland, 2002).[6] The employment coefficients are presented in Figure 3.3. We find that exports are more female labour intensive than imports, while for male labour, the employment coefficients for exports and imports do not differ significantly. In the aggregate, the structure of exports is marginally more labour intensive than that of imports. Thus, with relatively weak growth in labour intensive manufacturing exports in the 1990s, Kenya's increasing integration with the rest of the world has not led to any appreciable change in employment linked to international trade.

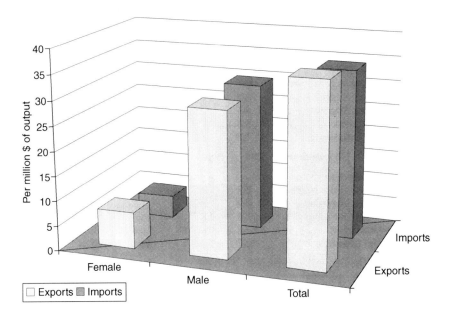

Figure 3.3 Employment coefficient of exports and import-competing domestic production (source: own elaboration from *International Economic Databank*
and UNIDO data).

Growth accounting

This methodology divides employment changes over a period of time into
that attributable to changes in domestic demand, exports, import penetration and productivity. The data used is the three-digit ISIC data for
imports and exports from the International Economic Database (IEDB) at
ANU, and UNIDO data on manufacturing output and employment also at
the three-digit level.

The results from the growth decomposition exercise are presented in
Table 3.8. Kenya shows a very different pattern in terms of manufacturing
employment in the 1990s compared to the period from 1975 to 1990.
Although the level of manufacturing employment has grown overall
during the whole period, the impact of trade flows on employment has
changed from positive to negative.

Between 1975 and 1990, employment generated by both exports and
import substitution increased. In contrast, in the 1990s employment fell as
a result of increased import competition and, since 1994, falling employment was associated with export decline. In the period 1994–98, industries
which observed a fall in employment due to a fall in exports were textiles,
wearing apparel and leather goods. During the same period, industries
which observed a fall in employment due to increased import penetration

Table 3.8 Decomposition of employment changes in Kenya, 1975–98

	1975–80	1980–85	1985–90	1990–94	1994–98
Domestic demand	53,239	44,760	46,250	7,183	−26,251
Export growth	4,141	5,281	2,728	5,039	−8,320
Import penetration	5,265	12,149	13,207	−9,929	−4,513
Productivity changes	−23,240	−42,575	−37,253	7,673	49,012
Total employment change	39,405	19,615	24,932	9,966	9,928
Net employment change from trade	*9,406*	*17,430*	*15,935*	*−4,890*	*−12,833*

Source: Manda and Sen (2004).

Note
The figures in the table are the absolute number of workers.

were wearing apparel, furniture, electrical machinery and transport equipment. An important aspect of the import liberalization measures undertaken in the 1990s was the lifting of restrictions on the imports of second-hand clothing and automobiles, and clearly the implementation of these measures have had a negative effect on employment in the garment and automobile industries.

A significant feature of employment changes in 1994–98 was the significant fall in labour productivity during this period which has mitigated the negative effects of international trade and falling domestic demand on total employment. The fall in labour productivity was observed mostly in the textiles and garments, electrical machinery and transport equipment sectors. In these industries, output fell sharply due to falling domestic demand, but employment did not decline in the same proportion. This seems to suggest that falling productivity in the late 1990s was a result of output contraction as a consequence of falling demand and, in the case of garments, electrical machinery and transport equipment, increased import penetration, with the labour force not being reduced to the same extent.

An economic approach

The previous two approaches examined the direct effects of international trade on employment via trade-induced adjustments in output. In this section, we study the indirect impact of trade reforms on employment via changes in the efficiency of labour use or the changing factor-intensity of output changes *within* the same industry (see Jenkins, 2004). To capture the indirect effects of trade, we estimate constant-output labour demand equations at the industry level, augmented by variables that measure the extent of integration of the industry with the world market. Thus, we estimate the following equation:

$$L_{it} = b_0 - b_1 W_{it} + b_2 Q_{it} + b_3 Z_{it} \tag{1}$$

where L_{it} is employment, W_{it} is real wage, and Q_{it} is real output, all in industry i at time t.[7] We will estimate the equation using the natural logarithms of variables, so that the coefficients on W and Q in these two equations can be interpreted as the wage and output elasticities of labour demand. The variable Z_{it} measures the degree of openness of industry i in time t. As is standard in the literature, we capture the degree of openness by the import penetration ratio (*IM*) and the export–output ratio (*EO*) defined at the industry level (Greenaway *et al.* 1999).[8] The use of these two variables also allows us to separate the effects of import competition from export orientation on the efficiency of labour use.

The equations are estimated using a pooled dataset drawn from the UNIDO's industrial statistics that provides data on output, employment and wages both at the ISIC three-digit and four-digit levels from the 1970s. In the case of Kenya, data at the ISIC four-digit level are not available, but the ISIC three-digit data are available for the 1980s and much of the 1990s. The number of industries included in the panel is 21, and the period of analysis is 1982–98 (the number of observations is 374).

In our estimation procedure, we also introduce industry-specific dummies to control for unobservable time-invariant differences across industries (such as in the rate of technological progress). We use one-year lagged values of *W*, *IM* and *EO*, given the short-run rigidities in adjusting employment in a given year, and to take into account possible concerns about simultaneity bias when current values are included in the regression. The regression results are presented in Table 3.9. In column 1, we present estimates of the standard labour demand equation without incorporating the openness variables. Column 2 reports the augmented labour

Table 3.9 Regression results – trade and manufacturing employment

Variables	Column 1	Column 2	Column 3	Column 4	Column 5
ΔQ	0.004	0.006	0.004	0.006	0.007
	(1.33)	(1.71)*	(1.33)	(1.70)*	(1.72)*
$\Delta W(-1)$	−0.09	−0.09	−0.09	−0.09	−0.09
	(1.92)*	(1.99)**	(1.92)*	(2.00)**	(1.97)**
$\Delta IM(-1)$	–	−0.0001	−0.00008	–	−0.0001
		(0.67)	(0.30)		(0.34)
$\Delta EO(-1)$	–	−0.0014	–	−0.001	−0.0013
		(1.42)		(1.42)	(1.15)
Industry dummies?	Yes	Yes	Yes	Yes	Yes
Time dummies?	No	No	No	No	Yes
R-square	0.09	0.11	0.10	0.10	0.14
S.E. of regression	0.1014	0.1014	0.1016	0.1012	0.1014
DW statistic	1.93	1.93	1.93	1.93	1.95

Notes
ΔL is the dependent variable.
* and ** denote statistical significance at the 10 and 5 per cent levels respectively.
All standard errors are White (1980) heteroskedasticity consistent.

demand equation with the import penetration and export orientation variables included together. In columns 3 and 4, we augment the labour demand equation by including the import penetration and export orientation ratios separately to incorporate concerns regarding the possible multicollinearity of the two openness variables. In column 5, we present the augmented labour demand equation, with time dummies included to control for economy-wide shocks to labour demand (structural adjustment programmes would fall into this category).

We find that the coefficients on output and the wage rate have the expected signs, though the coefficient on the latter is statistically significant while the former is not (column 1). A 1 per cent increase in the real wage rate leads to a fall in employment by 0.09 per cent. Including import penetration and export orientation, we find that there is little evidence of increased international trade having any discernible effect on employment in Kenyan manufacturing. With respect to export orientation, the coefficient is negative, but not statistically significant. Including *IM* and *EO* separately, and also including time dummies, does not lead to any change in the results (columns 3, 4 and 5). Thus, the evidence suggests that the Kenyan manufacturing sector's increasing economic integration with the rest of the world does not seem to have led to an appreciable indirect effect on employment, either through increased export orientation or greater import penetration.

Has trade-openness had an impact on poverty in the agricultural sector?

McCulloch and Ota (2002) examine the effect of trade reforms on poverty in the agricultural sector in Kenya, focusing on export horticulture. Horticulture is the most highly export-oriented activity in the Kenyan agricultural sector, and horticultural exports have seen a significant increase in both volume and value in the 1990s, which has seen greater integration with world markets in the post-reform period. McCulloch and Ota (2002) find that export horticulture contributed to improvements in the economic situation of rural households in two ways. First, employment was generated on farms owned by major exporters and on independent large farms producing for these exporters under contract. Second, smallholders producing for companies involved in the exportation of horticulture benefited both from higher incomes and also access to credit and extension services provided by these companies. Thus, export horticulture has led to an increase in employment and incomes among agricultural workers and smallholder farmers, and would have contributed to a fall in the incidence of poverty in the rural areas.

Conclusion

There is little doubt that Kenya has considerably opened up its economy since the early 1980s, when it embarked on a process of economic reform. The evidence presented in this chapter suggests that the response to these trade reforms does not seem to have had an appreciable positive impact on economic growth and has not contributed to a reduction in poverty, except in a limited manner for workers employed in the horticultural sector. The effects of increased trade-openness in Kenya on growth and poverty outcomes seem to differ from the cross-country evidence on the positive relationship between trade, growth and poverty alleviation presented by Dollar and Kraay (2002).

What explains the difference in outcomes in Kenya relative to the 'average' developing country? Two possible reasons may be offered in response to this question. First, the reforms in Kenya were 'stop–go' in nature, and may have led to a lack of credibility of the reforms themselves (Reinnika, 1996). Second, the reforms were implemented in the presence of significant macroeconomic uncertainty and in a political environment where the relationship between the government and major bilateral and multilateral donors has not been the most conducive (O'Brien and Ryan, 2000). Thus, trade reforms should not be expected to have a beneficial effect on growth and poverty alleviation if they are not seen to be credible and if accompanying conditions of macroeconomic stability and political commitment are not met.

Notes

1 The sequence of devaluations was in response to a possibility of capital flight following the coup attempt in August 1982.
2 'Kenya can be made to fit the mould of a reluctant reformer whose overall record has been no better than the (Sub-Saharan African) average' (O'Brien and Ryan, 2000: 494).
3 Dollar and Kraay (2002) estimate that Kenya's weighted average tariff rate fell from 39.4 per cent in 1985 to 13.5 per cent in 1995.
4 The data was obtained from the World Bank's *World Development Indicators* database.
5 We also experimented with the one period lag of the trade-openness measure to control for possible endogeneity of changes in trade-openness to economic growth. However, there was no change in the results. This may be because exports, one element of the denominator, are determined largely by world factors independent of Kenyan policy, as observed for Uganda in Chapter 4.
6 Due to lack of availability of International Standard Industrial Classification (ISIC) four-digit data, we use ISIC three-digit industry data. Also, we compute employment coefficients only for 1996, as disaggregated data on female and male employment is not available for all industries for other years.
7 In the absence of product specific price deflators, we use the GDP manufacturing deflator to deflate nominal output and nominal wage.
8 We define the import penetration ratio for a particular industry as its imports as a ratio of domestic demand (i.e. imports + output − exports); while the export orientation ratio is exports as a ratio of output.

4 Trade policy, economic performance, poverty and equity in Uganda

Oliver Morrissey, Nichodemus Rudaheranwa and Lars Moller

Uganda since the early 1990s has been one of the most successful African examples of economic liberalization, attaining macroeconomic stability and reducing policy-induced anti-export bias in its trade policy in the 1990s. Taxes on exports have been abolished, and import protection has been reduced considerably. It now has one of the most open trade regimes in Africa. In conjunction with trade liberalization, the government has liberalized much of the agricultural sector, notably coffee marketing, and this has been associated with increased prices and incomes for producers. Growth performance has been impressive. In rough terms, real per capita GDP doubled by the early 2000s compared to the early 1990s. Export growth, especially coffee in the mid-1990s but including non-traditional exports more recently, made a significant contribution to this growth performance; export earnings doubled in real terms during the 1990s. The evidence of successive household surveys is that poverty is being reduced, fuelled by increased agricultural incomes for most of the 1990s (first coffee, then food crops since 1997) and increasing non-farm incomes in recent years. The percentage of the population recorded as living below the poverty line (the poverty headcount measure) fell by some 20 per cent between 1992 and 1998, and has continued to fall until the early 2000s, when it appears to have stabilized.

There were several forces at play in the economy during the 1990s that impacted on poverty. These included trade liberalization and trade performance (which is only in part determined by Uganda's own trade policy), but there were also large aid inflows. Although we will make reference to other factors where appropriate, our concern is with identifying any ways in which trade policy and performance has affected the poor. Trade may affect poverty by contributing to increased or decreased incomes or opportunities, or by altering the prices, the poor face for the main commodities they consume. All of these linkages will be addressed. However, the gains of the past decade have not been evenly distributed; while the 'average' household gained, some households are likely to have suffered under liberalization and some groups remain rooted in poverty. This chapter aims to review the evidence to identify which types of households have, and which have not, benefited from trade under Uganda's more liberal economic regime, and to suggest what can be done regarding trade policy to spread the benefits more widely.

The major trade policy reforms tend to have a more immediate effect on imports than on exports, as Ugandan reforms directly affect import prices (by reducing restrictions or tariffs). Export revenues are largely determined by world prices, which are beyond Uganda's influence, while export performance is influenced by non-trade factors, such as marketing and transport. The effects for exports and imports will be examined separately, including reference to results from modelling exercises, in particular Computable General Equilibrium (CGE) studies for Uganda. An attempt is made to relate product effects (e.g. prices of food, imports) to consumption, especially of the poor, using evidence from household surveys. As export growth contributes to economic growth, trade can directly contribute to reducing poverty. Trade, imports and exports affect households in different ways, as producers or consumers, and we emphasize how such distribution effects should be allowed for when incorporating trade policy into any poverty reduction strategy.

Trade policy and economic performance[1]

Uganda has averaged real GDP growth of over 5 per cent per annum since the launch of the Economic Recovery Programme (ERP) in 1987. The key features of the ERP were market-oriented policy reforms, including liberalization of trade and the foreign exchange regime, and achieving macroeconomic stabilization. Uganda has undergone substantial structural transformation over the past decade with services and industry becoming more important at the expense of agriculture. Nevertheless, the Ugandan economy continues to be dominated by agriculture, contributing more than 90 per cent of export earnings, 80 per cent of employment and about 40 per cent of government revenue. The proportion of monetary in total GDP rose from 66 to 77 per cent in the same period, reflecting the transformation from a subsistence-based to a more market-based agricultural sector.

Trade performance, in particular exports, has been a fundamental factor in growth, and trade policy has made a contribution, although global market conditions are the major determinant of export earnings. As Uganda is a price-taker on world markets, it has little influence on the price received for its exports, especially for its major exports of coffee and, more recently, gold and fish. However, the high world prices for coffee during much of the 1990s is not the sole reason for increasing producer incomes – the share of the world price received by farmers also increased significantly following liberalization. Thus, domestic policies are important. In the early 1990s, Uganda had a strongly protectionist and highly distorted trade regime, with taxes on coffee (the major export) and high tariffs and restrictions on imports. By the end of the decade, a more liberal trade regime was in place.

The presence of import barriers or restrictions creates an anti-export bias by raising the price of importable goods relative to exportable goods. Removal of this anti-export bias through trade liberalization would induce a shift of resources from the production of import substitutes to the production of exports. The factors used intensively in the production of exports, land and rural labour in Uganda, should benefit most. On the other hand, factors employed in the production of import-competing goods, mostly urban capital and labour, can anticipate losses. Typically, import supply from the rest of the world responds more rapidly than domestic export supply, so liberalization imposes adjustment costs (losses tend to be immediate whereas export gains can take time). As we will see, this has not really been the case in Uganda. Although imports increased with growth, they remained a stable share of GDP; variations in export earnings drove the balance of payments.

Evolution of trade policy

The ERP aimed to improve the competitiveness of Ugandan exports by eliminating controls in the foreign exchange market. It aimed at restoring incentives for producers by abolishing most of the price controls and inefficient marketing monopolies. The ERP aimed at promoting investment by introducing investment incentives and guarantees and returning expropriated properties to their owners. Trade policy reforms implemented in Uganda since 1987, coupled with direct export promotion measures, other aspects of the ERP, reduced the bias against exports, and policy-induced barriers to trade have been reduced substantially. Table 4.1 provides a summary of the main reforms over 1987–2000, the most recent year for which reforms have been identified. Tariff rates have been reduced, often significantly, and many non-tariff restrictions (e.g. quotas, import bans) have been converted into tariff equivalents. The tariff schedule with rates of 0, 10, 20, 30 and 60 per cent in 1995 has been reduced to a standard schedule with rates of 0, 7 and 15 per cent in 2001, although some goods face higher rates.[2] Lower tariffs apply to imports from regional partners. The export tax on coffee, which generated up to a half of the government revenue in the 1980s, was abolished in 1992 and temporarily reintroduced in 1994 as a Coffee Stabilization Tax but eliminated in 1996. The main export duty is a 1 per cent levy collected by the Uganda Coffee Development Authority on coffee exports.

Trade performance

Trade policy reforms in Uganda have been aimed at poverty reduction, promoting employment, economic growth and promotion and diversifica-

Table 4.1 Ugandan trade policy reforms

Year	Reform
1987	• Dual trade licensing system introduced.
	• Duty exemptions on raw materials and capital goods suspended.
1988	• Some protective tariffs (sugar, soap) raised.
	• Open General License (OGL) scheme for imports implemented.
1989	• Retention account scheme for export earnings introduced.
	• Duty exemption on raw materials.
1990	• Export licensing system replaced with certification system.
	• Foreign exchange bureau/parallel foreign exchange market legalized.
1991	• Import licensing replaced with certification system.
	• Duty drawback scheme introduced.
1992	• Tariff structure rationalized (six rates in 10–60% range).
	• Several duties on raw material abolished.
	• Tax on coffee exports abolished.
1993	• Unified inter-bank foreign exchange market/floating exchange rate.
	• System of trade documentation reformed, pre-shipment requirements introduced.
	• Cross-border initiative (CBI) to promote regional trade introduced.
1994	• Further rationalization (10–50% range) of the tariff structure.
	• Import duties on some of the materials suspended.
	• Tax on coffee exports reintroduced.
1995	• Coffee tax reduced.
	• Narrow range of products only on negative import list.
	• Reduced exemptions from duties on raw materials and intermediate inputs.
1996	• Coffee tax abolished.
	• Further rationalization of tariffs, to three non-zero rates with maximum of 30% (though protective excise duty of 12% applies also on many tariff lines).
1998	• Tariff bands reduced to three – 0, 7 and 15% (although with some special excise duties) and almost all import bans removed.
	• Uganda qualifies for HIPC debt relief.
2000	• Fixed Duty Drawback Scheme and the Manufacturing Under Bond Scheme introduced for exporters.

tion of exports, particularly non-traditional exports. There are duty and tax exemptions and concessions as incentives to increase the volume and diversity of exports. The policy initiatives undertaken in recent years have provided incentives and increased producer prices. For example, the elimination of the monopoly of the Uganda Produce Marketing Board (PMB) has contributed to the growth and diversity of horticultural exports.

Trade performance during the 1990s has been volatile on the export side, but surprisingly stable on the import side (Table 4.2). Exports

Table 4.2 Exports, imports and trade balance, 1990–2001, selected years

Year	1990	1995	1996	1997	1998	1999	2000	2001
Exports/GDP (%)	7.0	10.9	11.9	15.0	12.1	11.8	11.7	11.6
Imports/GDP (%)	20.0	20.8	20.7	20.5	20.1	20.0	20.2	20.7
Balance/GDP (%)	−13.0	−10.1	−8.8	−5.5	−8.0	−8.2	−8.5	−9.1

Source: Economist Intelligence Unit, 2002.

increased from 7 per cent of GDP in 1990 to peak at 15 per cent in 1997, during the coffee boom, falling to a stable level of 11–12 per cent of GDP for the rest of the decade. Imports remained at 20–1 per cent of GDP throughout the decade. As a consequence, Uganda has run a chronic trade deficit of over 8 per cent of GDP for most of the period (this has been sustained by aid inflows).

The composition of Uganda's exports changed markedly during the 1990s, especially in the second half of the decade. One important trend is the fall in export revenue from traditional cash crops, notably coffee since 1999 and cotton in the early 1990s. In contrast, non-traditional exports, especially fish, experienced a boost in revenues in recent years. By 2000/01, non-traditional revenues surpassed those from traditional exports (Table 4.3).

Coffee has been by far the single most important export commodity over the decade (Table 4.4). Between 1992/93 and 1998/99, coffee contributed between 54 and 77 per cent of total exports, earning US$457 million at its peak in 1994/95. Uganda benefited tremendously from a boom in the world coffee prices in the mid-1990s combined with an increased supply response. But the boom was followed by bust as coffee export prices fell by almost 70 per cent in dollar terms between 1998/99 and 2001/02. Coffee's share of exports has fallen dramatically to only 18 per cent in 2001/02, earning US$85 million, some five times less than in 1994/95. Cotton, another traditional cash crop, also experienced a recent downturn. Tobacco, on the other hand, has grown steadily in importance,

Table 4.3 Traditional and non-traditional exports, selected years (US$m)

	1991–92	1993–94	1994–95	1995–96	1996–97	1998–99	1999–2000	2000–01
Traditional exports	131.4	202.3	477.4	435.6	424.2	363.1	258.4	172.0
Non-traditional exports	40.7	62.4	115.5	152.4	259.3	186.0	180.6	253.2
Total exports	172.1	264.7	593.0	588.0	683.5	549.1	438.9	425.2

Source: *Background to the Budget 2002/03* (MFPED, 2002).

Note
Excludes exports of services. 'Non-traditional' refers to commodities that have only featured in export trade over the last ten years.

Table 4.4 Composition of exports (% shares), 1990–2001, selected years

	1990	1992	1994	1995	1997	1998	1999	2000	2001
Traditional exports									
Coffee	79.0	65.0	74.6	66.9	52.0	55.1	60.1	31.2	21.6
Cotton	3.3	5.6	0.8	1.7	4.9	1.4	3.6	5.5	3.0
Tea	2.0	5.3	2.6	1.2	5.1	5.3	4.5	9.4	6.7
Tobacco	1.7	2.9	1.8	1.3	2.1	4.2	3.1	6.7	7.1
Non-traditional exports									
Maize	1.9	2.7	6.2	4.0	2.5	1.7	1.1	0.6	4.1
Beans and other legumes	2.3	1.9	2.8	2.8	2.0	1.2	1.8	1.1	0.5
Fish and fish products	0.8	4.4	2.3	5.6	4.7	7.4	5.2	7.7	17.3
Cattle hides	2.3	2.3	2.3	1.8	1.7	1.1	0.6	3.2	5.7
Sesame seeds	2.9	4.4	0.3	1.0	0.2	0.0	0.3	0.2	0.2
Soap	0.0	0.0	0.4	0.5	0.4	0.3	0.4	0.4	0.6
Electric current	0.7	1.0	0.5	0.4	2.0	2.2	2.8	4.6	2.3
Cocoa beans	0.3	0.2	0.1	0.1	0.2	0.3	0.3	0.4	0.4
Goat and sheep skins	1.2	0.5	0.1	0.0	0.0	0.0	0.0	0.0	0.0
Hoes and hand tools	0.1	0.3	0.2	0.3	0.0	0.0	0.1	0.1	0.1
Pepper	0.0	0.1	0.1	0.0	0.0	0.0	0.1	0.1	0.1
Fruits	0.0	0.0	0.1	0.0	0.1	0.1	0.0	0.2	0.0
Bananas	0.0	0.1	0.1	0.1	0.0	0.0	0.1	0.2	0.2
Roses and cut flowers	0.0	0.0	0.1	0.1	0.6	1.4	1.5	2.5	3.3
Gold and gold compounds	0.0	0.0	0.0	4.7	13.6	3.6	7.0	10.8	10.9
Other precious compounds	0.0	0.0	0.0	0.0	0.0	0.0	0.6	2.7	2.8
Other products	1.6	3.2	4.1	6.9	7.8	14.3	6.7	12.7	10.5
Traditional exports	85.9	78.7	79.8	71.1	64.2	65.9	71.3	52.6	38.3
Non-traditional exports	14.1	21.3	20.2	28.9	35.8	34.1	28.7	47.4	61.7

Source: Computed from *Background to the Budget* (MFPED, various years).

especially towards the end of the decade. Tea exports have also improved significantly, primarily due to an increase in volumes.

Fish is the current export success story in Uganda, increasing from only $4 million (2 per cent of exports) in 1992/93 to $48 million (9 per cent) in 1998/99. A temporary import ban imposed by the European Union caused a loss of foreign currency earnings in 1999/2000, as exports dropped to $19 million. When the ban was lifted, exports expanded further to a record $88 million (19 per cent of exports) in 2001/02, making fish the most important export commodity in Uganda in terms of revenue earned. The boom in fish exports can be attributed to increased prices as well as volumes. Hides and skins are other promising export commodities. Flowers and electricity show equally promising trends. Maize exports are also important, but volatile, as the produce is sold in bulk and depends on food shortages in other parts of the continent (to which transport is often a problem).

Non-trade factors and constraints

Trade policy barriers are only a component of the transactions costs associated with trade. Poor infrastructure, notably by increasing transport costs, and institutional inefficiencies can significantly increase trade costs. The implicit tax on exports due to transport costs and inefficiencies are often very high, in many cases representing a greater cost (tax) to exporters than trade policy. These high transaction costs make exporters less competitive in world markets. Many institutional reforms, especially dismantling state monopolies on marketing, complemented the trade reforms. However, institutional rigidities and infrastructure inefficiencies persist and these constrain trade performance.

The poor functioning of institutions that facilitate trade also constrains efforts to increase exports and may indeed result in reduced incomes and increased poverty. The lack of capacity in the Uganda National Bureau of Standards (UNBS) to monitor and enforce standards in the fish sector in the late 1990s illustrates this point. The EU ban on fish from Lake Victoria in the late 1990s resulted in a loss of income to fishermen and employees in the fish processing plants as a result of abrupt and massive lay-offs in the fish industry. Out of 100,000 people involved in various fishing activities, 32,000 lost their jobs, whilst others earned less than one third of their normal incomes. Families and other dependants (about 300,000 people) of the directly employed were also affected by the ban on Uganda's fish exports in 1999. This example suggests that weak institutions can have direct and indirect effects on efforts to reduce poverty. Stringent quality requirements and standards are of increasing importance in sectors into which Uganda is making attempts to diversify (Ruda-heranwa *et al.*, 2003). For example, maximum chemical residue limits are expected to come into force in 2003 and would affect products in the horticulture and flower industries, both of which are a major source of employment and current export earnings. Institutional capacity is required to ensure they do not have the same adverse experiences as in the fish sector.

Trends in poverty in the 1990s[3]

Although we recognize that poverty is a multi-dimensional concept, we limit our discussion here to its money-metric aspect using income- and consumption-based approaches because data on these are more readily available from household surveys and this allows us to identify recent trends. More importantly, it allows us to 'track' poverty in different regions and household-types, which can be related to the evidence on trade and economic performance by sector and commodity.

Since 1989, the government of Uganda has undertaken a series of household surveys that provide data to monitor poverty, notably the 1992

Integrated Household Survey (IHS). There have been four annual moni-
toring surveys since 1992, and the results of the Uganda National Household Survey (UNHS) of 1999/2000 have recently become available. The
national poverty line is the cost of obtaining 3,000 calories per day using
the food basket of the poorest 50 per cent of Ugandans in 1993 prices.
Non-food requirements are estimated as the non-food spending of those
households whose total consumption is just equal to the food poverty line.
The rationale for this is that if households are sacrificing the food expenditure needed to meet calorie requirements for non-food spending, then
this non-food spending must be considered vital. Results have been shown
to be robust to the choice of poverty line.[4] We review trends largely by
comparing the results of the 1992 and 1999/2000 surveys.

In 1992, poverty was widespread, with 56 per cent of the population
estimated to be below the poverty line. Although poverty was mainly a
rural phenomenon (with rural areas contributing 93 per cent to the
poverty headcount), 29 per cent of urban residents were poor. Regional
variations were significant, and poverty was significantly higher in the
North and lowest in the Central region, which includes Kampala (Table
4.5). Considering the entire period 1992–2000, a clear picture emerges.
Poverty declined substantially to only 35 per cent in 2000. The greatest
decline was in urban areas, from 28 per cent to 10 per cent, whilst in rural
areas the decline was from 60 per cent to 39 per cent (Table 4.5). The
performance in conflict-stricken northern Uganda, known for production
of cotton, groundnuts and sesame, was the worst. The maize and bean-
growing Eastern region registered a decline from 59 per cent to 37 per
cent, suggesting gains from non-traditional exports. As the West and
Central are the main coffee growing regions it is not surprising that most
of the gains from the coffee boom and liberalization in the coffee sector
accrued there, and they experienced the largest reductions in poverty

Sector variations in poverty help us to identify which sectors enjoyed the
greatest income growth, and therefore the greatest potential for poverty
reduction. In 1992, about 70 per cent of Uganda's population was employed
in the agriculture sector,[5] 47 per cent engaged in food crop agriculture and

Table 4.5 Incidence of consumption poverty in Uganda 1992–2000 (%)

	1992	1997	2000
Uganda	56	44	35
Rural	60	49	39
Urban	28	17	10
Central	46	28	20
East	59	54	37
West	53	43	28
North	72	60	66

Source: *Uganda Poverty Status Report 2001* (PMAU, 2002a).

20 per cent in cash crop farming. Government services accounted for some 8 per cent of employment. All the major socio-economic groups saw a reduction in poverty by at least one quarter in the period 1992–2000 (Table 4.6). The food crop sector contributed almost half (43 per cent) of the reduction in poverty over the whole period, but this was almost entirely between 1996 and 2000. The cash crop sector contributed some 27 per cent to the reduction, with gains primarily for the coffee farmers during the coffee boom and liberalization of the coffee sector in 1992–96. The decline in poverty among households employed in government and private sector services was more pronounced in the later period (1995–2000).

While nationally the proportion of the Ugandan population identified as poor fell from 56 per cent in 1992 to 35 per cent in 1999, with substantial poverty reduction occurring everywhere in the country except the Northern region, this provides no information on the dynamics of poverty change. Table 4.7 presents poverty dynamics based on panel subsamples

Table 4.6 Incidence of poverty by main occupation of household head (%)

	Rural			Urban		
	1992	1996	2000	1992	1996	2000
All	60	54	39	28	20	10
Food crops	60	63	46	–	–	–
Cash crops	63	47	34	–	–	–
Non-crop agriculture	57	43	44	–	–	–
Agriculture	–	–	–	55	36	23
Mining, manufacturing	45	40	35	38	36	23
Private sector services	40	31	22	16	12	7
Government services	41	36	22	26	22	6
Non-working	65	68	53	32	18	15

Source: *Uganda Poverty Status Report 2001* (PMAU, 2002a).

Table 4.7 Distribution of poor in Uganda 1992–99 (% households)

	Chronic poor	Moving out of poverty	Moving into poverty	Never in poverty	All
All	18.9	29.6	10.3	40.9	–
Rural/urban					
Urban	8.1	12.2	8.8	21.9	15.0
Rural	91.9	87.8	91.2	78.1	85.0
Region					
Central	23.4	32.0	26.3	37.2	31.9
East	19.6	28.0	21.9	19.9	22.5
North	30.1	11.3	25.4	6.8	14.5
West	26.8	28.7	26.3	36.1	31.1

Source: Calculations from raw survey data provided by David Lawson.

of the national surveys in 1992 and 1999, to identify households that remained either poor or non-poor and households that moved into or out of poverty. Almost 20 per cent of the panel households were chronic poor, i.e. poor in the two years for which they were surveyed, while 41 per cent were non-poor in both periods. The remainder moved into or out of poverty between these years, indicating substantial mobility.

Table 4.7 also shows how chronic and transient poverty is distributed across rural/urban areas and by region. Chronic poverty is particularly prevalent in both the Northern region and rural areas of Uganda. Considering the chronically poor as a whole, almost one-third (30.1 per cent) are in the Northern region. Households in the North also appear less likely to move out of poverty, with only 11 per cent of households escaping poverty being from the North, compared to 32 per cent from the Central region. It is clear that while there has been substantial movement both into and out of poverty, there appears to be a core of Ugandan households remaining in poverty. These 'chronic poor' are disproportionately located in rural areas (over 90 per cent), especially in the North. Evidently, growth has been associated with distribution effects and has not benefited a significant proportion of the population.

Trade and poverty: exploring the linkages

It is only within the last ten years that economists have started to address, in a rigorous manner, the ways in which trade may impact on the poor. Data permitting, the unit of analysis would be the household as producer and consumer. As a producer, the household earns income by selling the factors it possesses (e.g. renting land, wage labour) or by utilizing the factors directly for production (e.g. combining household land and labour to grow food, for sale or own-consumption). The distinguishing feature of poor households is that they possess few or low-value factors (e.g. they do not have access to land and their labour is of very low quality). Trade expands market opportunities and increases the demand for, and return to, factors. International trade provides access to (and competition from) a larger market, but also one that is more competitive, so success in exporting, or import competition, requires increased efficiency in producing high quality goods. The major share of the benefits from trade will accrue to those households owning the factors that are most in demand, and in general, these will not be poor households. This does not mean that trade will not benefit the poor, but rather suggests that the poor will derive the least direct benefit from trade. Insofar as trade expansion fuels economic growth, aggregate demand in the economy increases and this benefits all.

From the perspective of producers, exports are beneficial (increased demand leads to increased production and incomes) but imports pose a challenge. Increased competition from imports can lead to a reduction of production of import-competing sectors, at least in the short run. This means that the owners of factors supplied to those sectors will suffer a reduction in income; in a country like Uganda, this is mostly wage labour in manufacturing. If the economy is flexible it will adjust over time and, in the long run, the economy should become more efficient. However, most evidence relates to the short-term, so there will be winners and losers from trade. From the perspective of households as consumers, however, trade is generally beneficial. Import competition implies that imports and the products of import-competing sectors will be cheaper. Expansion of export sectors, if they also sell on the local market, should mean lower prices and/or higher quality. Thus, trade has interacting effects on households, some good and some bad. To disentangle how these effects may have impacted on different households in Uganda, we present results from simulations using a Computable General Equilibrium (CGE) model in the first subsection below. This helps to identify the types of households that benefited from trade and those that did not benefit.

It is important to distinguish trade policy from trade performance, especially as it is the latter that results in effects on poverty. Trade performance is an outcome, while trade policy is one of the inputs that influences that outcome. Trade policy reforms affect relative incentives, and the performance outcome depends on the ability of agents and sectors to respond to these altered incentives. The link between policy and performance is not a simple direct one. Policy reforms have economic effects on: (a) prices of traded products; (b) output, wages and employment opportunities in affected sectors; and (c) the government's fiscal position. We focus on economic effects, in particular those on export performance to address (b), as data on the effects on import prices are quite limited.

A brief comment on the fiscal effects is warranted. Import liberalization might be expected to reduce government revenue, as tariffs are typically an important tax. Despite the significant trade liberalization since the early 1990s, tariffs have continued to be a major source of tax revenue. Although tariff revenue fell by about a third in the 1990s, this decline was compensated by increased revenue from VAT on imports. Thus Uganda, in effect, substituted domestic sales taxes for tariffs.

The remainder of this section addresses three separate issues. First, we review some simulation evidence of how trade reforms impact on Uganda, taking into account distribution effects on types of household. Second, we look at the performance of the agriculture sector, as this is the mainstay of the economy. There is evidence that producer prices of some major crops increased and that farmers substituted into, and increased production of, those crops. Finally, we look at trends in prices of important consumption goods to see how these may affect the real incomes of the poor.

Model simulation evidence

Trade liberalization increases competition faced by domestic producers; while some firms may fail, others may respond by increasing efficiency (especially firms using imported inputs). There are welfare gains for consumers who can purchase an increasing variety of goods, potentially of better quality, at lower prices. The immediate effect of import liberalization is losses in some sectors, gains in other sectors, gains to consumers and possible revenue losses to government; the net impact is indeterminate. The longer-term impact will depend on how effectively the export sector responds to improved incentives: although trade liberalization does not usually affect actual export prices, it increases the return to exportables relative to the return to importables. An adequate export response is usually sufficient to ensure that the net impact of trade liberalization is favourable. Because there are so many different effects, some offsetting and others reinforcing, one cannot say *a priori* how trade reforms will affect household welfare. Even if one expects an aggregate gain for the economy, it is important to know which types of households or sectors are most likely to gain and which are most likely to lose. Computable General Equilibrium (CGE) models are useful in this respect, as they allow one to trace through how relative prices alter production and factor incomes, and how this in turn affects real incomes of specific types of households.

The results of simulations from CGE models of Uganda summarized in Table 4.8 show the distribution of impacts for ten types of households (the share of each type in the economy is given in the second column).

Table 4.8 Effects of trade on household welfare in Uganda (illustrative CGE simulations)

	Share	*Export growth*	*UR*
1 Urban wage earners	12%	0.00	0.08
2 Rural wage earners	10%	0.08	0.24
3 Agricultural, Central	14%	0.57	0.50
4 Agricultural, Eastern	14%	0.57	0.36
5 Agricultural, Western	15%	0.65	0.51
6 Agricultural, Northern	9%	0.51	0.29
7 Urban non-farm self employed	12%	0.87	1.20
8 Rural non-farm self employed	9%	0.80	0.87
9 Urban non-working	1%	0.00	−0.53
10 Rural non-working	3%	−0.07	−0.59
Total	–	0.46	0.42

Source: Blake *et al.* (2002).

Notes
The 'share' column is the share of each household type in total income (of all households). The two columns of results are simulations of the effect of the Uruguay Round (UR), first assuming only a 10% increase in the world price of Ugandan coffee exports and second assuming full implementation of UR (with only a mild increase in coffee prices).

The two cases refer to multilateral Uruguay Round (UR) liberalization, and therefore allow for changes in world prices (that arise from liberalization in other countries). The 'Export Growth' column simulates the effect of a 10 per cent increase in the world price of coffee *only* (no other adjustments are allowed). Although this may appear to be a large price increase, the simulation is intended to illustrate the impact of export expansion more generally; the estimated supply response of coffee farmers is quite low (output increases by 2.3 per cent), while labour and other factors are treated as fixed. Obviously, a lower price increase would have less of an impact, but greater supply response would have a greater impact. The aggregate effect is positive, there is an increase of almost 0.5 per cent in real household income (welfare) at the national level. Most households benefit but those that are most likely to produce or trade coffee benefit most. Interpreting the table, coffee-growing farmers (agriculture) gain, as do traders, processors and providers of inputs (including services) to the farmers (these will be in the urban and rural non-farm self-employed households). Rural wage earners derive some benefit, as wages increase, but urban wage earners are unaffected. The households that lose, the rural non-working, are those that are most likely to include the chronic poor.

In this 'export growth' simulation, even agricultural households in the Northern region benefit, although this is not a coffee growing area. The model generates this by allowing farmers in that region to substitute from other crops into coffee. Even if this is unrealistic, the simulation captures the broader benefits of export growth. In simple terms, a significant expansion of exports provides a direct benefit to households that do or can supply factors to the export sector (in production, processing, marketing or trading). Note that this simulation imposed severe rigidity on the economy – it did not permit factors (such as labour and capital) to move between sectors (e.g. from wage labour into export crops), nor did it permit any efficiency gains in the economy.

The second simulation (UR, all factors) relaxes this rigidity, allowing for import liberalization and some factor movement. This simulation assumes a much more moderate increase in world coffee prices (0.4 per cent), which as it happens would have no effect on aggregate welfare (although coffee producers and traders benefit). Thus, the second simulation adds factor mobility and tariff reductions to export price increases that would not affect aggregate welfare, and can be interpreted as the effects of the former only (this is why the aggregate welfare effect is lower than in the first simulation). It is evident that once flexibility for the economy to adjust is allowed, the net impact is positive – a 0.42 per cent increase in total household welfare (the measure of national income). All households accept the non-working gain, although the greatest gains are again to farmers and, especially, the non-farm self-employed. Non-working households lose in this simulation because tariff reductions reduce government revenues and this leads to a cut in transfers (to some extent this is an artifact of the structure of the model, but it serves to highlight the problem of those depending on transfers). A greater increase in export prices would generate greater benefits, but the distribution across households would follow the pattern shown here.

These results provide two broad conclusions. First, in a relatively inflexible and constrained economy such as Uganda's, trade liberalization is more likely to provide aggregate benefits if there are also efficiency gains and factors are mobile (this captures the ability of the economy to respond and adjust). In fact, the greatest benefits arise in the case of multilateral liberalization when the economy has some flexibility to respond to opportunities to export. Second, there are significant distribution effects of trade liberalization. In general, the largest proportional gains are to the urban self-employed, but there are also significant gains in agriculture. The benefits to agriculture are greater in the main food and coffee growing Central and Western regions, because the factors that benefit are more prevalent in those regions. This is consistent with the evidence that agricultural growth, and poverty reduction, in Uganda in the 1990s was concentrated in these areas (whereas the Northern region fared least well). In these simulations, the non-working households are the major losers. Although not all of these households are the poorest, these household types will tend to include the poorest (the chronically poor), those that do not own the factors that benefit.

These estimates of the effect of trade reform on Uganda suggest that the overall effect will be small, but on balance positive. As there are major benefits to agriculture/rural households, the impact is likely to be pro-poor. However, producers respond not so much to the prices they face for individual commodities, but the relative prices faced for substitute commodities. The CGE models address the effects associated with relative price changes. For example, if cash crop prices increase, farmers will substitute from food to cash crops, and food production will fall. However, if imports do not meet the demand for food, food prices may then rise. The net effect could be to increase the returns to farming in general, so more resources will be attracted to agriculture, or existing resources will be used more effectively. Consequently, outputs of most agricultural commodities, and incomes to farm households, can rise, as appears to have been the case in Uganda. Nevertheless, there are some households that may not benefit from trade or economic growth. Such households depend on transfers (from government in the model, but remittances or inter-household transfers may be more important in practice).

The aggregate impact on the economy will tend to be greater in sectors with higher value added. Primary exports benefit households supplying factors to produce them, but adding stages of processing spreads the economic benefits wider (although one would have to allow for the possibility of domestic processors offering producers prices lower than the potential export price). Uganda's comparative advantage is in primary commodities, but the economy can derive a greater benefit if exports are upgraded so that that more value added is domestic. Non-traditional exports often require more processing and/or packaging than traditional exports, so the shift into new products should broaden the economic benefits. Furthermore, if linkages are greater the benefits spread to more households and are more likely to contribute to poverty reduction.

Trade, agriculture and poverty[5]

The CGE models are no more than simulations of how trade reforms are likely to affect prices, and how this impacts on households via the linkages in the economy. It is relevant to consider what has happened to production and household incomes in particular sectors, and we focus on agriculture as being the single most important sector. The impact of trade liberalization on poverty depends on whether poor households are net consumers or net producers of the products whose prices have changed and the nature of the labour they supply. That is, price increases benefit net producers but hurt net consumers. In this section we focus on agriculture households as producers (the next section considers the perspective of consumers).

As noted, agriculture's share in GDP declined from over 50 per cent in the late 1980s to just over 40 per cent in the early 2000s, mostly accounted for by a decline in the share of food crops in GDP. However, this was during a period of dramatic GDP growth, and real growth rates in agriculture averaged about 5 per cent per annum during the 1990s. As agriculture is defined to include fishing, most of the growth in (non-traditional) exports emanated from the sector. The share of agriculture products in imports declined during the late 1990s, as did the volume of imports of most agricultural products (except cereals and sugar preparations among the major imports). Thus, agriculture was evidently a dynamic sector, and contributed to the reductions in household poverty reported above.

Actions to directly increase the ability of the poor to raise their incomes hinge on more targeted interventions in sectors where the poor are involved, and an increase in returns to the factors that the poor own. Survey results show that the agricultural sector is a key employer in Uganda and therefore the Plan for Modernization of Agriculture (PMA) is central to the fight against poverty while increased liberalization which will ensure increased returns to unskilled labour is critical. Table 4.9 gives changes in real prices received by producers for selected crops between 1992 and 1999, the response in terms of number of growers per crop, and changes in yield per farmer. Producer prices of coffee more than doubled reflecting both the liberalization of coffee marketing and favourable world prices. Prices of tea, maize, groundnuts and peas also rose significantly. On the other hand, the prices of beans and cassava, the two most

Table 4.9 Real producer prices and output growth, 1992–99

Crop	Price per kg (Ushs)			Growers (%)		Output
	1992	1999	Change (%)	1992	1999	Change (%)
Cash Crops						
Coffee	239	500	109.2	16.4	27.5	56.5
Cotton	510	230	−54.9	7.1	5.8	−31.7
Tea	185	510	175.7	0.3	0.1	1,289
Tobacco	1,005	1,013	0.8	2.3	2.4	−51.9
Starchy Crops						
Cassava	158	113	−28.5	59.7	58.5	27.6
Matoke	75	78	4.0	41.2	57.0	−0.8
Sweet Potatoes	113	114	0.9	61.9	56.8	354.9
Grains						
Maize	120	200	66.7	27.5	67.8	131.4
Millet	300	300	0	41.9	31.3	−31.7
Legumes						
Beans	320	256	−20	76.1	69.2	−0.1
Peas	300	400	33.3	9.9	19.8	94.9
Groundnuts	300	567	89	31.8	29.7	−27.0

Source: *Uganda Poverty Status Report 2001* (PMAU, 2000a), derived from Deininger and Okidi (2001).

Notes
All data based on a number of sample villages. The percentage of farmers growing the crops refers to the villages, not the national average. Similarly, the output growth is the mean per farmer in the sample villages.

widely grown crops (in terms of the percentage of farmers planting them), fell. The prices of three other widely grown crops remained stagnant – *matoke*, sweet potatoes and millet. This benefits consumers as these are mostly staple foods, but represents a loss to growers unless they substitute into crops that are more profitable.

It appears that farmers have substituted into crops that are more profitable. In general, the number of growers increased for those crops that saw an increase in prices, especially coffee, maize and peas. The main exceptions are tea, which accounted for very few growers, and groundnuts. Similarly, the percentage of growers declined for crops with falling prices, especially cotton and beans. There is evidence that substitution occurred mostly within types of food crops as relative prices changed. Within grains, the shift was from millet to maize; within starchy crops, there was a shift into *matoke*; and within legumes, from beans to peas.

The increase in output also tended to reflect changes in relative prices. The largest growth in output was generally in crops where prices increased – tea, maize, peas and coffee. The largest declines in output were in cotton, which recorded the largest fall in prices, and millet (the price relative to maize declined). Groundnuts are an exception, as output fell despite the significant increase in prices, and tobacco is also something of an exception. This merely serves to highlight the importance of non-price factors in determining yields.

Many of the commodities discussed above are included among the 'strategic export' commodities identified for Uganda – coffee, tea, cotton, and vegetables (Government of Uganda, 2001). The strategic commodities we have not addressed are fish, livestock, fruits, flowers and Irish potatoes. In terms of recent export growth, the most important of these are fish, cattle hides and cut flowers, which together accounted for some 27 per cent of exports in 2001. Cut flowers tend to be a commercial (market garden) rather than agricultural activity. Within agriculture, cash crops will continue to be very important but are susceptible to sudden and often dramatic changes in world prices. One strategy is to aim for high quality niche ends of the market, which is possible for coffee and perhaps tea but may not be viable for cotton, and another is to do more processing. Vegetables, especially legumes, and fruits, especially bananas, do offer export potential, but are unlikely ever to become very significant (given that, there is intense competition in these buyer-driven global markets).

A major factor in the reduction in rural poverty was the improved incomes and earnings from marketed agricultural produce. This is in part a reflection of trade policy reforms in crops with favourable world prices – producers of coffee and tea benefited during this period, although producers of cotton did not. The relevance of agriculture for poverty and the poor, however, is not limited to export crops. Food crop production is a larger sector, and staple foods are more likely to impact on the poor, as consumers if not producers. In this context, it is measures to increase yields and output that matter, not effects on prices. As emphasized earlier, the principal effect of trade policy, and often of trade, is on prices. Of greater importance than trade *per se*, however, is the ability of farmers to respond to opportunities, in particular to substitute crops as relative prices change. While the evidence is that farmers will respond to price incentives, it is also evident that they face major constraints in doing so. These are issues to be addressed in the PMA, and could be considered as necessary measures to enhance the potential of farmers to benefit from trade (internally, in the case of food crops, as well as external trade in cash crops).

Trade, imports and prices

Had adequate data been available we would have identified tariff reductions at a product level in Uganda during the 1990s and linked this to trends in import volumes and prices of those commodities. However, such detailed import data are not readily available. What we do in this section is to identify price changes in a range of commodities identified as the most important for poor households (from survey data). These are classified as primarily tradables or non-tradables (or, at least, not traded internationally), to ascertain how a more liberal trade regime might have affected the real incomes of the poor.

In principle, trade liberalization would not directly affect prices for non-tradables, but it may affect production and thus have an indirect effect on prices. Broadly speaking the price of non-tradables falls relative to exportables but increases relative to importables, so the net effect will depend on substitution possibilities in production and consumption. For example, staples such as cassava, *matoke* and sweet potatoes could be considered as non-tradables (they are produced primarily for household consumption and local markets) but are substitutes in consumption for foods such as rice, an importable, or maize, an exportable. If the price of rice falls due to cheaper imports and the price of maize falls due to increased production, then the price of staples relative to these alternatives increases. Demand for and prices of staples will fall, and it is possible that ultimately relative prices will remain the same. However, it is possible that there are segmented markets, e.g. primarily non-poor urban households consume rice whereas staples are most important in the consumption of poor rural households, in which case any effect of trade on staples will be dampened.

Four of the 12 goods can be deemed non-tradables – cassava, *matoke*, alcohol (homemade) and firewood. Fish, beans, vegetables, maize and sweet potatoes are exportables (and often significant exports), while sugar and soap are import, competing and clothes are typically imported. The fact that the import component of the expenditure of a poor household is relatively small implies that import liberalization would have a negligible direct effect on these households.

Table 4.10 illustrates the change in prices for the 12 goods in the 1992–99 periods. Prices can be obtained either directly from the household survey or on the basis of the consumer price index. This can produce conflicting observations, as is to be expected given that the quantity measure (units) and quality vary. Nevertheless, the data are indicative. The available data do not provide conclusive evidence as to whether the prices of tradables have increased less than for non-tradables. There is some tendency in this direction, as in the case of sugar, which has experienced very modest price increases, possibly due to potential competition from imports.

Food prices are among the most important factors affecting the real income of the poor, but are influenced by domestic production more than imports, especially in the case of the rural poor. While trade has been important in influencing opportunities to earn incomes, it has had only a slight effect on the prices paid by poor households for the major goods they consume.

Table 4.10 Consumption goods of an average poor household

Product	Expenditure share (%)	Type	Change in unit value 1992–99 Rural poor (%)	Consumer price index 1992–99 (%)
Cassava	10.3	Non-tradable	−20	+60
Beans	6.3	Tradable (export)	+133 (fresh) +5 (dried)	+52.2 (dried)
Vegetables	4.4	Tradable (export)	–	–
Alcohol	2.4	Non-tradable	+184	–
Firewood	12.5	Non-tradable	–	–
Washing soap	2.0	Tradable (import)	+107	–
Sweet potatoes	7.5	Tradable (export)	+100	+38
Maize	4.8	Tradable (export)	+11 to 15	+38 (meal)
Matoke	4.0	Non-tradable	+86	+40
Fish	3.0	Tradable (export)	+30 (fresh) +19 (dried)	– –
Clothes/ footwear	3.8	Tradable (import)	–	–
Sugar	2.4	Tradable (import)	+42	+16
Total	63.4	–	–	–

Source: Derived from Household Survey data provided by David Lawson.

Conclusion

There is clear evidence of a decline in poverty in Uganda during the 1990s, and this was associated with sustained economic growth in part due to growth of exports. Thus, trade was an important factor contributing to poverty reduction. The headcount poverty index fell from 56 per cent in 1992 to 46 per cent in 1996, due largely to growth in coffee production, and to 35 per cent by 2000, with the most recent reduction reflecting growth in food crop production. While the gains from trade and growth are widely distributed, with average incomes in most regions and types of households increasing, they are not evenly distributed (there is no evidence of a decline in income inequality). Some households have been unaffected, and some may even have suffered a loss of income (including some urban wage labour and especially households with a non-working head – AIDS is an important factor here).

The incidence of poverty is greater in more remote, and less secure, regions and among large families (often where relatives are caring for AIDS orphans). Through the Poverty Eradication Action Plan and the Poverty Action Fund (established through HIPC), Uganda has tried to tackle the problems. In the late 1990s, expenditure on primary education increased 307 per cent, on primary health care by 227 per cent, on agriculture by 186 per cent and on roads by 279 per cent (MFPED, 2001). Despite these achievements, the problem remains immense and many people and regions remain vulnerable (poor transport and lack of access to markets are a major problem).

The analysis presented here demonstrates that trade has made an important contribution to this reduction in poverty. In the first half of the 1990s, most of the gain from trade was through coffee exports. Since the late 1990s, however, significant export diversification has occurred, although exports are still largely of primary commodities. As export growth has contributed to economic growth, it has contributed to poverty reduction. The gains from trade are unevenly distributed, some households derived no benefits (and some even suffered losses). Even in sectors that are growing, the lowest paid workers may derive negligible benefits. Thus, while trade has benefited the Ugandan economy on aggregate and increased average incomes, almost a fifth of the population remains rooted in poverty. This is to be expected: trade and growth can reduce poverty, but trade alone will not eradicate poverty.

Future Ugandan trade policy should aim to consolidate the gains, i.e. support sectors that have experienced export growth, and also to support diversification, not only in emerging non-traditional exports but also in upgrading and processing. This is the 'export side' of trade policy, but the strategy must also recognize the pressures of trade liberalization on import-competing sectors. Furthermore, complementary government policies will be needed to target the poor in sectors or households that are marginalized from international trade. The summary below (Box 4.1) shows that the gains from trade (export growth) were widespread, although concentrated in households (producers or providers of services) and regions where cash and food crop agriculture predominated. Although not specified in the CGE model, households engaged in non-traditional exports, especially fish, will also have gained in years that are more recent. The growth in exports benefited not only the households engaged in export sectors but also provided a dynamic gain. The increase in incomes increased general demand for food and services and spread the benefits more widely throughout the economy.

The households that did benefit from trade, or that derived limited benefits in the 1990s, comprise three distinct types. First, the Northern region is remote from the dynamic parts of the economy, faces insecurity and is more vulnerable to droughts, and is relatively dependent on cotton (in the 1990s, production and world prices were low). This is the poorest region. While a recovery in world prices for cotton means that trade offers potential gains, in terms of poverty reduction the priority is to address the security problem. Nevertheless, improved transport and marketing infrastructure would integrate the North better with the rest of the country. This would facilitate increased exports and may reduce the price of food transported to the region.

Second, urban wage earners are likely to have borne the cost of increased competition from imports. To some extent, this is a short-term adjustment

Who gained from trade?	Channel(s)
Household types	*Principal factors*
Coffee farmers	Increased farm-gate prices; favourable world prices, liberalization of marketing.
Food crop farmers	Increased demand associated with growth in the economy, leading to higher prices.
Self-employed	Increased demand for the services they provide (e.g. trading, processing).
Rural wage labour	Increased demand for labour given growth of agriculture production.
Central region	Coffee and food crop production.
Western region	Coffee and food crop production.
Eastern region (less)	Food crop and tea production.
Who did not gain from trade?	
Household types	*Principal factors*
Non-working households	Received lower (transfer) incomes but faced higher consumer prices (especially food).
Wage earners (urban)	Increasing food prices relative to wages, and import competition reduced wages and/or employment.
Northern region	Poor performance of cotton and insecurity.

Box 4.1 Losers and gainers from trade.

cost. If food crop production continues to expand, food prices will decline and this will increase the real incomes (purchasing power) of urban workers. Policies to address employment and industrial development are central to increasing the incomes of workers. The development of processing industries can help, especially if these avail of the growth in production of primary commodities. More generally, investment is needed to increase efficiency, and education (general and vocational) can increase productivity.

The final groups are what are termed in the CGE model as non-working households, but are better thought of as the chronic poor. They lack assets and factors, and are therefore the least able to avail of any expansion in employment opportunities as the economy grows. They include the lowest skilled labour and female-headed 'AIDS-afflicted' households. Reducing poverty in such households will require targeted interventions. For example, public works schemes could provide employment opportunities (this may be practical in the North).

In general, the economic impacts of trade in Uganda have been favourable in the 1990s. The challenge for future trade policy is to sustain and consolidate these gains. In respect of traditional (cash crop) exports, the major issue is 'insulating' Uganda from declines in world prices. Producers should aim to increase productivity, requiring investment in new varieties and technology, and to upgrade quality (e.g. aiming for niche markets such as organic coffee). In respect of non-traditional exports, the need is to continue diversification, upgrading quality (to link into global marketing chains) and, where possible, adding processing to increase domestic value added. Some import-competing sectors are likely to face increased competition in the future, as further import liberalization is implemented (e.g. East African regional integration). Firms will need investment in technology to increase efficiency, and training and education to increase labour productivity.

Uganda could target two related areas for further export growth, food and processing. Uganda has considerable potential to increase productivity and production in agriculture and expand exports of, for example, maize, vegetables and fruits. If investment in expanding food crop production aims to penetrate export markets this will encourage quality upgrading; any surplus above export demand can be supplied to the domestic market. Producers aiming to export will want to increase productivity, and this could reduce prices of food in domestic markets. Investment in infrastructure (transport, storage and distribution) and in agriculture supports exports and domestic sales. Expansion of agriculture provides the inputs to develop domestic processing industries, which in turn create employment. In this way, trade policy can be a dynamic element of the poverty reduction strategy.

Acknowledgements

This chapter is derived from a paper prepared for the Uganda Trade and Poverty Project, part of the Africa Trade and Poverty Program coordinated by Maxwell Stamp for DFID. The views expressed here are those of the authors alone and should not be attributed to their respective institutions, DFID, Maxwell Stamp or any other body.

Notes

1 General information on Uganda's economic performance can be found in *Statistical Abstract* (e.g. UBOS, 1999, 2000) and *Background to the Budget* (e.g. MFPED, 1999, 2000, 2002); information on trade policy is in WTO (2001).

2 Some imports are subject to an import licence commission of 2 per cent, a withholding tax of 4 per cent as well as excise duty – normally 10 per cent except on cigarettes (13 per cent), alcoholic beverages (70 per cent) and soft drinks (15 per cent). The 17 per cent value added tax (VAT) applies equally to imports and domestic products.

3 Our discussion is based on Appleton (2001), Appleton *et al* (1999) and PMAU (2002a).

4 This is true for both the national price index and regional indices (see PMAU, 2002b). However, regional indices are constructed using food-based indices for urban and rural areas that omit *matoke*, an important staple, due to lack of data.

5 Households are allocated to the sector in which the household head is employed, data provided in Appleton (2001).

6 This section draws on Deininger and Okidi (2001, 2002), Larson and Deininger (2001).

5 Equity implications of reforms on living standards and child health in post-apartheid South Africa

Pushkar Maitra and Ranjan Ray

The international community recently celebrated an important milestone, namely, a decade of non-racial democratic governance in South Africa following the end of apartheid in that country. Not surprisingly, this period has witnessed a large literature on the behaviour and welfare of South African households. This was aided in large part by the availability of good quality data sets based on household surveys carried out by international agencies such as the World Bank and the International Food Policy Research Institute (IFPRI) with the cooperation and support of local institutions.

Apart from the political developments, the reasons for the recent upsurge of interest in South Africa are primarily threefold:

i Because of the importance of remittances sent by the migrant worker to her/his family in the homelands, a practice that owes its existence largely to apartheid, the South African data set provides an ideal basis for an evaluation of the impact of private transfer on household behaviour and welfare.

ii The South African pensions system is quite unique in its coverage of the population and as a form of redistributive transfer. It has undergone a remarkable transformation from one that existed as a system of public support for unemployed Whites during the apartheid era to one that is based on racial parity and directed at the elderly who have lived through years of White minority rule.

iii For historical reasons, the economic and social demarcation between the races are nowhere as distinctive as in South Africa. During the era of apartheid, South Africa's ruling National Party officially classified all individuals as falling into one of four races: Black (African), Coloured (Mixed Race), Indian (Asian) and White (Caucasian). To maintain consistency with the existing literature, this paper will stick to this terminology.

Today, ten years on from the end of apartheid, is an opportune moment to look at certain aspects of living standards in post-apartheid

South Africa. This paper provides evidence on two such features with significant policy content: (a) expenditure pattern and poverty, and (b) child health. With respect to (a), we compare the expenditure pattern of different socio-economic groups, and provide evidence on its determinants and changes during 1993–98. In this context, we summarise recent econometric evidence on the "crowding out" of private transfers by public pensions, a result with significant welfare and policy implications. With respect to (b), we exploit the availability of panel data on households in Kwazulu-Natal province to provide evidence on changes to health infrastructural facilities and child health over the period 1993–98.

Data sets and principal features

An analysis of household survey data reveals a disturbing picture of poverty, inequality and deprivation in South Africa. Fifty-three per cent of South Africans reside in the poorest 40 per cent of the households and this includes 60 per cent of the country's children (i.e. 60 per cent of South African children are growing up poor). Poor households are more likely to be Black and made up of pensioners living with children and working age adults. The average size of a poor household is around eight, compared to six for the country as a whole. The South African social security system therefore needs to be examined in the context of this kind of poverty and deprivation, which are essentially a result of the policies of apartheid followed by successive governments in South Africa before 1994.

There are three main social security programmes in South Africa: the State Old Age Pension programme, the Disability Grant Scheme and the Child Support Grant. Recently there has been a vigorous debate in the country regarding the potential benefits of a basic income support grant.

The State Old Age Pension programme (or the Social Pension programme) is the largest social assistance programme with about 1.9 million beneficiaries (in April 2001 around 3.5 million South Africans received some form of social assistance grant). Much has been written in the literature on the effects of the Social Pension programme on household outcomes: see, for example, Maitra and Ray (2003) on the effects of this programme on household expenditure patterns; Bertrand *et al.* (2003) on the effects on unemployment; Jensen (2004) on the effects on private inter-household transfers; and Duflo (2003) and Maitra and Ray (2004a) on the effects on child health. The programme indeed has a significant effect: if we exclude per capita pension income from per capita household income, all households without a wage income drop below the subsistence level and 60 per cent of households with at least one earner drop below the subsistence level. It reduces the poverty gap of pensioners by 94 per cent. Poor households that include pensioners are less poor compared to poor households that do not.

The Disability Grant Scheme is the second largest programme in terms of aggregate expenditure (though not coverage). Eligibility is determined on the basis of a medical test, to diagnose difficulty, and a means test. An individual can apply for a disability grant after the age of 18. More than 600,000 South Africans received the disability grant in 2001.

The Child Support Grant, introduced in 1998, is regarded as one of the most important reforms introduced by the government since transition to democracy in 1994. Initially the programme paid the carers R100 per month, per child for children below the age of seven. In April 2001, the benefit was raised to R110 to account for inflation. In 2001 more than 800,000 carers received this grant. One important feature of this grant programme is the concept of "follow the child" so that the benefit is independent of the family structure in which the child is born and resides. Other programmes include the Foster Care Grant, which provides benefits for families that have adopted a child and the Care Dependency Grant, which supports parents taking care of a disabled child at home.

Despite all intentions, the effect of the social security grants (with the exception of the Social Pension programme) on South African households is quite negligible. One could argue that these programmes have failed to provide adequate social protection to those who needed it most. One of the main reasons for that is the fact that the take-up rate for most of the programmes is quite low. Approximately, 43 per cent of the eligible individuals/households actually received the grants: the take-up rate was of course much higher for the Social Pension programme, close to 80 per cent and at the other extreme only 20 per cent of the eligible households actually receive the Child Support Grant, with quite obvious negative consequences.

Two different data sets are used in the paper: the 1993 South Africa Integrated Household Survey data set (henceforth called the SIHS 1993 data set) and the 1998 Kwazulu-Natal Income Dynamics Survey data set (henceforth called the KIDS 1998 data set). While the former data set was used by Ray (2000) in a comparison of South African and Pakistani expenditure patterns and by Klasen (2000), both these data sets featured in Maitra and Ray (2003, 2004b) and in Maitra (2002).

The SIHS 1993 data set was obtained from a survey conducted jointly by the World Bank and the South Africa Labour and Development Research Unit (SALDRU) at the University of Cape Town as a part of the Living Standard Measurement Study (LSMS) in a number of developing countries. The complete sample consists of approximately 9,000 households drawn randomly from 360 clusters. Households in the SIHS data set that resided in the Kwazula-Natal province were reinterviewed in 1998 and constituted the KIDS data set. The KIDS data set is the outcome of a collaborative project between the researchers at the University of Natal, the University of Wisconsin at Madison and the International Food Policy Research Institute (IFPRI). Details of the KIDS data set can be obtained from May *et al.* (2000), Maluccio *et al.* (2000), Maluccio (2000) and Maluccio *et al.* (2003).

Table 5.1 presents the sample means of the key household variables for the four races in South Africa from the SIHS 1993 data. The figures vary a good deal between races and are consistent with Engel's law on the inverse relation between household affluence and food share of the budget. The food budget shares confirm the ranking of Black, Coloured, Indian and White households in increasing order of affluence. This is confirmed in Table 5.2 which presents the poverty estimates in South Africa under P_0 (headcount ratio) and P_1 (income gap ratio). This table also shows the sensitivity of the poverty estimates to the inclusion or otherwise of economies of household size. The legacy of apartheid is clear. Regardless of which poverty measure one adopts, the majority Blacks form the poorest racial group in the population. Female-headed households face higher poverty rates than the male-headed for all the non-White races in South Africa.

Table 5.3, from Maitra and Ray (2004b), shows the change in the expenditure allocation of households in Kwazulu-Natal between 1993 and 1998. The fact that the budget share of food fell significantly and that of non-food rose significantly is indicative, via Engel's law, of a rise in living standards in Kwazulu-Natal between 1993 and 1998. This is confirmed by Table 5.4 which presents the various resource inflows (at sample mean) in the two years. Over the period 1993–98, the average income has increased from R454 to R820, a sizeable increase even when we account for inflation. As discussed later, the improvement in living standards is consistent with the results of Maitra and Ray (2004a) who find an improvement in the health of Black children residing in Kwazulu-Natal over 1993–98. The resource components that are primarily responsible for this improvement are: female income (earned and unearned) and male unearned income. The importance of pensions as a source of income is clear from this table. Note, however, that unlike female income, the average amount of social pension received in Kwazulu-Natal has remained static over 1993–98. The importance of private transfer (i.e. remittance) and social pension in poverty alleviation for the South African population as a whole is further underlined in Table 5.5 which calculates the headcount poverty rates based on income, gross and net of transfer, and pension. Transfers are more important for Black than non-Black households as seen from the size and statistical significance of the drop in poverty rates for these racial groups due to transfer and pension groups.

Further analysis of the SIHS 1993 and KIDS 1998 data sets is provided in Maitra (2002) which uses panel data to examine the effect of household characteristics on poverty and living standards and how they have changed over the five years following the dismantling of apartheid. This study shows that the gender and educational attainment of the household, ethnicity and region of residence have significant effects on both the

Table 5.1 Sample means of key variables in South Africa

Variables	Household Categories[a]						
	A	B	C	D	E	F	G
Budget share of:							
1 Food	0.455	0.434	0.514	0.519	0.396	0.320	0.201
2 Drinks and tobacco	0.035	0.039	0.023	0.037	0.037	0.023	0.025
3 Entertainment	0.004	0.005	0.003	0.003	0.005	0.010	0.011
4 Health	0.010	0.011	0.008	0.007	0.010	0.020	0.026
5 Education	0.024	0.023	0.025	0.023	0.015	0.018	0.031
6 Fuel	0.086	0.082	0.097	0.084	0.115	0.100	0.081
7 Adult clothing	0.042	0.042	0.041	0.042	0.051	0.051	0.032
8 Child care	0.005	0.005	0.004	0.004	0.007	0.001	0.006
9 Food eaten outside home	0.013	0.013	0.013	0.013	0.004	0.011	0.017
10 Other items	0.326	0.347	0.271	0.267	0.362	0.447	0.571
No. of boys in age group:							
(0–4 years)	0.31	0.31	0.32	0.36	0.28	0.19	0.12
(5–14 years)	0.62	0.60	0.68	0.69	0.62	0.53	0.28
(15–17 years)	0.16	0.15	0.17	0.18	0.16	0.15	0.08
No. of girls in age group:							
(0–4 years)	0.30	0.30	0.31	0.35	0.27	0.22	0.12
(5–14 years)	0.60	0.58	0.66	0.68	0.59	0.42	0.27
(15–17 years)	0.17	0.16	0.21	0.20	0.15	0.17	0.08
No. of male adults	1.33	1.49	0.92	1.38	1.32	1.31	1.08
No. of female adults	1.52	1.34	1.98	1.59	1.54	1.50	1.16
Household size	5.01	4.92	5.26	5.42	4.93	4.48	3.18
No. of households	8,508[b]	6,194	2,335	6,298	663	248	1,299
Monthly expenditure per capita (Rand)	541.0	595.0	398.0	291.0	504.0	798.0	1,723.0
Monthly expenditure per adult equivalent (Rand)	747.55	829.11	530.61	408.87	743.91	1,219.60	2,301.30

Notes

a A: All households. B: Male-headed households as reported in the survey. C: Female headed households as reported in the survey. D: Black households. E: Coloured households. F: Indian households. G: White households.

Table 5.2 Poverty estimates (P_α) of various household groups[a] in South Africa

α[b]	Poverty line: 8 Rand a day per capita							Size economies						
	No size economies													
	A	B	C	D	E	F	G	A	B	C	D	E	F	G
0	0.425	0.374	0.563	0.546	0.259	0.020	0.003	0.530	0.471	0.689	0.687	0.379	0.044	0.002
1	0.184	0.161	0.247	0.240	0.086	0.003	0.0004	0.248	0.216	0.334	0.330	0.137	0.007	0.0006

Notes
a A: All households.
B: Male-headed households.
C: Female-headed households.
D: Black households.
E: Coloured households.
F: Indian households
G: White households.
b P_0 denotes headcount ratio, while P_1 denotes income gap ratio.

Table 5.3 Sample means for expenditure shares

	SIHS 1993: all households	SIHS 1993: households in in Kwazulu-Natal only	KIDS 1998	t-test for difference
Food	0.4551	0.5158	0.3982	5.472***
Clothing	0.0426	0.0393	0.0362	0.379
Health	0.0100	0.0122	0.0118	0.065
Non-food	0.0446	0.0305	0.0553	−2.835***
Education	0.0233	0.0209	0.0322	−1.633
Personal expenses	0.0733	0.0657	0.0881	−1.948*
Transportation	0.0450	0.0448	0.0646	−2.015**
Energy	0.0861	0.0903	0.0673	1.983**
Other expenses	0.2201	0.1806	0.2463	−3.713***

Notes
* significant at 10%; ** significant at 5%; *** significant at 1%.
t-test for difference: Average (1993) − Average (1998), for Kwazulu-Natal households only.

poverty status and standard of living of the household. Consistent with the results of Klasen (2000) and Ray (2000), the study by Maitra (2002) found that female-headed households experienced lower living standards than male-headed ones.

Determinants of expenditure pattern

Table 5.6 from Ray (2000) presents evidence on the impact of various household and regional characteristics on the expenditure pattern of all households in the SIHS 1993 data set. The statistical significance of the coefficient of both log expenditure (LX) and its square (LX^2) in the food equation suggests that food exhibits rank three demand. *Ceteris paribus*, Black households, female-headed households (FHH) and those living in the rural areas experience higher budget share for food, consistent with their inferior living standards. A result with some policy significance is that households with better educated female adults spend a higher share of their total expenditure on education and child care. Another result worth noting is that, unlike in South Asian societies, none of the items exhibits "gender bias" in its allocation, with the gender bias variable measured as the difference between the number of boys (n_b) and girls (n_g) in the household divided by the total number of children ($n = n_b + n_g$).

Maitra and Ray (2003) used the SIHS 1993 data to provide disaggregated evidence on the impact of public and private transfer (i.e. social pensions and remittances) on each other and on the budget shares. Space considerations prevent us from reporting the results in detail but let us summarise the main results.

Table 5.4 Sample means for resource inflows

	Resource[a]				Share of resource[b]			
	SIHS 1993: all households	SIHS 1993: households in Kwazulu-Natal only	KIDS 1998	t-test for[b] difference	SIHS 1993: all households	SIHS 1993: households in Kwazulu-Natal only	KIDS 1998	t-test for[b] difference
Male earned income (E_m)	446.5905	239.7445	248.7583	0.254	0.3876	0.3247	0.2686	−2.848[c]
Female earned income (E_f)	170.9411	92.4285	155.2831	4.731[c]	0.1991	0.1935	0.1750	−1.014
Male unearned income (U_m)	100.4745	37.8058	224.4416	4.108[c]	0.0982	0.1093	0.1717	4.161[c]
Female unearned income (U_f)	21.6547	19.4187	122.4681	1.834	0.0453	0.0629	0.1305	5.293[c]
Male social pension received (P_m)	27.1081	12.1647	11.4142	0.353	0.0456	0.0353	0.0336	−0.218
Female social pension received (P_f)	42.2471	29.6781	31.2218	0.540	0.0997	0.1208	0.1073	−0.985
Male remittance received (R_m)	3.2841	2.2678	3.5247	1.527	0.0182	0.0109	0.0119	0.222
Female remittance received (R_f)	17.7799	20.3809	23.4423	1.450	0.1065	0.1427	0.1014	−2.926[c]
Total	830.0800	453.8889	820.5541	4.289[c]	–	–	–	–

Source: Maitra and Ray (2004b).

Notes

a All the eight resource inflows are expressed in terms of "per adult equivalent in the household".

b t-test for difference: Average (1993) − Average (1998), for Kwazulu-Natal households only.

c Indicates statistical significance at 1% level.

Table 5.5 Impact of transfer and pension on poverty disregarding distribution sensitivity; proportion of households classified as poor ($\phi = 0.656$)

Household category	Income excluding transfer and pension	Income including transfer and pension	Difference[a,b]
All households	53.10 (4,459)	46.34 (3,892)	8.75[c]
Black households	67.02 (4,163)	58.47 (3,632)	9.85[c]
Non-Black households	13.54 (296)	11.89 (260)	1.64[d]

Source: Maitra and Ray (2003).

Notes
a t-test for the difference in proportion below the poverty line.
b Figures in parentheses indicate the number of households below the poverty line.
c Indicates statistical significance at 5% level.
d Indicates statistical significance at 10% level.

i   In a departure from conventional demand analysis, Maitra and Ray (2003) allowed both a discrete effect (through a poverty dummy) and a continuous effect of changing household resources on its expenditure pattern. In case of several items, most notably food and fuel, both effects are significant. With respect to these items, therefore, the poor have a fundamentally different expenditure pattern from the non-poor, something that is not adequately captured by the income variable.

ii Pensions, transfer and other income have quite different impacts on budget shares and in particular transfer and non-transfer income are not spent in the same way.

iii Race does not have any impact on social pensions. This is a result of some concern since, if public transfer is to be viewed as an instrument for making positive discrimination in favour of the Black households to overcome the legacy of apartheid, then it is not serving such a role.

iv Public pensions and private transfers are generally regarded as substitutes, with the former crowding out the latter. However, in a major departure from other studies, Maitra and Ray (2003) found evidence of crowding out only in the case of households below the poverty line. In fact, for the non-poor households, private and public transfers actually complement each other. This raises important questions regarding the effectiveness of the targeting of the public pensions programmes because such programmes are designed to improve the welfare of the poor.

Changes to health facilities and analysis of child health in post-apartheid South Africa[1]

Has the dismantling of apartheid led to improved health status of Black children in South Africa? As that country came out of White minority rule

Table 5.6 OLS estimates^a of budget share equations for South Africa

Item	Interdependent variables^c													
	LX	LX2	Gender bias (d)	FHH	RUR	URB	WI	FEMED	Gender bias FHH	Blacks	Coloured	Indian	Constant	R^2
1 Food	13.89^b (1.51)	-2.03^b (0.13)	-1.13 (0.69)	2.26^b (0.42)	4.33^b (0.43)	0.43 (0.43)	0.41 (0.42)	-0.37^b (0.04)	1.73 (1.22)	3.84^b (0.64)	-0.05 (0.76)	1.38 (0.97)	34.39^b (4.43)	0.551
2 Drinks and tobacco	3.72^b (0.60)	-0.32^b (0.05)	-0.15 (0.28)	-1.7^b (0.17)	-0.98^b (0.17)	0.02 (0.17)	0.13 (0.17)	-0.23^b (0.02)	0.28 (0.49)	0.44 (0.25)	0.01 (0.30)	-0.97 (0.39)	-5.10^b (1.77)	0.063
3 Entertainment	-0.69^b (0.15)	0.08^b (0.01)	0.09 (0.07)	0.07 (0.04)	-0.25^b (0.04)	-0.19^b (0.04)	-0.09 (0.04)	-0.00 (0.00)	0.01 (0.12)	-0.00 (0.06)	-0.05 (0.08)	0.33^b (0.10)	1.77^b (0.44)	0.086
4 Health	-0.56 (0.28)	0.06 (0.02)	-0.14 (0.13)	-0.12 (0.08)	0.31^b (0.08)	0.18 (0.08)	0.12 (0.08)	0.03^b (0.01)	-0.11 (0.22)	-1.69^b (0.12)	-1.34^b (0.14)	-0.48^b (0.18)	3.30^b (0.81)	0.084
5 Education	0.03 (0.51)	0.00 (0.04)	0.34 (0.23)	0.06 (0.14)	-0.07 (0.14)	-0.35 (0.14)	-0.10 (0.14)	0.28^b (0.01)	-0.36 (0.41)	0.32 (0.21)	-0.88^b (0.26)	-1.06^b (0.32)	0.30 (1.49)	0.063
6 Fuel	-11.83^b (0.68)	0.64^b (0.06)	-0.30 (0.31)	0.08 (0.19)	0.82^b (0.19)	1.38^b (0.19)	0.63^b (0.19)	0.03 (0.02)	0.53 (0.55)	-6.40^b (0.29)	-0.88^b (0.34)	-0.31 (0.44)	59.81^b (2.0)	0.247
7 Adult clothing	3.00^b (0.45)	-0.19^b (0.04)	0.16 (0.21)	0.14 (0.13)	0.36 (0.13)	0.62 (0.13)	-0.33^b (0.13)	0.09^b (0.01)	0.03 (0.37)	2.16^b (0.19)	2.57^b (0.23)	1.93^b (0.29)	-9.55^b (1.33)	0.045
8 Child care	0.78^b (0.21)	-0.05^b (0.02)	0.02 (0.10)	0.04 (0.06)	-0.13 (0.06)	-0.15 (0.06)	-0.11 (0.06)	0.03^b (0.01)	0.07 (0.17)	0.18 (0.09)	0.24 (0.11)	-0.37^b (0.14)	-2.43^b (0.63)	0.012
9 Food eaten outside home	-2.12^b (0.60)	0.20^b (0.05)	0.28 (0.27)	0.18 (0.17)	-0.03 (0.17)	-0.38 (0.17)	-0.00 (0.17)	-0.02 (0.02)	-0.68 (0.48)	0.53 (0.25)	-0.43 (0.30)	0.07 (0.38)	6.24^b (1.76)	0.009
10 Other items	-6.23^b (1.61)	1.60^b (0.13)	0.84 (0.74)	-1.02 (0.45)	-4.37^b (0.46)	-1.55^b (0.46)	-0.66 (0.45)	0.16^b (0.04)	-1.49 (1.30)	0.62 (0.68)	0.81 (0.81)	-0.52 (1.03)	11.28 (4.73)	0.534

Notes

a The estimates of coefficients and standard errors (in brackets) have been multiplied by 100.

b Indicates statistical significance at 1% level.

c Variable names: LX = log of total household expenditure, LX2 = (LX)^2, Gender bias = $\dfrac{n_b - n_g}{n_b + n_g}$ where n_b = no. of boys, n_g = no. of girls in the household, FHH, RUR, URB denote, respectively, the dummy for female-headed households, rural and urban residence (with city residence as the default) and FEMED = years of education of the most educated female in the household.

in the early 1990s, there was widespread hope and anticipation that the end of apartheid and the restoration of democratic governance would lead to a rapid advance in the welfare of the dispossessed Black majority. One of the principal components of that welfare is the health of children. This section presents tentative evidence on this, based on panel data of households in Kwazulu-Natal over the period 1993–98, that provides pointers to the wider issue of the welfare of Black households in post-apartheid South Africa.

The evidence presented here is based on the data for Kwazulu-Natal households from SIHS, 1993 and the KIDS 1998 data set described earlier. More than 84 per cent of the original sample of Black households from the SIHS data set residing in Kwazulu-Natal in 1993 were successfully reinterviewed in 1998. The anthropometric data, namely the Z scores, is available for children that were less than (or equal to) 60 months of age at the time of the survey.

Table 5.7 provides evidence on the changing picture of health care facilities in Kwazulu-Natal province between 1993 and 1998. Clearly, in most cases where comparable figures are available, we see a marked improvement in health care facilities. For example, there has been a manifold increase in the availability of dispensaries, pharmacies and maternity clinics.

Tables 5.8 and 5.9 present the summary evidence on changes to child health in Kwazulu-Natal during the five years, 1993–98, as measured by

Table 5.7 Proportion of clusters in Kwazulu-Natal with the specific personnel/ facility

	1993	1998
Hospital	0.80	–
Public hospital	–	0.73
Private hospital	–	0.35
Dispensary	0.13	0.78
Pharmacy	0.17	0.72
Maternity clinic	0.13	0.67
Doctor	0.49	0.90
Family planning clinic	0.45	0.86
Doctor	0.40	–
Private doctor	–	0.57
Nurse	0.55	–
Pharmacist	0.19	–
Midwife	0.28	–
Family planning worker	0.36	0.30
Health worker	0.32	–
Traditional healer	0.24	0.91

Source: Maitra and Ray (2004a).

Note
Sample consists of panel households from Kwazulu-Natal.

Table 5.8 Change in child anthropometric status, 1993–98[a]

	1993			1998			Difference between 1998 and 1993	
	Count	HAZ	WHZ	Count	HAZ	WHZ	HAZ	WHZ
All children	792	−1.06	0.23	675	−0.72	0.58	0.34[b] (3.64)	0.35[b] (4.18)
Girls	397	−1.03	0.33	333	−0.67	0.55	0.36[b] (2.77)	0.22 (1.95)
Boys	395	−1.08	0.12	342	−0.77	0.60	0.31[b] (2.39)	0.48[b] (3.90)
Black children	713	−1.14	0.29	649	−0.71	0.61	0.43[b] (4.44)	0.32[b] (3.68)
Indian children	79	−0.29	0.32	26	−0.89	0.58	−0.60 (−1.78)	0.26 (0.40)

Source: Maitra and Ray (2004a).

Notes
a t-values in parenthesis
b Indicates statistical significance at 1% level.

Table 5.9 Changes in the percentage of children by Z-score categories, 1993–98

Z-score interval	Degree of malnutrition	1993			1998			Difference between 1998 and 1993	
		All	Black	Indian	All	Black	Indian[a]	All	Black
Height for age (HAZ)									
<−3	Severe	0.1199	0.1318	0.0127	0.0874	0.0832	0.1923	−0.0325 (−2.027)	−0.0486[c] (−2.880)
(−3, −2)	Moderate	0.1263	0.1374	0.0253	0.1378	0.1356	0.1923	−0.0115 (−0.650)	−0.0019 (−1.000)
(−2, −1)	Mild	0.2639	0.2679	0.2278	0.2385	0.2450	0.0769	−0.0254 (−1.115)	−0.0229 (−0.966)
>−1	Normal	0.4899	0.4628	0.7342	0.5363	0.5362	0.5385	0.0464 (1.772)	0.0734[c] (2.705)
Weight for height (WHZ)									
<−3	Severe	0.0379	0.0407	0.0127	0.0119	0.0108	0.0385	−0.0260[c] (−3.128)	−0.0299[c] (−3.434)
(−3, −2)	Moderate	0.0543	0.0533	0.0633	0.0222	0.0185	0.1154	−0.0321[c] (−3.142)	−0.0348[c] (−3.412)
(−2, −1)	Mild	0.1124	0.1024	0.2025	0.0696	0.0663	0.1538	−0.0427[c] (−2.814)	−0.0361 (−2.386)
>−1	Normal	0.7955	0.8036	0.7215	0.8963	0.9045	0.6923	0.1008[c] (5.276)	0.1008 (5.229)

Source: Maitra and Ray (2004a).

Notes
a Sample size is very small.
b Figures in parenthesis are t-values.
c Indicates statistical significance at 1% level.

the mean Z-scores (Table 5.8) and by the distribution of children in the various categories of malnutrition (Table 5.9). Following Kassouf and Senauer (1996) we categorise children according to the following classification of malnutrition: (1) severe: Z-score <3; (2) moderate: Z-score lies in the interval (−3, −2); (3) mild: Z-score lies in the interval (−2, −1); (4) normal: Z-score >1.

It is clear that there has been a definite and significant improvement in the state of child health of Black children, as confirmed by the statistically significant t-values reported in the last two columns. This is true of both boys and girls in the Black households. Note, for example, from Table 5.9 that the percentage of Black children in Kwazulu-Natal who do not suffer from malnutrition has increased significantly on account of both height for age (HAZ) and weight for height (WHZ).[2] The indifferent or unsatisfactory performance of Indian children, in contrast, possibly reflects the small sample size, and should not be taken to be conclusive evidence.

Figure 5.1 presents the Kennel density estimates of the height to age (HAZ), and Figure 5.2 presents the corresponding density estimates of weight to height (WHZ) for the Black children residing in Kwazulu-Natal in 1993 and 1998. The kernel density estimates show that the distributions are quite different between the two years. This is confirmed using the Kolmogorov-Smirnov equality of distribution test. In both cases the equality of distributions is rejected. The associated p-values are 0.0001 (for HAZ) and 0.000 (for WHZ). Clearly therefore, not only has the mean state of child health changed but so has the distribution during the period, 1993–98.

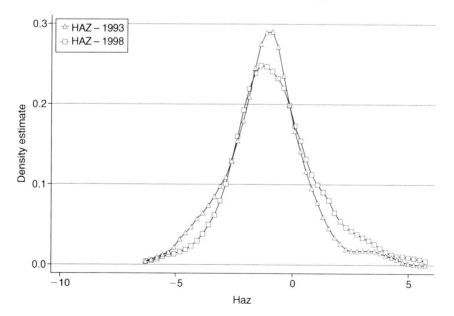

Figure 5.1 Kernel density estimates of HAZ – Black children.

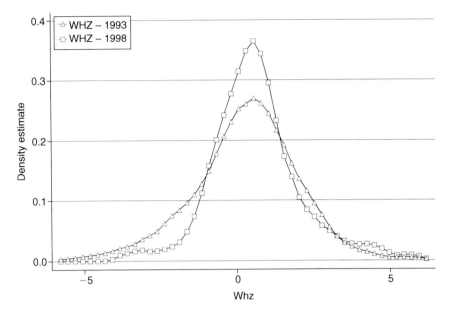

Figure 5.2 Kernel density estimates of WHZ – Black children.

This leads us to the important policy question: which variables are the principal contributors to this improvement in the health status of Black children in Kwazulu-Natal during the first five years of post-apartheid South Africa? Maitra and Ray (2004a), on which this section is based, contains detailed empirical evidence on this issue. We quote the principal results of that study.

i   Increase in household resources has contributed significantly to the improvement in child health in Kwazulu-Natal over this period. Male remittance and female social pensions record the highest positive contribution to the improvement in child health in both size and significance.

ii Children in male-headed households and those with large numbers of working age adults have done better than other children in the age group 0–5 years in improving their long-term nutritional status during the post-apartheid period.

iii The education of the household head has, also, made a positive contribution to improvements in child health in post-apartheid South Africa. With the dismantling of apartheid, there is now much greater opportunity for Black adults to benefit from education and for the health of Black children to improve as a consequence.

iv The health service variables, namely, the number of dispensaries and clinics in the cluster have, also, contributed significantly to the improvement in child health.

Conclusion

The end of apartheid and the restoration of democratic governance in South Africa have provided an opportunity to improve the welfare of the Black households who suffered under decades of White minority rule. In South Africa much of the differences in living standards among different segments of the population are the direct result of apartheid policies that denied equal access to education, employment, services and resources to the non-White population of the country. Following the dismantling of apartheid, such official policy of classifying individuals on the basis of race no longer exists. However, the legacy of years of injustice is apparent in the form of wide divergences in the standard of living of the different segments of the population. While much has been achieved in the ten years following the dismantling of apartheid, as this brief review has shown, a good deal more needs to be done to achieve social and economic equality among the different segments of the South African population.

Acknowledgements

The authors acknowledge financial support provided by an Australian Research Council Large Grant and an Australian Research Council Discovery Project for the research reported in this paper. Helpful comments from Dr Kishor Sharma and an anonymous referee are also gratefully acknowledged. This disclaimer applies.

Notes

1 The material in this section is a summarised version of our study (Maitra and Ray 2004a). For more details, the interested reader should consult this paper.
2 Note that while height for age (HAZ) is a measure of the child's long-term, nutritional status, weight for height (WHZ) is a measure of her short-term nutritional status.

Part III

Experience of centrally planned Asian countries

6 Global integration, growth and equity in Kazakhstan

Richard Pomfret

In the second half of 1991, Kazakhstan suffered a huge and unexpected political and economic shock. With very little warning, the Union of Soviet Socialist Republics (USSR) dissolved and Kazakhstan became an independent country in December 1991. With no previous history of state-hood and a precarious ethnic composition, the country faced huge challenges in state- and institution-building. The Soviet economy was without regard for internal borders, and Kazakhstan's role had been mainly that of a primary product supplier, mainly oil, minerals, grain and cotton. Within the Soviet Union, Kazakhstan had an open economy, but it had almost no direct contact with the global economy.

Given the structure of its economy, Kazakhstan's economic future after independence clearly lay as an open trading nation integrated into the global economy. The process of opening up to global integration was, however, fraught with difficulties in the face of the massive economic shocks accompanying the dissolution of the USSR. The country suffered negative economic growth for much of the 1990s, and experienced unprecedented increases in inequality.

The purpose of this chapter is to examine the growth and equity implication of global integration. The first section reviews Kazakhstan's post-independence development strategy, with particular emphasis on trade policy. Despite some major hiccups, the overall pattern has been one of increasing liberalization of the economy and, despite great outlays of policymakers' time in negotiating regional arrangements, the basis of Kazakhstan's trade policies has been liberal multilateralism. The second section evaluates Kazakhstan's economic performance since independence, stressing the uneven incidence of the post-Soviet transitional recession; households in areas with tradable resources or services weathered the storm better than households in areas without ready opportunities for earning export revenue. Since 2000 Kazakhstan's economy has been enjoying rapid growth, primarily on the basis of booming oil revenues, and the third section analyzes the prospects for growth and equity as the economy becomes more tightly integrated into the global economy.

Development strategy and trade policies since 1991

After the dissolution of the USSR in 1991, Kazakhstan and the other Soviet successor states all experienced a severe negative economic shock. None had seriously anticipated the dissolution of the Soviet Union before its final months, and all were unprepared for the severing of Soviet ties. Demand and supply networks quickly collapsed in the early 1990s, and all of the new countries in Central Asia suffered from disrupted supply chains and higher prices for imports. Imminent economic collapse was signaled in falling output and rising prices in 1991, but it would become much worse after formal dissolution of the USSR removed residual central control over the Soviet economic space and the ruble experienced hyper-inflation in 1992 and 1993. The shift to world prices notionally benefited the energy exporters such as Kazakhstan,[1] but in the short term, the country was unable to realize these gains due to dependence on Russian pipelines.

Kazakhstan adopted fairly radical reforms after independence. In January 1992, for example, Kazakhstan followed Russia's radical price reforms more closely than did other Central Asian successor states (Pomfret, 1995). The liberalization process slowed, however, in the mid-1990s.[2] Already in the currency debates of 1993, Kazakhstan was one of the more reluctant countries to abandon the ruble, and after the national currency was eventually introduced in November 1993, the monetary authorities were slow to use monetary policy to control inflation; annual inflation was not reduced to below 50 percent until 1996. This macroeconomic policy failure undermined support for other reform efforts, as the market economy could scarcely perform well when incentives from relative price changes were masked by high inflation. The privatization process, on paper a radical and equitable voucher-based system despite being biased in favor of rural (i.e. ethnically Kazakh) households, turned into a distorted distribution of public resources such that a few people gained ownership of the country's valuable oil and mineral resources while the majority received essentially valueless state assets.[3]

Since mid-1996, Kazakhstan has had a liberal trade policy when export duties were removed and the average tariff on imports fell to twelve percent. The average tariff had fallen below 8 percent by 2002 (Elborgh-Woytek, 2003: 18 – reporting IMF calculations), but there are recurring complaints of *ad hoc* impositions which make actual trade policy less predictable. Kazakhstan suddenly raised duties on intra-Central Asian trade in response to its 1998 crisis.[4] In October 1999, Kazakhstan passed legislation requiring labeling of all imports in both Russian and Kazakh, which could become a significant non-tariff barrier, although its implementation has been postponed.

The 1998 Russian Crisis and its spillover effect on Kazakhstan's economy was the major turning point in the country's post-independence economic history. Although Kazakhstan had been diversifying its trade away from the overwhelming share of the Commonwealth of Independent States (CIS) in the early 1990s, the CIS still accounted for half of the country's international trade in 1997 (Table 6.1). The largest single trading partner was Russia, and the August 1998 Russian Crisis had large contagious effects on Kazakhstan. After the initial protectionist reactions described in the previous paragraph, in April 1999 the Kazakh tenge was floated, which led to an effective 50 percent devaluation. This coincided with an upturn in world oil prices and in the early 2000s Kazakhstan experienced an export boom (Table 6.2).

In its external trade policies, Kazakhstan has pursued both multilateral and regional paths. Kazakhstan applied for membership in the World Trade Organization (WTO) in January 1996 and a Working Party was established on 6 February 1996. Bilateral market access negotiations in goods and services commenced in October 1997, and are continuing based on revised offers in goods and services. The process slowed down in 1998 following the Russian Crisis and its contagious effects on Kazakhstan,[5] but has been revitalized since 2001 in part because Russian accession negotiations have gathered steam.

In terms of diplomatic activity, Kazakhstan's president has been more visibly involved in negotiating regional arrangements. As early as December 1991 President Nazarbayev emerged as the key broker in ensuring that the USSR was followed by a regional organization covering the entire Soviet space apart from the Baltics. The Commonwealth of Independent States, however, has never played a significant role as an economic organization, despite many paper agreements to create payment areas, free trade areas, customs unions and other integrated economic spaces (Sakwa and Webber, 1997: 386–90; Pomfret, 2000b). In practice, the freedom of intra-CIS trade has deteriorated as the poorly monitored national borders of the early 1990s gave way to formal customs posts, and by the early 2000s

Table 6.1 Share of exports and imports with the CIS, 1991–99 (percentages)

	1991	1992	1993	1994	1995	1996	1997	1998	1999
Exports	91	88	84	58	53	56	46	40	26
Imports	86	94	90	61	69	70	54	47	43

Source: Islamov (2001: 173).

Table 6.2 Total exports and imports, 1993–2002 (millions of US dollars)

	1993	1994	1995	1996	1997	1998	1999	2000	2001	2002
Exports	1,107	3,227	5,256	5,926	6,497	5,511	5,598	9,138	8,647	9,930
Imports	1,704	3,285	3,807	4,247	4,302	4,373	3,686	5,052	6,363	6,809

Source: Elborgh-Woytek (2003: 4, 5), based on IMF *Direction of Trade Statistics*.

several CIS members (including Russia) were imposing visa requirements on citizens from other CIS countries.

Frustrated by lack of implementation of the many agreements signed by CIS members, President Nazarbayev has, since the collapse of the ruble zone, advocated a customs union among those CIS member countries wishing to retain a formal regional trading arrangement in the ex-Soviet space. In December 1994, Kazakhstan signed a customs union treaty with Russia and Belarus, which came into effect on 15 July 1995, and the accession of the Kyrgyz Republic in 1996 and Tajikistan in 1999 made it a Union of Five. Despite the formal agreements between 1994 and 2000, there was little evidence of implementation; echoing Nazarbayev's earlier reservations about the CIS, the Kyrgyz Republic's President Akaev was quoted in 1999 as saying that the customs union agreements existed 'on paper only"(Zhalimbetova and Gleason, 2001: 4).

In October 2000 the Union of Five was renamed the Eurasian Economic Community and a new treaty was signed in Astana, which came into effect in May 2001. In contrast to its predecessor organizations, the Eurasian Community is intended to operate as a regional international organization rather than as an inter-state agreement. The institutional framework has been strengthened in a bid to ensure better implementation, although the functional areas of the new Community differ little from those agreed within the earlier frameworks. The emphasis is on free intra-Community trade as well as a common market for labor and capital, common policies towards migration and more general policy harmonization. A specific intention is to coordinate WTO accession negotiations (but even this attempt at a common external trade policy is dubious given that the Kyrgyz Republic is already a WTO member and that Belarus appears to have differing WTO goals from Russia). At the political level, the Eurasian Community has strong support from Kazakhstan, but the attitude of the other signatories is lukewarm. Kazakhstan's ambitious aspirations are reflected, for example, in statements by the governor of Kazakhstan's central bank that the Community should aim to have a single currency and that preliminary procedures for the introduction of a single currency might take only five to seven years." [6] In practice, however, Eurasian Community integration plans stalled in 2003.[7]

An alternative grouping among CIS countries emerged in February 2003 when the leaders of Russia, Belarus, Ukraine and Kazakhstan reached a tentative agreement to create a United Economic Space (UES). Russia promoted the UES concept, but the other three countries have bridled at suggestions of establishing supranational institutions. Both the Eurasian Community and the UES reflect a more assertive Russian stance in leading regionalism in the former Soviet space, but so far, none of the intra-CIS arrangements has had any impact on trade relations.[8]

Kazakhstan has joined other regional organizations since independence. In 1992 Kazakhstan, together with Afghanistan, Azerbaijan, the

Kyrgyz Republic, Tajikistan, Turkmenistan and Uzbekistan became members of the Economic Cooperation Organization (ECO). With the three original members, Iran, Pakistan and Turkey, ECO now contained over 300 million people, and included all non-Arab Islamic countries west of India. The ECO heads of state have met frequently since 1992, and the summits have typically included grand declarations, but the implementation record is poor (Pomfret, 1999; Afrasiabi, 2000). A similar fate has beset a succession of Central Asian regional organizations, where lofty declarations have contrasted to feeble practical achievements (Rumer and Zhukov, 1998; Pomfret, 2000a). Another overlapping configuration, dubbed the Shanghai Five, emerged from a meeting in 1996 of China, Russia, Kazakhstan, the Kyrgyz Republic and Tajikistan intended to demilitarize borders. At a summit in Dushanbe in July 2000, the Shanghai Five, with Uzbekistan as an observer, took up a number of themes related to trade facilitation as well as discussing issues such as countering Islamic terrorist groups; the extension into economic areas was a fresh departure, and the group changed their name to the Shanghai Forum and invited other countries to join them. At the June 2001 summit Uzbekistan became the sixth member and the group was renamed the Shanghai Cooperation Organization (SCO). Despite the intention to cover matters such as trade facilitation, the subsequent history of the SCO has centered on political rather than economic matters.

The regional arrangements described above have often been in implicit competition, reflecting differing and mutually exclusive political pacts. The evolving patterns have incorporated concerns for closer or more arm's-length relations with Russia and, to a lesser extent, China, and competition with Uzbekistan for leadership within Central Asia. Such ebbing and flowing of interest in alternative regional permutations has inhibited the institutional development of any regional organization involving Kazakhstan. Although most have an economic content, at least in their stated goals, their economic impact has been minimal. None has reached a stage of seriously discussing preferential trade policies, and none has posed a threat to multilateralism in Kazakhstan's trade policies. In sum, despite the far greater presidential attention to regional trading arrangements, economics and external politics have driven Kazakhstan's global integration along the path of multilateralism.

Economic performance since independence

Kazakhstan suffered a severe recession in the first half of the 1990s as GDP fell by over two-fifths between 1991 and 1995. The decline halted in 1996 and 1997, before GDP suffered a further drop in 1998. Anemic performance in 1999 ended a decade of poor macroeconomic performance (Table 6.3a). This could not be explained by war as in most of the CIS

Table 6.3a Output growth and inflation (percent)

	1991	1992	1993	1994	1995	1996	1997	1998	1999	2000	2001	2002	2003	2002; 1989 = 100
Growth in real GDP	−11	−5	−9	−13	−8	1	2	−2	3	10	14	10	9	86
Inflation	79	1,381	1,662	1,892	176	39	17	7	8	13	8	6	6	–

Source: European Bank for Reconstruction and Development: *Transition Report*, 2003: 56, 58.

Notes
2002 = preliminary actual figures from official government sources.
2003 = EBRD estimates.

economic disasters.[9] Indeed, with its high initial income and human capital and its abundant natural resources, Kazakhstan might have been expected to do much better.

The most plausible explanation is in terms of disorganization (Blanchard, 1997). The government moved quickly towards price liberalization in January 1992, but it failed to follow up with the institutions required for a well-functioning market economy. Thus, the functioning, albeit inefficiently, coordinating mechanisms of central planning were followed by a coordinating void. Tardiness in bringing the hyperinflation of 1992–93 down to moderate inflation levels also contributed to the poor functioning of the market economy, although inflation was more or less under control by 1997 (Table 6.3a).

Physical disintegration was exacerbated because, among the Soviet republics, Kazakhstan was one of the most tightly integrated into the Union economy. In particular, its mineral wealth was associated with single-enterprise towns dependent on production chains involving suppliers, smelters and end-users elsewhere in the Soviet Union (usually in Russia). The fledgling oil industry in western Kazakhstan relied on Russian pipelines, but Kazakhstan's own major refineries in Pavlodar in the northeast and Shymkent in the south were linked by pipeline to Siberian oilfields. The chaotic privatization of large enterprises in 1995–96 added to the confusion, although in the longer run providing clearer ownership rights may have encouraged reduction of the physical problems.[10]

Kazakhstan experienced high emigration during the 1990s, as its population fell from over 17 million at the time of independence to less than 15 million a decade later. According to the final Soviet census in 1989 the population consisted of roughly two-fifths Kazakhs, two-fifths Russian and one-fifth other ethnic groups. The Russians, who had been the largest group in the republic a decade earlier, were concentrated in the capital city, Almaty, and in northern and eastern regions bordering the Russian Federation. Among the öther"groups were large contingents of ethnic Germans and Koreans who had been shipped to Kazakhstan by Stalin who feared their potential to be a fifth column supporting invaders from the west and east. Most of the Germans took advantage of German citizenship laws to immigrate to Germany in the early 1990s. Together with Russian emigration, both of which contained a disproportionate number of the country's well-educated and skilled people, this constituted a substantial brain drain in the early post-independence years.

Emigration complicates assessment of Kazakhstan's economic performance because output comparisons across transition countries are usually by total output rather than per capita GDP; so that Kazakhstan's relative performance may look worse than it was. In addition, the biases of all GDP estimates for transition economies probably overstate the extent of the initial recession. Other indicators of well-being reinforce the impression that Kazakhstan did not perform as poorly as the GDP estimates suggest, and that this gap between estimates and reality was bigger for Kazakhstan than for neighboring CIS countries (Pomfret, 2003b). Nevertheless, whatever its absolute or relative magnitude, Kazakhstan's output performance in the 1990s was well below potential.

The creation of a market-based economy was accompanied by increasing economic inequality. The Gini coefficient increased from 0.26 in 1987/88 to 0.33 in 1993/95 (Milanovic, 1998).[11] The best data on the distribution of expenditure are contained in the 1996 Living Standard Measurement Study (LSMS) survey and they reveal strong patterns of gainers and losers (Anderson and Pomfret, 2002, 2003). The college-educated were best placed to deal with the huge shock of the collapse of the centrally planned economy, and large households with many children were, other things being equal, the worst hit. A less self-evident feature of the transition was the emergence of large regional differences during the 1990s, as otherwise identical households experienced large differences in per capita consumption depending on their geographical location. The districts in the north and east, and to a lesser extent those in the west and the financial center of Almaty, fared much better than districts in the south and center of the country. These patterns are strongly related to regions' potential to engage in international trade. Residents of those regions with little export potential found that necessities became unattainable and living standards deteriorated drastically.

By anecdotal accounts, the winter of 1997/98 was the nadir of Kazakhstan's transition from central planning in many towns, as power supplies were uncertain. In the second half of 1998, however, the economy went through a recession following the Russian Crisis. Although this was an exogenous negative shock, Kazakhstan's susceptibility to contagion reflected to some extent the failure to create a vibrant market economy, which could withstand such a shock. The government responded with a large devaluation, which, as in Russia, helped to kick-start the economy in 1999 and 2000.

Since 2000 Kazakhstan has enjoyed rapid economic growth. To an important extent this was led by the oil sector (Table 6.4). A number of developments led to oil production beginning to increase substantially just as world oil prices started to soar. Disputes over the organization of the oil sector were gradually sorted out during the 1990s as the major international oil companies obtained access to Kazakhstan's oilfields, and this is reflected in the upturn in foreign direct investment over the second half of the 1990s (Table 6.3b), which was overwhelmingly in the energy sector. Increased exploration hit a bonanza in 2000 with the discovery of a huge offshore field in the northern Caspian Sea. The pipeline constraints on oil exports, which had been hampered by the monopsony position of Transneft's Russian route, were eased by the opening of a commercial pipeline in 2001 offering an alternative to the sea.

Table 6.3b Foreign direct investment (million US dollars)

	1992	1993	1994	1995	1996	1997	1998	1999	2000	2001	2002	2003
FDI	100	473	635	964	1,137	1,320	1,143	1,584	1,278	2,796	2,138	2,500

Source: European Bank for Reconstruction and Development: *Transition Report 2003*.

Table 6.4 Output and exports of oil and gas

	1998	1999	2000	2001	2002
Oil production (mmt)	25.6	29.4	35.4	39.3	47.3
Oil exports (mmt)	20.4	23.7	29.4	31.7	39.5
Oil exports ($m)	1,650	2,164	4,429	4,463	5,157
World oil price ($/bbl)	13.1	18.0	28.2	24.3	24.9
Natural gas production (bcm)	7.9	9.9	11.5	11.6	13.1

Source: International Monetary Fund, "Republic of Kazakhstan: Selected Issues and Statistical Appendix", *IMF Country Report No. 03/211*, July 2003: 8 (oil), 72 (gas).

Note
The source projects oil production in 2010 of 96.7 mmt and natural gas production of 39.3 bcm.

Global integration, growth and equity

In the twenty-first century, Kazakhstan is starting to fulfill its destiny as a major oil exporter. Unexplored areas of the north Caspian are expected to contain large fields, adding to the long-term bonanza. World energy prices are difficult to predict, but the IMF is forecasting annual oil exports of 84 million metric tons earning $10 billion, and natural gas production of around 40 billion cubic meters by 2010 and, although government revenue from product sharing is always back-loaded, it could amount to around $165 billion over the next 45 years.[12] Unless these forecasts turn out to be far above the mark, the coming decades will see a huge stimulus to the economy and potential for economic development. Will this benefit from integration into the global economy lead to growth with equity or will it benefit a wealthy few?

A more rigorous debate on the old topic of whether natural resource abundance is a boon or a curse was reignited by Sachs and Warner (1995), who found a negative relationship between resource abundance and economic growth in cross-country regressions. Subsequent contributions have refined the debate, establishing that the relationship is conditional (on variables proxying for institutions or on democracy) and that the negative relationship is stronger for oil and minerals than for agriculture.[13] Identification of the transmission mechanisms has focused on three links: through relative prices (Dutch disease effects), through volatility, and through rent seeking and distortion of institutions.[14] In Kazakhstan, it is difficult to assess the actual significance of the first two mechanisms due to the short time period, but it is possible to comment on the third mechanism. The existence of rent seeking is well documented in Kazakhstan, and has been especially associated with the oil sector.

Although much of the alleged malfeasance dates from the large-scale privatizations of 1995–96, it became increasingly publicized around the turn of the century. Even earlier, in October 1994, the Prime Minister,

Tereschenko, had been forced to resign amidst a scandal surrounding two of his ministers, but there were no convictions. Stories of pay-offs began to circulate more widely during the term of the next Prime Minister, Kazhegeldin.[15] The sale of state assets in 1996 involved many deals which were speedily concluded at apparently bargain prices.[16] Especially controversial was the sale of the Pavlodar and Aksu aluminum facilities to the Trans-World Group, whose leading figures included men closely associated with members of the Kazakhstan government (Olcott, 2002, 161–3); the Group's influence waned as Kazhegeldin's star faded after 1997, but it received substantial compensation.[17] Balgimbayev, who was appointed Prime Minister in October 1997, was former head of the oil ministry and had already been involved in deals to sell oil exploration rights.

The highest profile case involves pay-offs associated with oil deals made in 1996–97 through the intermediation of a US banking company, Mercator Corp. The legal proceedings started in the courts of England and judges' offices in Switzerland, before moving to US courts, where a former senior Mobil executive has been sent to jail for 46 months and an American investment banker potentially faces jail sentences of up to 88 years. The numbers involved in this case, associated with $1.05 billion paid by Mobil for a 25 percent stake in the Tengiz oilfield, dwarfed earlier documented bribes.[18] Other major oil companies, Amoco, Texaco and Phillips, have been mentioned in the US indictments in connection with bribes paid in 1996–97.[19]

In Transparency International's 2003 corruption perceptions index, Kazakhstan ranked 100th out of 133 countries covered – down from 65th, out of 90, in 2000. The external dimension of the corrupt practices is, however, of secondary importance. Outside the oil and minerals sectors, corrupt practices may deter foreign companies from operating in Kazakhstan. Oil and mining companies are, however, used to working under tough conditions, but they go where the oil is, and the drive for reserves is pushing all the major oil companies to seek stakes in the Caspian Basin.

The domestic consequences are more insidious. Although the indictments in the US courts do not name the Kazakhstan officials involved – they are identified only as KO1 and KO2 – they are widely believed to have been the president and a former prime minister.[20] The wider sense of scandal surrounding the government and the president's family are domestically referred to as "Kazakhgate", and have had two opposing impacts on domestic institutional quality.

The positive aspect was the emergence of a domestic opposition party offering a potential alternative to the incumbent regime and emphasizing the importance of the rule of law. Whether this will in fact be a step towards political pluralism remains to be seen. Kazakhstan was, after independence, viewed as one of the more liberal CIS countries, but President Nazarbayev's rule became more autocratic during the 1990s. He was, however, never able to assert centralized authority to the extent that his counterparts in neighboring Uzbekistan and Turkmenistan did. This reflected in part the delicate ethnic balance, and also the three-horde division among Kazakhs. Connected to these ethnic and tribal divisions, substantial regional independence limits the power of the center. These centrifugal forces are exacerbated by the regional differences in economic performance described in the previous section and by the geographical concentration of oil and mineral deposits.

During the early 2000s, the degree of centralized repression fluctuated, but the prospects for a more democratic system have not been extinguished. A feature of Kazakhgate has been the ability of non-governmental forces to keep the charges against the government in the limelight and to elicit responses to their charges. When the main opposition group in Kazakhstan stepped up allegations of corruption, Prime Minister Tasmagambetov admitted the possible existence of secret accounts in Switzerland but alleged that they had been set up by former Prime Minister Kazhageldin, who was by then a leading opposition figure. President Nazarbayev subsequently disclosed the existence of a Swiss account holding $1 billion that he was holding as a reserve fund to be used in a national emergency. In April 2002, the president formally reported to parliament the existence of accounts abroad, which were based on proceeds from the sale of shares in oilfields to foreign investors in 1996, and which had been drawn upon to finance the budget and for construction of the new capital in Astana. According to information provided to the February–March 2003 IMF mission, $321 million had been transferred from these accounts to the National Fund for the Republic of Kazakhstan (NFRK) in May 2002, and all government accounts held abroad in March 2003 amounted to just over $0.5 million.[21] In April 2003, $1 billion was transferred from a Swiss account to the NFRK.[22]

The negative aspects of high-level corruption are more obvious, even though their long-term effects remain difficult to measure. Rent seeking undermines entrepreneurship, as high returns to socially unproductive activities discourage people from putting their energies into directly productive activities. Corruption in high places validates corruption at lower levels, and Kazakhstan's public service is now filled with officials whose expected incomes consist of bribes as well as official salary. Such rent seeking undermines the efficiency of provision of public services from health-care to law and order. Trade with neighbors and transit trade are diminished by the venality of customs officials and traffic police. The erosion of law and order and of public morality undermines the efficiency of any economic system, because even in a market economy based on self-interest the invisible hand requires acceptance of behavioral mores such as instinctive honesty or avoidance of fraud in order to reduce transactions costs.

Whether global integration will produce growth with equity in Kazakhstan over the next decade depends critically upon the relative impact of these two countervailing forces. Democracy, as shorthand for an inclusive and fair civil society, would curb economic rent seeking and provide a basis for building good institutions. Reinforcement of a corrupt despotic regime would take Kazakhstan along the path of nations such as Nigeria or Venezuela, where oil has been a curse for the majority of the population.

Conclusion

The story of global integration, growth and equity in Kazakhstan can be divided into two post-independence phases. During the 1990s, the economy was transformed from a centrally planned economy within the Soviet Union to a market-oriented economy in the global trading system. This decade was characterized by dismal economic performance, including negative economic growth and increased inequality, although this had more to do with the transition from central planning and the dissolution of the Soviet Union than with the global integration that was the corollary of these seismic changes.

Since 2000, the country has enjoyed rapid economic growth, the main source of which was increased oil production by consortia involving foreign corporations, better pipeline options for exporting the oil and soaring oil prices. The economic growth is clearly associated with the global integration of Kazakhstan's economy, but will it produce long-term growth with equity? The process of allocating oil exploration and exploitation rights and selling other state assets created fabulous wealth for a few entrepreneurs and officials. A key issue for Kazakhstan's near future is whether oil will turn out to be a blessing or a curse for the population as a whole.

Notes

1 Tarr (1994) estimated, on the basis of 1990 trade flows, terms of trade gains of 19 percent for Kazakhstan. Russia (79 percent gain), Turkmenistan (50 percent gain) and Kazakhstan were the only two Soviet successor states expected to benefit significantly from replacing Soviet prices by world prices.
2 For general assessments of Kazakhstan's post-independence economy see Kalyuzhnova (1998) and Olcott (2002).
3 Privatization in Kazakhstan resembled that in Russia in key aspects. The early privatizations and the voucher scheme ended up distributing only small or valueless enterprises in the early 1990s. The most valuable state assets, i.e. viable large enterprises, mines and oil exploration rights, were mostly sold in 1995–97, creating a wealthy elite of the new owners and officials enriched by the sales.
4 After the August 1998 Russian crisis, Kazakhstan introduced a 20 percent value added tax on all personal imports from Russia, the Kyrgyz Republic and Uzbekistan, and then in December 1998 enacted a law on "Measures to Protect the Domestic Market from Imported Goods". Under this law special tariffs as high as 200 percent were imposed on a number of goods imported from the Kyrgyz Republic and Uzbekistan in February 1999, when a number of other restrictions such as quotas on cement imports from the Kyrgyz Republic were also

introduced. In April 1999 the 200 percent February tariffs were eliminated, but new licensing procedures, transit fees and mandatory deposits on imports from the Kyrgyz Republic and Uzbekistan were introduced.

5 After the third WTO Working Party meeting on Kazakhstan in October 1998, there were no further meetings until July 2001. Another example of the hiatus in trade liberalization was the failure to implement trade reform commitments included in 1998 EFF-supported IMF programs. Kazakhstan, however, maintained its commitment to current account convertibility, unlike Uzbekistan and Turkmenistan who responded to economic difficulties by introducing draconian exchange controls in 1996 and 1998 respectively.

6 The quotation by the governor of the National Bank of Kazakhstan, Grigori Marchenko, is from a sponsored section in *International Herald Tribune*, 24 April 2002. Later in 2002 Russian Prime Minister Kasyanov expressed hope that the Eurasian Community would adopt the Russian ruble as a common currency.

7 See Tomiuc (2002) and, for a more optimistic analysis of the Community's prospects, Zhalimbetova and Gleason (2001).

8 Even as Russia was promoting the UES concept at a political level, in 2002–03 Russia was raising tariffs and non-tariff barriers on specific imports from CIS countries, such as steel from Ukraine (Yudaeva, 2003). By the end of 2003 the UES appeared to have joined the list of defunct schemes; the concluding communiqué of the January 2004 Astana summit between presidents Putin and Nazarbayev made no mention of the UES.

9 The worst CIS performers during the 1990s, measured by the level of real GDP in 1999 relative to 1989, were Moldova, Georgia, Ukraine, Tajikistan and Azerbaijan, all of whom saw their GDP cut by over half (**EBRD**, *Transition Report Update April 2001*, p. 15).

10 Table 6.3a, however, illustrates the lack of short-term benefits at the macroeconomic level.

11 Milanovic's Gini coefficients are based on the Soviet-era household budget surveys, whose sampling techniques left much to be desired. The expenditure Gini of 0.35 from the 1996 Kazakhstan LSMS survey suggests that the HBS-based income Gini of 0.33 in 1993/5 is too low, because income-based Ginis are normally substantially higher than expenditure Ginis.

12 IMF staff estimates reported in International Monetary Fund, "Republic of Kazakhstan: Selected Issues and Statistical Appendix", *IMF Country Report No. 03/211*, July 2003, pp. 15–16.

13 See, for example, the literature review and regression analysis in the first two sections of Sala-i-Martin and Subramanian (2003).

14 The Dutch disease literature has a lengthy theoretical pedigree (Corden, 1984), but appears to be the empirically least important link. Sala-i-Martin and Subramanian (2003) reject Dutch disease explanations of Nigeria's dismal growth record and emphasize the institutions link. The deleterious effects of volatility was emphasized in the case studies in Gelb (1988). Tornell and Lane (1999) analyze competition for, and dissipation of, rents as the source of the resource curse. Other authors have suggested other links, e.g. resource abundance reduces the incentive to invest in human capital, but these have not received much attention in the empirical literature.

15 According to a widespread rumor in 1996, a $500 million signing bonus was "lost" in an oil sector transaction. In the same year, the Chief Justice, Malakhov, was dismissed for taking over $100,000 in bribes.

16 Sander Thoenes "Kazakhstan's Sale of the Century", *Financial Times*, 25 October 1996.

17 See, "Trans-World settles with Kazakhstan", *Financial Times*, 8 February 2000,

and, more generally on TransWorld, Richard Behar "Capitalism in a Cold Climate", *Fortune*, 12 June 2000).

18 This case was featured in Transparency International's 2004 *Global Corruption Report*, pp. 204–5. For a juicier account of the escalating demands of the Kazakhstan officials, see Seymour M. Hersh "The Price of Oil; What was Mobil up to in Kazakhstan and Russia?" *New Yorker*, 9 July 2001, pp. 48–65.

19 As a result of subsequent mergers in the oil industry this involves some of the world's largest companies: Exxon-Mobil, BP-Amoco, ChevronTexaco, and ConocoPhillips. Other Kazakhstan-related cases of corrupt practices or money-laundering have been or are in the courts of Belgium and Canada.

20 Several commentators, including the *New York Times* report, identified the top official described in the indictment as having signed the sale to Mobil as President Nazarbayev. The *Wall Street Journal* (23 April 2003) identified KO1 and KO2 as Nazarbayev and Balgimbayev.

21 International Monetary Fund, *Staff Report for the 2003 Article IV Consultation*, 7 May 2003, p. 18.

22 The NFRK is primarily an oil fund, but it has also been used to support pension reform, and Kazakhstan officials claim that most of the $1 billion went to pay off pension arrears.

7 Reform, growth and equity in Kyrgyz Republic

Kishor Sharma

With the disintegration of the former Soviet Union (FSU), the Kyrgyz Republic (also known as Kyrgyzstan) together with four other Central Asian land-locked countries gained independence in the early 1990s.[1] Independence from the FSU brought more challenges than opportunities mainly because being a part of the FSU for about 70 years Kyrgyzstan (and many other Central Asian countries) did not have institutions and infrastructure to manage its economy independently. Despite this, Kyrgyzstan embraced an outward-oriented policy by lowering barriers to trade and investment, liberalizing prices and privatizing public enterprises. It even went forward and joined the WTO in December 1998. It was the first country in the region to be the WTO member despite the fact it was known as a non-market economy for about 70 years. While these achievements towards global integration are remarkably good for a newly independent country, there has not been any attempt to examine its implications for growth and equity, and identify development challenges in the post-reform period. The aim of this chapter is to fill this gap in the literature.

Reforms since the early 1990s

The Kyrgyzstan reform process has gone through three distinct phases. In the first phase (1991–95), it focused on privatization of small-scale enterprises, liberalization of prices and introduction of Enhanced Structural Adjustment Facility (ESAF) of the International Monetary Fund (IMF). During this phase, it also eliminated most export taxes and introduced the full current account convertibility. In the second phase (1996–99), it introduced the value added tax (VAT), reformed banking sector and privatized medium-scale enterprises. It was during this period that Kyrgyzstan became a member of the WTO. The third phase which is being implemented (2000–05), focuses on privatization of large enterprises (such as telecommunications, one energy distribution company, the national airlines and two commercial banks) and the development of physical infrastructure.

Trade policy regime

The Kyrgyz Republic is one of the most open economies in the region (Table 7.1). Since independence, it has adopted a comprehensive reform agenda to remove policy-led distortions inherent under the Soviet policy. Kyrgyzstan has one of the lowest import tariffs in the region and has continued to refine its tariff structure after joining the WTO in 1998. Kyrgyz Republic does not regulate exports through export restrictions. In addition, exporters are not required to sell a certain percentage of output to government at lower prices nor are they required to sell through the marketing board. As such, there is no marketing board for any export commodity and exporters are free to sell their products. An export licence is required only for electricity export, which is issued by the State Agency for Energy (SAE) – a state owned agency. An import licence is not required for most products. While Tajikistan has a very low tariff and it does not exercise quantitative restriction (QRs), it seems to restrict trade through time consuming customs formalities. For example, exporters and importers have to obtain several documents from various departments in order to meet customs formalities.

Table 7.1 A comparative perspective of trade restrictiveness in Baltic Republic countries 1999 and 2002

	1999		2002	
	Average tariff	*Overall rating*[1]	*Average tariff*	*Overall rating*[1]
Armenia	3.7	1.0	4.0	1.0
Azerbaijan	12.0	5.0	10.8	2.0
Belarus	12.6	8.0	12.2	8.0
Estonia	0.0	1.0	3.1	1.0
Georgia	10.0	2.0	10.9	2.0
Kazakhstan	7.8	4.0	7.8	4.0
Kyrgyz Republic	9.2	1.0	5.1	1.0
Latvia	5.3	1.0	4.3	1.0
Lithuania	4.5	1.0	5.3	1.0
Moldova	8.9	1.0	6.9	1.0
Tajikistan	12.6	5.0	5.0	5.0
Turkmenistan	8.0	1.0	8.0	1.0
Ukraine	0.5	7.0	0.0	7.0
Uzbekistan	14.7	5.0	12.7	5.0
	29.0	10.0	15.3	10.0

Source: International Monetary Fund (IMF) (2000, 2003).

Notes
1 The overall rating consists of a 10-point scale, which weighs a country's simple average tariff and the extent of non-tariff barriers. Countries with a scale of one to four are considered to have broadly open trade regimes. A rating of five or six indicates moderate trade restrictions. Countries with ratings of seven to ten are considered to have restrictive trade regimes.
Central Asian countries are highlighted.

Foreign exchange regime

Following independence, Kyrgyzstan faced a payment crisis. To address this, the government exercised tight exchange control, including foreign exchange surrender requirements under which exporters were required to surrender a certain percentage of their earnings at the Central Bank at a lower exchange rate. This acted as a tax on exports, which prompted over-invoicing of imports and under-invoicing of exports. To combat this, the government exercised tight valuation processes and frequent inspections of production sites, leading to delay and corruption. In 1993, the government abolished export earning surrender requirements and adopted a unified exchange rate regime. In the same year, Kyrgyz introduced its own currency (som). To reverse the shortage of foreign exchange, the government relaxed restrictions on foreign exchange transactions and introduced a market-based exchange rate regime in 1995. In the same year, its currency was made fully convertible for current account transactions. Presently, there are no restrictions in foreign exchange transactions.

Privatization

The Kyrgyz government has privatized a large number of public enterprises, deregulated business activities and gradually removed sector-specific subsidies, particularly in the energy and water sectors. Privatization has proceeded in three stages. Small-scale enterprises were privatized in the first stage, which was completed by the mid-1990s. In the second stage, medium-scale enterprises were privatized, which were completed by late 1990s. Privatization of large-scale enterprises is currently under way and almost 50 per cent of these enterprises have been privatized so far. Within large-scale enterprises, progress in privatizing natural monopoly enterprises, namely energy and transportation, has been slow. Some competition has been introduced in the telecommunications sector by permitting mobile phone companies to operate in the domestic market. The private sector is allowed to generate electricity, but it appears that government still maintains control in the distribution line. It means all power generated by the private sector will have to be sold to SAE at much lower prices than what it would charge from customers. The number of privatized state-owned enterprises from 1993 to 1999 is presented in Table 7.2. Most of these enterprises are trade and catering (1,916), followed by communal services (1,907) and manufacturing (529).

Although privatization has transferred the ownership structure, these enterprises have not gone through a major restructuring. With the exception of agricultural farms, there has not been any significant improvement in productivity in manufacturing, trade and catering. Table 7.3 reports type of privatization. As of 1999, 6,658 units were privatized, of which 18 per cent and 8 per cent were privatized through commercial competition and auction respectively. Over 70 per cent of privatized units were either

Table 7.2 Number of privatized units by economic sectors

	1993*	1994	1995	1996	1997	1998	1999	Total*
Total	4,428	702	703	327	177	175	146	6,658
Manufacturing	259	57	137	23	46	3	4	529
Light manufacturing	42	6	9	1	–	1	1	60
Food manufacturing	77	31	87	4	–	1	1	201
Machinery and metal rolling	56	3	9	1	2	–	–	71
Construction materials	37	5	14	2	2	–	–	60
Others	47	12	18	15	42	1	2	137
Agriculture	235	84	22	10	1	1	3	356
Construction	223	76	74	39	5	15	23	455
Transport	82	21	33	7	14	4	4	165
Communal services	1,811	37	19	15	6	16	3	1,907
Trade and catering	1,626	123	50	87	15	11	4	1,916
Supplies	–	12	30	6	59	2	2	111
Public utilities	–	24	31	23	8	36	28	150
Health care, sports and social security	–	174	170	7	–	6	23	380
Education	–	7	2	2	3	7	3	24
Culture and arts	–	4	6	7	3	7	10	37
Science and scientific research	–	1	–	–	–	–	–	1
Others	192	82	129	101	16	67	39	626

Source: Kyrgyz Republic official website.

Note
* Cumulative.

Table 7.3 Number of privatized units by type of privatization

	1993*	1994	1995	1996	1997	1998	1999	Total*
Total	4,428	702	703	327	177	175	146	6,658
Conversion to joint stock company	778	281	364	75	124	31	20	1,673
Rented to subsequently purchase	67	–	7	21	2	9	7	113
Sale through commercial competition	1,079	35	16	51	5	30	5	1,221
Conversion to limited joint stock company	99	66	10	9	4	10	6	204
Sale to private parties and workers' collectives	2,147	280	205	91	36	64	98	2,921
Auctioned	257	40	100	80	5	31	10	523

Source: Kyrgyz Republic official website.

Note
* Cumulative.

converted into joint stock company, with the government being the major shareholders or rented to the employers working in the company. Since the government still has direct interventions in these entities, this may have restricted competition.

Foreign investment policy

In an attempt to attract export-oriented investment, the government created four export-processing zones (EPZs), but only one is currently in operation, the Bishkek EPZ. Industries that operate in the EPZ have duty free access to intermediate inputs. In addition, they are exempt from import duties and taxes, pay lower turnover tax (less than 2 per cent depending on industry), but pay payroll tax (about 37 per cent) which is applied to all industries regardless of their location. Customs formalities for industries that operate within the EPZ are performed by the customs office of the Bishkek EPZ. Any industry that exports over 75 per cent of its output can be established in the zone, but in reality, most industries sell about 50 per cent of their output locally. With pressure from the international finance institutions, the EPZ law was amended in 2000 and 2001, which requires the EPZ enterprises to pay duties and taxes on goods sold locally. Despite these lucrative incentives, very few export-oriented industries have emerged in the Bishkek EPZ mainly due to the poor business climate (see the last section of this chapter). It appears that industries that have come to the EPZ are motivated by the duty free access to intermediate inputs and tax avoidance rather than exports.

In an attempt to attract foreign investment, the Kyrgyz government offers several financial incentives. These include tax holidays of between two and five years depending on the sector. Export-oriented industries tend to get income tax holidays for a longer period. Foreign firms are allowed to repatriate 100 per cent of their profit and there are no restrictions as to the foreign share holding. Also, there are no local content and technology transfer requirements. Despite these incentives, foreign investment remains very low. The cumulative foreign director investment during 1993–2001 was about US$414 million. Among the CIS countries, Kyrgyzstan is the second least popular destination for foreign investment after Tajikistan. The lower level of foreign investment appears to be linked with poor governance, weak enforcement of commercial law and inefficient infrastructure rather than the weakness in investment policy.

Growth, structural change and equity

Structure of the economy and growth performance

Kyrgyzstan's economy relies heavily on agriculture. In the post-independence period, its share in GDP rose from 33 per cent in 1990 to 52 per cent by the mid-1990s and reached about 55 per cent by early 2000 (see Table

7.4), thanks to privatization of farm and land reform, which significantly improved agricultural productivity in the post-independence period. Agriculture contributes about 55 per cent to GDP and employs 53 per cent of the work force (Table 7.5). The industry sector, which includes mining, manufacturing, electricity, gas and water, contributes less than 20 per cent to GDP and employs about 9 per cent of the work force. Its share in GDP has fallen since the early 1990s. The service sector, which includes trade, transport, communication and finance, contributes just over 18 per cent to GDP and employs about 37 per cent of the work force (in 2001).

Like most other Central Asian economies Kyrgyzstan experienced a significant fall in GDP. While this was somehow arrested by the mid-1990s, the 1997 Russian financial crisis did not help sustain the growth in GDP. In fact, growth in real GDP fell from 7.1 per cent in 1996 to 1.8 per cent by 1998, although since the early 2000s it has achieved an average annual growth of about 5 per cent (see Table 7.4). Kyrgyzstan has not yet fully recovered the lost output since disintegration from the FSU. Even by 2002, it recovered only about 76 per cent of the lost output. For example, GDP at constant 1990 market price was 39.4 million soms on the eve of independence (1991) which did not even exceed 30 million soms by 2002 (Table 7.5). Poor growth performance resulted in a fall in per capita income, which declined, from U$751.7 in 1992 to US$342.7 by 2001 (Table 7.5).

Loss in subsidies from the FSU, on the one hand, and poor growth performance, on the other, has increased Kyrgyz reliance on foreign debt, which increased from about 33 per cent of GDP in 1990 to 110 per cent by 2001 (Table 7.6). Kyrgyz's commitments towards market-oriented reform helped attract a significant amount of foreign aid to the country. In fact, among the CIS countries it has attracted the highest amount of foreign assistance in the post-independence period. If it was not for external assistance, the Kyrgyz economy would not have seen its ten years of independence and

Table 7.4 Macroeconomic indicators and performance

	1990	1992	1994	1996	1998	2000	2001
Growth in real GDP	0.3	−19.0	−20.0	7.1	1.8	5.4	5.3
GDP per capita in US$	–	751.7	249.1	398.4	350.2	263.8	342.7
Share of agriculture in GDP (%)	33.5	37.5	46.2	52.0	52.7	54.1	54.6
Share of industry in GDP (%)	27.1	25.4	18.3	14.2	18.5	17.2	17.4
Share of service in GDP (%)	19.1	18.0	18.8	20.0	17.7	17.2	18.1
Inflation (change in CPI %)	170.0*	1,259.0	95.7	35.0	10.4	18.7	6.9
Central government budget balance (% of GDP)	0.3	−17.4	−11.6	−9.5	−4.6	−10.0	−4.0
Current account balance (% of GDP)	–	−1.8	−11.3	−23.6	−16.7	−5.6	−0.7

Sources: ADB (2002a) and EBRD (1999), 'Transition Report 1999 Ten Years of Transition'.

Note
* 1991.

Table 7.5 Kyrgyzstan key indices: production

Item	1991	1992	1993	1994	1995	1996	1997	1998	1999	2000	2001	2002
Population (million: as of July 1)	4.39	4.49	4.48	4.47	4.62	4.69	4.76	4.83	4.90	4.97	4.95	4.98
GDP at 1990 constant market prices *Labour force* (thousand: calendar year)	39.4	34.0	28.7	22.9	21.7	23.2	25.5	26.0	27.0	28.5	30.0	29.8
Employed	–	–	1,710	1,716	1,741	1,791	1,792	1,811	1,901	1,911	1,926	–
Agriculture	1,754	1,836	1,681	1,645	1,641	1,651	1,689	1,705	1,764	1,767	1,774	1,775
Manufacturing	623	70	669	686	771	778	816	837	924	938	944	–
Others	466	414	359	318	271	241	228	219	204	202	182	–
Unemployed	665	722	653	641	599	632	645	649	636	627	648	–
Unemployment rate (%)	–	–	29	71	100	140	103	106	137	144	152	–
Production (thousand metric tons: calendar year)												
Agriculture, crop year	–	–	1.7	4.1	5.7	7.8	5.7	5.9	7.2	7.5	7.9	–
1 Wheat	434	634	831	566	625	964	1,274	1,204	1,109	1,039	11,190	–
2 Barley	557	582	477	288	159	166	152	162	180	150	140	–
3 Potatoes	326	362	308	311	432	562	678	774	957	1,046	1,168	–
4 Maize	365	281	184	129	116	182	171	228	308	338	443	–
5 Vegetables (fresh, frozen, etc.)	399	404	259	266	318	369	479	556	719	747	815	–
6 Meat	230	228	214	197	180	186	186	191	196	196	197	201
7 Milk	1,131	961	946	872	864	885	912	973	1,064	1,105	1,142	1,173

Production indexes period averages

Agriculture (1985/1989–91 = 100)	107.0	100.6	97.0	88.0	81.2	89.8	97.9	100.8	106.3	107.7	111.2	113.0
Industry (1985/1995 = 100)	118.0	87.0	65.0	47.0	100.0	108.8	163.6	178.0	170.5	185.7	194.1	142.0

Energy (annual values)

Coal ('000 m.t.)

Production	–	2,151	1,721	848	463	410	522	432	417	419	475	498
Exports	–	1,024	531	171	171	100	78	23	11	22	19	101
Imports	–	1,339	1,028	1,355	500	844	290	806	764	726	343	883
Consumption	–	2,465	2,218	2,032	792	1,154	734	1,215	1,170	1,123	801	–

Electricity (mn kWh)

Production	14,171	11,892	11,091	12,932	12,349	13,758	12,637	11,618	13,119	14,886	13,667	11,902
Exports	–	–	–	–	1,622	2,881	2,417	998	2,011	3,153	2,165	1,062
Imports	–	–	–	–	254	815	715	394	184	321	322	385
Consumption	8,814	8,616	8,467	8,189	10,981	11,678	10,854	10,893	11,262	12,054	11,797	–

Source: Asian Development Bank (2002c, 2003).

would have collapsed by now. The current level of external debt is unsustainable without a significant improvement in growth performance, which requires reforms in domestic fronts as well as cooperation from neighbouring countries. Given its land-locked position and the small size of its domestic market, regional cooperation is important to accelerate its growth.

The government in Kyrgyzstan is operating under the severe resource constraint. Despite a huge requirement for developmental investment, gross fixed capital formation has been declining. From the period 1990 to 2001, gross fixed capital formation as a percentage of GDP fell from 24 per cent to 16 per cent (Table 7.6). Foreign investment remains very low despite liberalization in trade and investment policies. It is obvious that in the absence of good governance, efficient infrastructure, and simplified customs and cross-border formalities, liberal trade and investment policies have failed to attract private investment.

In the immediate transition period, the Kyrgyz Republic experienced hyperinflation and a huge budget deficit. By the early 1990s, inflation was over 1,200 per cent and the central government budget deficit was about 17 per cent of GDP (Table 7.4). This was reversed by the mid-1990s mainly through tight monetary and fiscal policies. By 2001, inflation was brought down to 6.9 per cent and the central government deficit to 4 per cent of GDP. The high current account deficit remained a problem until the end of the 1990s. It was only in early 2000s that the current account deficit was brought under control (about 6 per cent and 1 per cent of GDP in 2000 and 2001 respectively). Although macroeconomic stability has been achieved mainly through tight monetary and fiscal policies, progress towards diversification of the production base has been very limited in the absence of efficient institutions, infrastructure and an easy access to regional and international markets as discussed in more detail below.

Trade performance

While the Kyrgyz Republic's exports almost doubled during the 1993 to 1997 period, it was not sustained after 1998 mainly due to the Russian finan-

Table 7.6 Key economic indicators

	1990	*2001*
Gross fixed capital formation % of GDP	24.29	16.41
Exports of goods and services % of GDP	29.20	36.54
Per capita FDI (US$)	3.03	4.43
External debt % of GDP	33.00[a]	110.00
External debt % of export	86.50[a]	148.20[b]

Source: ADB (2002a) and EBRD (1999), 'Transition Report 1999 Ten Years of Transition'.

Notes
a 1993.
b 1994.

cial crisis of August 1997, as Russia and other FSU countries were the major destinations of its exports. The share of exports in GDP fell from about 39 per cent in 1993 to 31 per cent by 2001, reflecting a fall in purchasing power of the nation as a whole. As exports fell, imports also declined. The share of imports in GDP fell from 51 per cent in 1993 to about 31 per cent in 2001. Since its imports are dominated by oil, gas and machinery, this fall had a significant impact on output growth. As imports fell faster than exports, trade deficit as a percentage of GDP declined from 12 per cent in 1993 to 6 per cent in 1997 and less than 1 per cent by 2001 (Table 7.7).

As shown in Table 7.8, Kyrgyzstan's exports are dominated by electricity, mining, machine building, light industries and food processing. In recent years, exports of light manufacturing as well as food products have sharply fallen. These two industry groups together had about a 40 per cent share in total manufacturing export earnings in 1994, which fell to about 19 per cent by 2002. The Kyrgyz Republic has a huge potential in hydroelectricity exports, but it has not fully exploited its water resources. In fact, production and exports of electricity have been fluctuating and the country still imports electricity. The share of electricity in manufacturing exports fell from 19 per cent in 1994 to 5 per cent by 2002. This appears to be due partly to the poor pricing strategy and partly to the poor management of the electricity authority. It appears that privatization of electricity production and its distribution network can significantly raise the production and exports of electricity.

Exports of agricultural products dramatically increased after privatization of farms in the mid-1990s, although there have been some fluctuations from year to year. The share of agricultural exports in total export earnings rose from 3 per cent in 1994 to about 12 per cent by 2002. Privatization of farms helped increase agricultural productivity, leading to an improvement in export competition. Given the importance of the agriculture sector in the country, this is a pleasing development.

Kyrgyz's imports consist of a large number of manufactured goods, contributing about 97 per cent of total imports in 2001 (Table 7.9). Three commodities, namely, oil and gas, chemicals and machines together had over

Table 7.7 Performance of foreign trade in post-independence Kyrgyz Republic

	1993	1995	1997	1998	1999	2000	2001
Merchandise exports (million US$)	339.6	408.9	603.8	513.6	453.8	504.5	476.1
Merchandise imports (million US$)	447.8	522.3	709.3	841.5	599.7	554.1	467.2
Trade deficit % GDP	12.4	7.6	6.0	19.9	11.7	3.6	0.6
Exports % of GDP	38.9	27.4	34.1	31.3	36.3	36.8	31.2
Imports % of GDP	51.3	35.0	40.1	51.3	48.0	40.4	30.6

Source: ADB (2002a).

Table 7.8 Exports of goods by economic sectors (in thousand US$)

	1994	1995	1996	1997	1998	1999	2000	2001	2002
Total	340,056.1	408,938.5	505,396.6	603,807.9	513,635.8	453,835.6	504,489.2	476,151.6	485,544.0
Manufacturing	329,349.4	366,058.4	442,112.9	558,594.0	461,075.0	396,878.7	457,515.3	430,827.1	429,238.9
	(96.9)	(89.5)	(87.5)	(92.5)	(89.8)	(87.4)	(90.7)	(90.5)	(88.4)
Electricity	63,391.2	40,967.8	73,550.5	83,218.0	25,581.0	52,042.3	79,782.7	46,821.9	22,039.8
	(19.2)	(11.2)	(16.6)	(14.9)	(5.5)	(13.1)	(17.4)	(10.9)	(5.1)
Oil and gas	9,129.6	4,615.5	4,197.0	4,122.1	3,374.4	1,598.2	2,749.3	7,666.8	36,121.2
	(2.8)	(1.3)	(0.9)	(0.7)	(0.7)	(0.4)	(0.6)	(1.8)	(8.4)
Ferrous metallurgy	9,256.5	10,398.8	6,872.3	2,981.1	2,897.6	1,570.8	5,399.3	5,970.6	5,242.8
	(2.8)	(2.8)	(1.6)	(0.5)	(0.6)	(0.4)	(1.2)	(1.4)	(1.2)
Non-ferrous metallurgy	52,446.6	62,665.3	56,680.3	215,979.1	220,992.2	217,226.7	234,375.5	247,173.9	197,621.4
	(15.9)	(17.1)	(12.8)	(38.7)	(47.9)	(54.7)	(51.2)	(57.4)	(46.0)
Chemicals	5,058.5	18,919.5	12,436.3	13,515.1	7,606.5	6,579.3	9,004.2	7,112.7	8,473.9
	(1.5)	(5.2)	(2.8)	(2.4)	(1.6)	(1.7)	(2.0)	(1.7)	(2.0)
Fuels	1,650.5	1,381.7	1,326.7	1,240.9	982.0	300.9	415.2	181.8	300.0
	(0.5)	(0.4)	(0.3)	(0.2)	(0.2)	(0.1)	(0.1)	(0.0)	(0.1)
Machine building	33,814.3	44,472.5	56,187.5	61,603.7	70,072.9	46,811.1	53,712.2	59,100.1	55,535.9
	(10.3)	(12.1)	(12.7)	(11.0)	(15.2)	(11.8)	(11.7)	(13.7)	(12.9)

Lumber and paper	1,149.9	1,812.5	2,369.9	3,564.1	4,589.8	742.9	942.5	565.3	1,162.5
	(0.3)	(0.5)	(0.5)	(0.6)	(1.0)	(0.2)	(0.2)	(0.1)	(0.3)
Construction mats	17,604.9	11,619.1	21,802.6	26,857.0	24,016.2	8,188.5	8,417.4	8,381.7	12,736.7
	(5.3)	(3.2)	(4.9)	(4.8)	(5.2)	(2.1)	(1.8)	(1.9)	(3.0)
Light industry	77,569.9	82,547.0	74,416.3	60,667.6	40,793.9	32,282.1	43,853.9	32,094.6	64,883.6
	(23.6)	(22.6)	(16.8)	(10.9)	(8.8)	(8.1)	(9.6)	(7.4)	(15.1)
Food industry	55,361.9	79,054.8	127,034.2	79,616.2	54,544.9	19,136.5	13,454.5	12,350.3	16,923.2
	(16.8)	(21.6)	(28.7)	(14.3)	(11.8)	(4.8)	(2.9)	(2.9)	(3.9)
Medical industry	1,066.3	3,778.4	2,471.7	1,769.4	1,918.2	1,530.4	780.7	600.0	884.6
	(0.3)	(1.0)	(0.6)	(0.3)	(0.4)	(0.4)	(0.2)	(0.1)	(0.2)
Other manufacturing	1,849.3	3,825.4	2,767.5	3,459.6	3,705.3	8,869.1	4,627.8	2,807.4	7,313.0
	(0.6)	(1.0)	(0.6)	(0.6)	(0.8)	(2.2)	(1.0)	(0.7)	(1.7)
Agriculture	*10,588.9*	*42,869.7*	*63,223.4*	*45,213.5*	*52,542.0*	*56,786.4*	*46,890.8*	*45,262.7*	*56,110.1*
	(3.1)	*(10.5)*	*(12.5)*	*(7.5)*	*(10.2)*	*(12.5)*	*(9.3)*	*(9.5)*	*(11.6)*
Others	*117.8*	*10.4*	*60.3*	*0.3*	*18.8*	*170.5*	*83.1*	*61.9*	*195.0*
	(0.0)	*(0.0)*	*(0.0)*	*(0.0)*	*(0.0)*	*(0.0)*	*(0.0)*	*(0.0)*	*(0.0)*

Source: Kyrgyz Republic official website.

Note

Figures in parentheses are percentage shares.

Table 7.9 Imports of goods by economic sectors (in thousand US$)

	1994	1995	1996	1997	1998	1999	2000	2001
Total	*316,985.0*	*522,334.9*	*837,688.2*	*709,304.9*	*841,504.1*	*599,739.8*	*554,113.7*	*467,242.1*
Manufacturing	*288,494.7*	*505,347.1*	*809,946.1*	*674,697.4*	*822,875.6*	*568,291.5*	*513,220.2*	*453,068.8*
	(91.0)	*(96.7)*	*(96.7)*	*(95.1)*	*(97.8)*	*(94.8)*	*(92.6)*	*(97.0)*
Electricity	0.0	8,579.0	26,717.9	23,836.8	7,907.1	2,840.6	7,568.7	9,843.1
	(0.0)	(1.7)	(3.3)	(3.5)	(1.0)	(0.5)	(1.5)	(2.2)
Oil and gas	128,122.5	179,542.1	212,746.8	182,889.8	198,990.7	118,711.9	120,814.1	110,995.3
	(44.4)	(35.5)	(26.3)	(27.1)	(24.2)	(20.9)	(23.5)	(24.5)
Ferrous metallurgy	7,659.1	17,773.3	15,021.6	9,944.4	21,618.1	9,481.3	11,094.1	9,621.6
	(2.7)	(3.5)	(1.9)	(1.5)	(2.6)	(1.7)	(2.2)	(2.1)
Non-ferrous metallurgy	4,537.5	11,266.3	9,074.3	22,366.8	30,608.0	22,862.3	13,084.7	24,946.6
	(1.6)	(2.2)	(1.1)	(3.3)	(3.7)	(4.0)	(2.5)	(5.5)
Chemicals	14,698.1	21,482.9	37,200.4	42,095.6	41,233.2	24,510.8	30,499.1	30,982.3
	(5.1)	(4.3)	(4.6)	(6.2)	(5.0)	(4.3)	(5.9)	(6.8)
Fuels	4,298.6	8,571.7	13,804.6	17,728.1	34,295.7	14,239.4	17,671.2	13,613.4
	(1.5)	(1.7)	(1.7)	(2.6)	(4.2)	(2.5)	(3.4)	(3.0)
Machine building	58,084.5	103,617.2	230,487.3	153,999.4	219,267.0	202,444.9	150,612.9	103,426.4
	(20.1)	(20.5)	(28.5)	(22.8)	(26.6)	(35.6)	(29.3)	(22.8)

Lumber and paper	4,982.0	19,795.4	26,209.6	29,230.9	35,319.2	19,138.0	25,588.3	20,926.6
	(1.7)	(3.9)	(3.2)	(4.3)	(4.3)	(3.4)	(5.0)	(4.6)
Construction materials	4,903.5	10,064.9	15,838.7	13,256.9	16,022.0	11,000.8	8,729.1	9,979.1
	(1.7)	(2.0)	(2.0)	(2.0)	(1.9)	(1.9)	(1.7)	(2.2)
Light industry	17,310.2	23,204.6	16,624.6	48,357.7	60,286.2	38,614.7	38,786.2	32,380.5
	(6.0)	(4.6)	(2.1)	(7.2)	(7.3)	(6.8)	(7.6)	(7.1)
Food industry	32,742.1	84,256.2	162,019.3	83,314.1	106,616.3	54,244.1	46,913.4	54,696.6
	(11.3)	(16.7)	(20.0)	(12.3)	(13.0)	(9.5)	(9.1)	(12.1)
Medical industry	9,829.9	12,476.5	36,383.2	36,302.2	27,839.6	42,264.6	28,115.9	26,629.8
	(3.4)	(2.5)	(4.5)	(5.4)	(3.4)	(7.4)	(5.5)	(5.9)
Other manufacturing	1,326.7	4,717.1	7,817.9	11,374.7	22,872.6	7,938.1	13,742.5	5,027.5
	(0.5)	(0.9)	(1.0)	(1.7)	(2.8)	(1.4)	(2.7)	(1.1)
Agriculture	*28,301.1*	*16,987.8*	*27,742.1*	*34,607.5*	*18,616.0*	*31,447.9*	*40,892.9*	*14,172.3*
	(8.9)	*(3.3)*	*(3.3)*	*(4.9)*	*(2.2)*	*(5.2)*	*(7.4)*	*(3.0)*
Others	*189.2*	*0.0*	*0.0*	*0.0*	*12.5*	*0.5*	*0.6*	*1.1*
	(0.1)	*(0.0)*	*(0.0)*	*(0.0)*	*(0.0)*	*(0.0)*	*(0.0)*	*(0.0)*

Source: Kyrgyz Republic official website.

Note
Figures in parentheses are percentage shares.

50 per cent share in manufacturing imports in 2001, although it fell from about 69 per cent in 1994. This fall in imports of developmental goods coincides with a fall in export earnings during the same period. Despite potential in hydro-electricity, Kyrgyz relies on imports of natural gas from Uzbekistan. It is a net importer of gas and oil from Uzbekistan and Kazakhstan respectively.

Tables 7.10 and 7.11 present the direction of Kyrgyzstan's exports and imports. In both exports and imports, shares of Russian and the FSU countries of Central Asia have fallen, while that of Asian and European countries have increased. Kyrgyz's exports to and imports from America, Australia and Oceania, and Africa remain very small (just over 2 per cent share in total exports). Europe is a major destination for Kyrgyzstan's exports (54 per cent) followed by Russia and the FSU countries of Central Asia (34 per cent) and Asia (11 per cent). Europe has emerged as a popular destination for Kyrgyz's exports as reflected by the rising share of its exports to these countries. Europe's share of Kyrgyz's exports rose from 37 per cent in 1997 to 54 per cent by 2001. Although the share of Russian

Table 7.10 Direction of exports (thousand US$)

Destination	1997	1998	1999	2000	2001
Europe	223,708.1	248,828.4	215,987.1	227,522.2	257,817.9
	(37.0)	(48.0)	(48.0)	(45.0)	(54.0)
Asia	59,256.6	39,835.3	51,275.3	73,882.1	50,115.7
	(10.0)	(8.0)	(11.0)	(15.0)	(11.0)
America	18,030.8	7,689.6	11,624.2	2,937.3	8,339.8
	(3.0)	(1.0)	(3.0)	(1.0)	(2.0)
Africa	6.8	19.7	453.6	1,983.8	39.1
	(0.0)	(0.0)	(0.0)	(0.0)	(0.0)
Australia and Oceania	121.7	4.8	1.8	12.8	9.6
	(0.0)	(0.0)	(0.0)	(0.0)	(0.0)
Russia and FSU	302,683.9	217,258.1	174,493.6	198,151.0	159,829.6
countries of	(50.0)	(42.0)	(38.0)	(39.0)	(34.0)
Central Asia					
Russia	98,844.9	83,679.3	70,713.1	65,125.1	64,510.2
	(16.0)	(16.0)	(16.0)	(13.0)	(14.0)
Kazakhstan	87,094.0	85,516.4	44,960.1	33,393.8	39,032.2
	(14.0)	(17.0)	(10.0)	(7.0)	(8.0)
Tajikistan	12,666.3	8,299.2	9,463.0	7,489.2	6,743.3
	(2.0)	(2.0)	(2.0)	(1.0)	(1.0)
Turkmenistan	2,566.5	1,220.8	2,788.7	2,729.3	1,546.3
	(0.0)	(0.0)	(1.0)	(1.0)	(0.0)
Uzbekistan	101,512.2	38,542.4	46,568.7	89,413.6	47,997.6
	(17.0)	(0.08)	(10.0)	(18.0)	(10.0)
Total	*603,807.9*	*513,635.9*	*453,835.6*	*504,489.2*	*476,151.7*

Source: Kyrgyz Republic official website.

Note
Figures in parentheses are percentage shares.

Table 7.11 Direction of imports (thousand US$)

Destination	1997	1998	1999	2000	2001
Europe	125,855.7	170,989.0	137,359.4	93,503.5	79,368.2
	(18.0)	(20.0)	(23.0)	(17.0)	(17.0)
Asia	123,622.3	167,573.9	131,722.3	109,261.7	101,744.5
	(17.0)	(20.0)	(22.0)	(20.0)	(22.0)
America	44,884.8	81,789.6	85,235.5	65,631.7	41,437.3
	(6.0)	(10.0)	(14.0)	(12.0)	(9.0)
Africa	150.2	3,271.4	1,483.6	89.9	275.5
	(0.0)	(0.0)	(0.0)	(0.0)	(0.0)
Australia and Oceania	322.2	1,692.4	102.6	467.9	350.9
	(0.0)	(0.0)	(0.0)	(0.0)	(0.0)
Russia and FSU	414,469.7	416,187.8	243,836.4	285,160.9	244,065.7
countries of	(58.0)	(49.0)	(41.0)	(51.0)	(52.0)
Central Asia					
Russia	190,799.2	204,057.8	109,366.1	132,614.6	85,052.1
	(27.0)	(24.0)	(18.0)	(24.0)	(18.0)
Kazakhstan	69,602.8	75,297.7	72,679.9	57,399.7	81,801.4
	(10.0)	(9.0)	(12.0)	(10.0)	(18.0)
Tajikistan	9,992.3	6,375.8	4,041.3	1,908.9	1,501.5
	(1.0)	(1.0)	(1.0)	(0.0)	(0.0)
Turkmenistan	15,463.4	8,214.5	7,780.6	18,664.6	8,977.3
	(2.0)	(1.0)	(1.0)	(3.0)	(2.0)
Uzbekistan	128,612.0	122,242.0	49,968.5	74,573.1	66,733.4
	(18.0)	(15.0)	(8.0)	(13.0)	(14.0)
Total	*709,304.9*	*841,504.1*	*599,739.8*	*554,115.6*	*467,242.1*

Source: Kyrgyz Republic official website.

Note
Figures in parentheses are percentage shares.

and the FSU countries of Central Asia as a group have fallen from 50 per cent in 1997 to 34 per cent share by 2001, it is the second most popular destination for Kyrgyzstan's exports.

Russia remains a major trading partner for Kyrgyzstan's exports, although its share has fallen from 16 per cent in 1997 to 14 per cent by 2001. Among the FSU countries of Central Asia, Uzbekistan remains a major market for its exports, but its share has been fluctuating from 17 per cent in 1997 to 10 per cent by 2001. Protectionist sentiment in Uzbekistan and deteriorating bilateral relations appear to have contributed to a fall in Kyrgyzstan's exports to and imports from Uzbekistan. Kyrgyzstan's exports to Kazakhstan have significantly fallen in recent years. For example, the share of latter's in the former's total exports fell from 14 per cent in 1997 to 8 per cent by 2001. The shares of other countries in the region remain very small. Table 7.11 presents the direction of Kyrgyz's exports.

About 50 per cent of Kyrgyzstan's imports originate from Russia and the FSU countries of Central Asia, although its share has fallen since 1998 from 58 per cent in 1997 to 52 per cent in 2001 (Table 7.12). Among this

Table 7.12 Poverty, inequality and human development in Kyrgyzstan

% of population below the national poverty line*		% of population below $2.15 per capita per day	Income ratio of highest 20% to lowest 20%	Gini coefficient	Human Development Index			
1988	1999	1999	2001	2001	1980	1990	2000	Rank in 2000
37	55	49	4.2	0.32	na	na	0.712	102

Source: IMF and World Bank (2002) for percentage of population below the national poverty line and percentage of people below $2.15 per capita per day. Other data come from ADB *Key Indicators* 2003.

Note
* The national poverty line is defined as percentage of population earning a per capita income lower than the minimum consumption basket. For 1988, a per capita income of 75 roubles per month was used as the conventional poverty line.

group of countries, Russia and Kazakhstan are the major suppliers, each accounting for an 18 per cent share in Kyrgyzstan's total imports in 2001. During 1997–2001, Russia's share fell from 27 to 18 per cent, while that of Kazakhstan rose from 10 per cent to 18 per cent. Uzbekistan's share in Kyrgyzstan's total imports fell from 18 per cent in 1997 to 14 per cent by 2001. Other Central Asian countries are marginal players in Kyrgyzstan's imports.

Poverty and inequality in post-independence Kyrgyzstan

A fall in national income and loss in subsidies from the FSU have significantly increased poverty and inequality in post-independence Kyrgyzstan (Table 7.12). Rising unemployment in the absence of a strong growth in the private sector, caused by poor business climate, has further contributed to this. As national income declined and budget deficit surged, the government was forced to cut its expenditures in several areas including health and education. Despite a need for greater investment in health and education, the government expenditures on these areas continued to decline in order to bring budget deficit under control, making the poor even more worse off. It declined from 10.5 per cent of GDP in 1995 to 6.4 per cent by 1999 (Table 7.13). Decline in social expenditure particularly on health has been problematic given that Kyrgyzstan has one of the highest adult mortality rates in the region, estimated at 303 per 1,000 adults in 1998. As shown in Table 7.12, the percentage of people living below the poverty line has increased from 37 per cent in 1988 to 55 per cent by 1999. In terms of the human development index (HDI), Kyrgyzstan has one of the lowest rankings in the region after Tajikistan. It was placed in 102nd position in 2000.[2] As unemployment and economic hardship had risen in the post-independence period, cases of frequent crime and violence are on the rise.

To reduce human suffering Kyrgyzstan needs to create a business climate for private sector development, which requires an efficient transport network, good governance and enforcement of law and order in the country (more about this in the next section). Private sector development is crucial not only for creating employment opportunities and raising the income level of the poor, but also in generating revenue for maintaining government expenditures on infrastructure, health and education. Unless revenue is raised through private sector-led growth, it is difficult for the government to increase its investment in health, education and infrastructure, especially when its debt-servicing obligation is on the rise. Kyrgyzstan is one of the highly indebted countries in the region and as shown in Table 7.6 its debt percentage of GDP reached 110 per cent of GDP by 2001.

Table 7.13 Non-monetary indicators of poverty and inequality

	1991	1992	1993	1994	1995	1996	1997	1998	1999	2000
Expenditure on health and education (% of GDP)	na	na	6.8	9.6	10.5	8.4	8.1	7.7	6.4	?
Mortality rate (per 1000 male adult)	na	na	na	na	na	na	305.0	303.0	na	?
Basic school enrolment (%)	90.6	90.3	89.7	89.0	89.2	89.4	89.4	89.7	?	?
Earning inequality (Gini coefficient)	na	30.0	44.5	44.3	39.2	42.8	43.1	na	?	?

Source: EBRD (1999).

Development challenges

A key question Kyrgyzstan is facing today is how to create a business climate for private sector development. To do this, it needs to address several challenges, which include both domestic and regional issues.

Trade and transit issues

While Kyrgyzstan has significantly reduced tariffs, it seems to restrict trade through cumbersome and time consuming customs procedures, which restrict trade flows. Traders are required to submit several documents obtained from at least five different agencies for customs clearance, which takes up a considerable amount of time and money. Lack of basic customs infrastructure at customs offices also contributes significantly to delays. For example, in the absence of automatic weighing and scanning machines at customs, goods are checked manually. In many cases, consignments are re-checked. In the absence of electronic data exchange between the shippers and customs, the pre-clearance system, that can significantly facilitate customs clearance, does not exist.

Being a land-locked country, Kyrgyzstan's exports and imports have to go through at least two countries' territories (Kazakhstan and Uzbekistan) before reaching their final destination. The existing cross-border procedures for the movements of goods and people are costly and time consuming. For example, at each country's entry and exit borders, consignments are checked. Consignments are even checked while goods are in transit. To avoid delays, shippers are forced to pay unofficial charges in several locations. Clearly, these practices are not consistent with GATT article V which outlines the freedom of transit for land-locked countries (Appendix 7.1). In addition, visa requirements and the transit permit system also contribute to delays and increase the costs of transportation.[3] These restrictions and charges appear to have discouraged trade flows. In the current situation, trade in vegetables in which Kyrgyzstan has a comparative advantage has not yet fully developed, because trade in such commodities demands better logistics, including trucks with refrigeration facilities and unrestricted access to the final destination. Dismantling the transit permit system and simplifying the visa requirements at the regional level will facilitate trade not only in Kyrgyzstan but also in other CIS countries.

Governance and infrastructure issues

Like other Central Asian countries, law enforcement is very weak in Kyrgyzstan. Also, there is a lack of coordination between departments and considerable delays occur in getting information from other departments. For example, there is no 'one window system' where exporters and importers can obtain all required documents. Traders have to run from one department to another just to obtain documents, which results in delay and encourages rent seeking behaviour. While exporters are entitled to value added tax (VAT) refunds, it takes several months to get them. This acts as a tax on exports in two ways. First, owing to inflation, the value of refunds is much lower than was paid. Second, exporters will keep on paying interest to the bank until they receive the full refund.[4] Poor governance and lack of transparency have significantly deterred private sector development. The governance indicators show that corruption is high, law enforcement is weak and political stability remains a problem (Table 7.14).

Kyrgyzstan mainly relies on road and rail networks for its international trade transactions. However, the condition of the road network is poor inside the country, and also throughout the region. Only about 40 per cent of domestic road networks are paved, making access from one region to another difficult in poor weather conditions. This has hindered rural–urban integration and discouraged trade potential between regions within the country.

Institutional issues

Small and medium sized enterprises (SMEs) are the major sources of employment in an agrarian economy like Kyrgyzstan. Their development requires a simple registration process, easy access to finance as well as assistance with product development and marketing. While SMEs face problems in all these areas, access to banking sector finance is a major problem due to the security-driven lending policy of the banking sector. Borrowers are required to show as high as 200 per cent collateral security in order to secure finance, which is extremely high for SMEs. This has significantly discouraged growth of SMEs, leading to lower employment outcomes. Also, in the absence of trade promotion agency in the country, SMEs' ability to develop and market new products has been very limited. Information about export markets and export potential are rarely available.

Regional cooperation

All CIS countries are land-locked, have a small domestic market and they lack resources to maintain transport networks as well as to utilize their resources effectively (namely electricity, mining, agriculture and manufacturing). In this context, regional cooperation can be a powerful mechanism and it should be viewed as an opportunity rather than a threat. Although a number of regional agreements currently exist very little progress has yet been made despite the annual meeting of the Heads of State when they agreed to harmonize procedures for deeper integration. Poor achievement appears to be mainly due to the lack of political willingness.

Table 7.14 World Bank Institute governance indicators for Kyrgyzstan

Governance indicator	Year	Percentile rank (0–100) in %	Estimate (−2.5 to +2.5)	Standard deviation	Number of surveys/polls
Voice and accountability	2000–01	31.6	−0.57	0.19	3
Political stability/no violence	2000–01	39.5	−0.32	0.48	2
Government effectiveness	2000–01	31.9	−0.61	0.31	3
Regulatory quality	2000–01	20.7	−0.63	0.37	4
Rule of law	2000–01	26.5	−0.72	0.22	4
Control of corruption	2000–01	20.5	−0.85	0.23	4

Source: Kaufmann *et al.* (2002): *Governance Matters II: Updated Governance Indicators for 2000–01* quoted in Gleason (2003).

Cooperation should first begin by simplifying and harmonizing cross-border procedures for the movements of goods and people. The current procedures for regulating goods, vehicles and people between the countries have made international trade transactions very costly and time consuming. This has deterred private sector investment, and discouraged export potential and employment growth not only in Kyrgyzstan but also in other Central Asian countries. Harmonization of tariffs, cross-border procedures and documentary requirements is necessary to reduce costs and delays, which will facilitate trade and investment in the region. Due to the land-locked position of CIS countries, harmonization of tariffs will discourage the possibility of smuggling from the low to high tariff countries, which significantly reduces the need for tight border and customs formalities and checking. Harmonization of cross-border formalities and documentary requirements will help reduce corruption and delays, while elimination of the transit permit system will not only lower transit costs and time, but also give a greater degree of certainty to all transiting countries. Since Central Asian countries are land-locked, this will benefit all in the form of increased trade flows and investment.

Regional cooperation among the Central Asian countries is feasible due to diversity of resources and similarity in culture among the countries. Apart from harmonization of cross-border procedures and tariffs, areas for cooperation should also include utilization of natural resources, and the development of railways and road transport. The regional management of roads and railways can narrow down the problems of transit and customs procedures.

Conclusion

The Kyrgyz Republic introduced market-oriented reform in the immediate post-independence period to arrest poor macroeconomic outcomes and facilitate global integration. The reform programme included liberalization in trade, investment and payment regime, and privatization of public enterprises. It even went further and joined the WTO: Kyrgyz is the first country in the region to be a member. Despite this, it has not yet recovered from the economic impact of disintegration, although some progress has been made in achieving macroeconomic stability. Poverty and unemployment is high and rising, and Kyrgyz's reliance on external debt is unsustainable, which all appear to be mainly due to internal and regional rather than external factors. These include cumbersome and time consuming customs formalities, transit problems in neighbouring countries, inefficient transport networks, poor governance and lack of banking sector finance. It is obvious that liberalization *per se* in the absence of a comprehensive reform package fails to generate the desired benefits.

In this context, Kyrgyzstan should view regional cooperation as a means of accelerating growth and alleviating poverty. Since all CIS countries have a small domestic market and they lack resources to maintain transport networks as well as to utilize their water resources, mining and agriculture, regional cooperation should be viewed as an opportunity rather than a threat. Regional cooperation can also be a powerful tool in gaining experience in export production and marketing. Having a closed economy for a long time, Kyrgyzstan and other CIS countries lack experience in these areas, which are essential ingredients for a market economy. Regional cooperation would provide these experiences in familiar regional markets before going into a complex global market. Regional cooperation should also be viewed as a means of resolving issues relating to cross-border movements of goods and people. The current procedures for handling these movements have significantly discouraged inter- and intra-regional trade flows, making Kyrgyzstan's transition to a market economy painful.

Acknowledgements

I thank Prema-chandra Athukorala and Richard Pomfret for providing useful suggestions on an earlier version of this chapter. However, all remaining errors are mine. Data presented in this chapter were collected while I was working on a related project for the Asian Development Bank. I thank the Bank for financial assistance.

Appendix 7.1   The General Agreement on Tariff and Trade (GATT 1947)

Article V

Freedom of Transit

1   Goods (including baggage), and also vessels and other means of transport, shall be deemed to be in transit across the territory of a contracting party when the passage across such territory, with or without transshipment, warehousing, breaking bulk, or change in the mode of transport, is only a portion of a complete journey beginning and terminating beyond the frontier of the contracting party across whose territory the traffic passes. Traffic of this nature is termed article 'traffic in transit'.

2   There shall be freedom of transit through the territory of each contracting party, via the routes most convenient for international transit, for traffic in transit to or from the territory of other contracting parties. No distinction shall be made which is based on the flag of vessels, the place of origin, departure, entry, exit or destination, or any circumstances relating to the ownership of goods, of vessels or other means of transport.

3   Any contracting party may require that traffic in transit through its territory be entered at the proper custom house, but, except in cases of failure to comply with applicable customs laws and regulations, such traffic coming from or going to the territory of other contracting parties shall not be subject to any unnecessary delays or restrictions and shall be exempt from customs duties and from all transit duties or other charges imposed in respect of transit, except charges for transportation or those commensurate with administrative expenses entailed by transit or with the cost of services rendered.

4   All charges and regulations imposed by the contracting parties or traffic in transit to or from the territory of other contracting parties shall be reasonable, having regard to the conditions of the traffic.

5   With respect to all charges, regulations and formalities in connection with transit, each contracting party shall accord to traffic in transit to or from the territory of any other contracting party treatment no less favorable than the treatment accorded to traffic in transit to or from any third country.

6   Each contracting party shall accord to products, which have been in transit through the territory of any other contracting party treatment no less favorable than that which would have been accorded to their destination without going through the territory of such other contracting party.

7   The provisions of this Article shall not apply to the operation of aircraft in transit, but shall apply to air transit goods (including baggage).

Source: World Trade Organization (1994),
Results of the Uruguay Round, Geneva, pp. 492–3, 545.

Notes

1 Other Central Asian countries are Kazakhstan, Tajikistan, Turkmenistan and Uzbekistan. The region is surrounded by China in the east, the Caspian Sea in the west, central Siberia in the north, and Afghanistan and Iran in the south. Five Central Asian countries together cover about 3,995,000 square kms and provide shelter for about 52 million people (less than 1 per cent of the world's population). Kyrgyzstan is surrounded by Kazakhstan in the north, Republic of China in the east, Tajikistan in the south and Uzbekistan in the west. It spreads in about 200,000 square kms and provides shelter for less than five million people. Among the CIS, Kyrgyzstan is the smallest country in the region.

2 Among the CIS countries, Tajikistan has the lowest HDI (ranked 112), while Kazakhstan has the highest HDI.

3 The main problem with the transit permit system is that it creates uncertainty among traders in transiting countries and discourages private sector investment in export-oriented activities that need frequent access by road to regional and/or international markets. In addition, transit permits issued by Kazakhstan to the Kyrgyz Republic are far less than its requirements, hindering trade flows.

4 For example, consider this. The annual inflation and interest rates are 14 per cent and 10 per cent respectively. An exporter is expecting a VAT refund of US$100. Due to red tape, he/she gets the refund in six months. Hence, the real value of the refund is US$88, after making allowance for interest paid and inflation. If one considers time spent in meeting VAT requirements, the actual refund is even lower than US$88. Delays in VAT refunds act as a tax on exporters.

south essex college
FURTHER & HIGHER EDUCATION
SOUTHEND CAMPUS

8 Trade, growth and equity in Myanmar

Peter Warr

The economic experience of Myanmar (formerly Burma)[1] is often contrasted with neighbouring Thailand. Since the Second World War, the economic policy positions of these two countries have been radically different and policies with respect to international trade and investment have been central to this difference. Whereas Thailand has welcomed globalization, opening its economy to greatly expanded trade and foreign investment, Myanmar has adopted an ultra-cautious, almost closed economy stance. The outcome for Thailand has been rapid growth and declining poverty, along with some instability. For Myanmar, the result has been stagnation and continued impoverishment. In 1960, all of the countries of Southeast Asia were poor. Out of Indonesia, the Philippines, Thailand and Malaysia, only one – Malaysia – had an average income per person greater than US$500 at 2002 prices. In 2002, only one of these countries still had an income per capita below this threshold. That was Myanmar. Leaving aside the Indo-China states of Vietnam, Cambodia and Laos, which were devastated by war and then by communism, Myanmar is the poor performer of Southeast Asia.

Agriculture is central to Myanmar's poor economic performance and to the lack of reform. Agriculture represents 58 per cent of GDP, employs 63 per cent of the population and accounts for at least that proportion of Myanmar's poor people. The performance of the agricultural sector has been deteriorating over a long period. The discussion in this chapter focuses on the problems of agriculture within the Myanmar economy and the prospect that recent reforms may produce badly-needed relief.

Macroeconomic performance

Output growth

Table 8.1 presents data on the long-term economic performance of five Southeast Asian countries: Myanmar, Indonesia, Thailand, the Philippines and Malaysia. The data to 1995 are based on calculations summarized in Khin Maung Kyi *et al.* (2000), which drew on the World Bank's *World*

Table 8.1 Southeast Asia: real GDP per person, 1960 to 2002 (US$ per person, 2002 prices)

	Myanmar	Indonesia	Philippines	Thailand	Malaysia	Myanmar to Thailand (%)
1960	252	243	498	415	870	60
1965	260	255	512	506	1,017	51
1970	268	266	610	695	1,290	38
1975	288	290	790	795	1,485	36
1980	300	410	920	1,008	1,929	29
1985	390	507	730	1,202	2,180	32
1990	307	621	815	1,810	2,706	16
1995	388	808	792	2,448	3,592	15
2000	434	770	829	2,201	3,811	19
2002	455	802	832	2,295	3,732	19

Sources: World Bank, *World Tables*, various years, cited in Khin Maung Kyi *et al.* (2000) and Institute of Southeast Asian Studies (2002), Figure 1.1 for growth rates since 1995.

Tables. The data since 1995 are drawn from the Institute of Southeast Asian Studies (2002). Concerning Myanmar's performance, the data speak for themselves. In 1960, income per person in Thailand was about 60 per cent higher than in Myanmar. In 2002, average incomes in Thailand were five times as high. Concerning Indonesia, in 1960 income per person was slightly lower than in Myanmar. In 2002 it was 75 per cent higher.

Comparisons between national income in Myanmar and other countries are made difficult by two points: Myanmar's distorted exchange rate structure, and the dubious nature of official data for Myanmar, including those relating to international trade. Regarding the first point, if the official exchange rate of 6.7 kyats (Kt) per US$ was used to calculate income per person in US dollars, then Myanmar's GDP per person in 2002 of roughly 50,500 kyats would be the absurd US$7,217. This would make Myanmar the second richest country in Southeast Asia, after Singapore. The artificiality of this calculation is that the official exchange rate is nowadays relevant only for state enterprise transactions.[2] On the other hand, using the market exchange rate of 620 kyats per US$ (mid-2002) gives the result shown in Table 8.2, as calculated in a recent publication of the Economist Intelligence Unit. Income per person is then US$78. But this estimate is also unreasonable because internationally traded goods, for which the market exchange rate is relevant, comprise a very small and isolated proportion of the goods and services actually exchanged in Myanmar's insular economy.

This point is shown by a further calculation, also discussed by the Economist Intelligence Unit, of trade as a share of GDP. If the official exchange rate is used to calculate GDP in US$ and then compared with trade data (already in US$) then exports plus imports relative to GDP

Table 8.2 East Asia: comparative economic indicators, 2001 (Economist Intelligence Unit)

	Myanmar	Thailand	China	Indonesia	Vietnam	Laos
GDP US$ billion	3.9[a]	115	1,180	145	33	484
GDP per head US$	78[a]	1,860	928	688	417	470
CPI inflation (%)	21.1	1.7	0.7	11.5	−0.4	3.7
Export of goods (US$)	2.3	65.1	265.9	56.5	15.1	43.8
Import of goods (US$)	2.6	62.1	243.9	31.0	16.0	49.8
Foreign trade[b] (% GDP)	0.8	110.6	42.4	60.3	94.2	19.3

Sources: Economist Intelligence Unit, *Country Profile, Myanmar*, 2002.

Notes
a According to Economist Intelligence Unit "calculated at the free-market exchange rate".
b Merchandise exports plus imports.

would be a ridiculous 125 per cent, implying that Myanmar was one of the most open economies in the world, more open than any of the countries shown in Table 8.2, including Thailand. Myanmar officials report that total trade as a share of GDP is about 20 per cent. This seems reasonable, making the Myanmar economy slightly more open than India and about half as open as China. If GDP in US$ is five times total trade, then GDP per person is around $485, approximately the same as the calculation shown in Table 8.1, above.

A second problem in calculating national income per person in Myanmar is that, for recent years at least, few observers believe the officially announced GDP growth data for Myanmar. It is agreed by virtually all analysts that in recent years actual growth rates have been well below the announced rates. Even government officials have made similar statements.[3]

The overstatement of real growth rates could, of course, be deliberate. But a less insidious and less obvious mechanism could also be at work. Real"GDP growth is calculated as a residual – the growth of nominal GDP, at current prices, minus the growth of the GDP price deflator. In circumstances of high inflation, as at present, deficiencies in the statistical calculation of the GDP deflator can lead to large errors in the resulting estimate of the residual – real GDP growth. For example, if official, controlled prices are used for some output items in the calculation of the deflator, rather than the prices actually received by firms, as used in the calculation of nominal GDP, the growth of the deflator will be understated relative to nominal GDP and the resulting residual will be overestimated. The more rapid the inflation, the greater the overestimation of real growth. Other sources of under-estimation of the growth rate of the price deflator will have the same effect. Recent inflation has clearly exceeded the government's officially declared rate of consumer price inflation and the measured increase in the GDP deflator is presumably underestimated as well, biasing upwards the official estimates of real GDP growth.

Real GDP growth rates since 1989 are summarized in Figure 8.1. The data from 1997 to 2002 use the Institute of Southeast Asian Studies estimates, as shown in the third row of Table 8.2. Myanmar was only negligibly affected by the Asian crisis of 1997–98. The short-term capital outflows that caused such havoc elsewhere in Southeast Asia did not occur in Myanmar because (i) the inflows of short-term capital which had accumulated elsewhere in Southeast Asia had not occurred in Myanmar and (ii) capital controls would have obstructed any desired capital outflow in any case. The small reduction in growth that did occur in 1998 was primarily caused by reduced demand for Myanmar's exports.

Real GDP growth by expenditure categories is summarized in Table 8.3. The interesting point is the moderate contribution of fixed investment to overall growth of demand. During the decade of boom in Thailand, Indonesia and Malaysia from the late 1980s to 1997 investment accounted for at least 40 per cent of the growth of aggregate demand. The picture for Myanmar is more like the post-crisis period of sluggish recovery in those countries, where slow growth of demand has constrained output growth and where investment demand has been particularly small. The Myanmar picture of low levels of investment as a proportion of national income is not consistent with an economy reportedly growing at over 10 per cent.

Table 8.4 shows output growth by sector, using official data. The striking feature of these data is the surge of reported growth of agricultural output

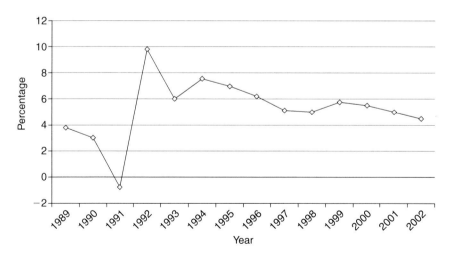

Figure 8.1 Myanmar: annual growth rate of real GDP, 1989 to 2002 (sources: Ministry of National Planning and Economic Development, Yangon and Institute of Southeast Asian Studies (2002)).

Table 8.3 Myanmar: selected economic data, 1997 to 2002

	1997	1998	1999	2000	2001	2002
Growth of real GDP (% change per year)						
Official	5.7	5.8	10.9	13.6	7.2	7.2*
EIU	5.7	5.8	10.9	6.2	5.3	5.2
ISEAS	5.1	5.0	5.8	5.5	5.0	4.5
Sectoral growth, real, official data (% change per year)						
Agriculture	3.7	2.8	2.5	10.5	3.4	3.0
Industry	8.9	6.6	13.7	20.6	14.7*	14.7*
Services	6.6	6.7	9.2	13.3	9.0*	9.0*
Trade (US$ million per year)						
Exports	975	1,065	1,125	1,309	2,300	2,900
Imports	2,107	2,451	2,116	2,355	2,600	2,200
Inflation, CPI (% change per year)	33.9	49.1	11.4	4.3	50.9	59.0
Exchange rate at year end, kyats per US$						
Official	6.2	6.2	6.3	6.3	6.7	6.7
Market	241	334	341	374	620	971

Sources: ISEAS (2002); EIU (2001); EIU (2003); IMF (2001).

Note
* Ministry of National Planning and Economic Development, Programme of Action for 2002–10, May 2001.

Table 8.4 Myanmar: GDP growth by sector, 1996/97 to 2000/01 (official data) (units: % change, year on year)

	1996/97	1997/98	1998/99	1999/2000	2000/01[a]
Agriculture	3.8	3.0	3.5	10.5	9.5
Livestock and fisheries	11.9	7.1	9.3	16.8	17.8
Forestry	2.1	2.8	3.2	4.6	3.3
Energy	−2.1	2.3	53.6	66.5	30.8
Mining	12.4	29.7	7.0	30.0	25.5
Manufacturing	4.6	5.0	6.2	14.5	23.4
Power	12.8	17.8	−5.4	14.2	13.9
Construction	24.6	9.8	6.3	4.4	11.9
Services	6.5	6.7	7.0	9.2	13.7
Transport	6.0	6.5	5.7	12.0	22.5
Communications	21.7	28.1	11.6	11.0	23.8
Financial institutions	21.9	14.4	17.0	12.6	14.2
GDP at factor cost	6.4	5.7	5.8	10.9	13.6

Source: Central Statistical Organisation, Statistical Yearbook 2001, Yangon.

Note
a Provisional.

for 1999/00 and 2000/01. As discussed below, there is reason to suspect that some increase in agriculture's contribution to total output may have occurred during this period, but not the very large increase reported in the data. As shown in Table 8.5, agriculture continues to dominate the Myanmar economy, both in contribution to GDP (value-added share) and total employment. A significant difference between the economic structure described by these data and that for other Southeast Asian countries, such as Thailand and Indonesia, is that output per worker is not much different in agriculture and industry. Based on the experience of other developing countries, output per worker would be expected to be much higher in industry than in agriculture. If these data are even approximately correct, Myanmar industry is *extremely* labour intensive.

The structure of GDP by ownership is summarized in Table 8.6. The data indicate a very high rate of state ownership in energy, power and

Table 8.5 Myanmar: structure of GDP and employment, 2000/01 (%)

	GDP share (%)	Employment share (%)	Value-added per worker (index)
Agriculture	58	63	0.92
Industry	10	12	0.83
Services	32	25	1.28

Source: Economist Intelligence Unit (2002).

Table 8.6 Myanmar: gross domestic product by ownership and sectoral contribution

Sector	GDP by ownership 1998/99			Share of GDP (%)
	State	Cooperatives	Private	
Crops	0.2	1.9	97.9	34.5
Livestock and fishery	0.3	1.1	98.6	7.2
Forestry	46.2	0.6	53.2	1.0
Energy	99.9	0.1	–	0.2
Mining	10.8	1.0	88.2	1.6
Manufacturing	28.2	0.9	70.9	9.2
Power	99.9	0.1	–	1.0
Construction	45.8	0.2	54.0	4.9
Transportation	29.8	1.0	69.2	4.3
Communications	100.0	–	–	1.9
Financial institutions	54.8	14.4	30.8	2.0
Administrative services	88.8	0.5	10.7	6.8
Rental services	3.9	2.9	93.2	4.3
Trade	21.3	2.4	76.3	21.1
GDP	*21.8*	*1.9*	*76.3*	*100.0*

Source: Planning Department, Ministry of National Planning and Economic Development, Yangon (unpublished).

communications. These outcomes are not unusual for developing countries, but the data also indicate surprisingly high levels of state ownership
in the manufacturing, construction, transport and trade sectors.

Trade

Myanmar's chronic current account deficits, as shown in Table 8.7, have
been eased in recent years by revenues from gas exports to Thailand (Table
8.8). There are two principal fields, Yadana and Yatagun. The demand

Table 8.7 Myanmar: current account, 2000 (US$ millions)

Merchandise exports f.o.b.	1,618.8
Merchandise imports f.o.b.	−2,135.0
Trade balance	−516.1
Services balance	12.1
Income balance	−36.1
Current transfers balance	297.2
Current-account balance	−243.0

Source: IMF (2001).

Table 8.8 Myanmar: exports by value, 1997/98 to 2001/02 (kyat, million, *fob*)

	1997/98	1998/99	1999/2000	2000/01	2001/02[a]
Unspecified items[b,c]	2,864.7	3,158.5	5,368.8	7,341.3	6,928.9
Gas	0.0	4.9	31.2	1,110.5	4,247.1
Hardwoods[c]	852.9	789.2	924.9	802.7	1,898.1
Teak	697.6	640.2	726.7	650.9	1,422.5
Other hardwoods	155.3	149.0	198.2	151.8	475.6
Pulses[d]	1,403.3	1,135.2	1,178.9	1,658.0	1,897.9
Marine exports	867.1	902.4	762.4	889.6	828.5
Prawns	565.4	574.8	530.5	598.3	518.6
Fish and fish products	301.7	327.6	231.9	291.3	309.9
Rice	37.7	166.8	64.9	207.6	754.1
Base metals and ores	30.1	73.7	288.5	323.8	275.9
Plywood & veneer	34.4	119.6	94.7	98.7	106.2
Raw rubber	133.6	100.3	75.2	66.6	75.9
Sesame seeds	175.6	164.2	81.8	119.2	40.1
Total inc. other	6,446.8	6,755.8	8,947.3	12,736.0	17,130.7
Government	1,655.3	2,102.7	2,026.1	3,775.7	8,172.7
Private	4,791.5	4,653.1	6,921.2	8,960.3	8,958.0

Sources: Central Statistical Organisation, Selected Monthly Economic Indicators, various issues,
Statistical Yearbook 2001, Yangon; Ministry of National Planning and Economic Development,
Review of the Financial, Economic and Social Conditions for 1997/98 (unpublished).

Notes
a Preliminary.
b Includes ready-made garments.
c Includes border trade.
d Includes pulses.

within Thailand is primarily for electricity generation, but demand for electricity has slowed following the 1997 crisis. The main generating plant involved, in Rajburi province of Thailand, adjacent to Myanmar, is not yet operating and cannot use the gas which is contracted. Thai sources report that they are obliged to pay for gas deliveries to this plant even though the gas is not actually being received. Contract re-negotiations are ongoing. In any case, the foreign exchange received by Myanmar to date has made a large difference to its current account balance. Rice exports have also increased since 1999 to approach one million tons. The circumstances under which these increased exports have occurred are controversial and are discussed further below. On the import front, imports of intermediate inputs and capital goods have marginally increased since the late 1990s while consumer goods imports remain very low (Table 8.9).

International economic relations

Myanmar has been governed by military or quasi-military regimes since 1962. The State Law and Order Restoration Council (SLORC), consisting entirely of military personnel, assumed power in 1988.[4] It called an election for May 1990 but then refused to accept the results when its own

Table 8.9 Myanmar: imports by value, 1997/98 to 2001/02 (kyat, million, c.i.f.)

	1997/98	1998/99	1999/2000	2000/01	2001/02[a]
Capital goods	6,172.1	7,358.0	5,335.1	4,060.6	5,557.8
Intermediate goods	3,350.1	4,171.3	5,132.0	4,579.8	7,410.0
Consumer goods	4,843.9	5,342.4	5,797.7	6,432.7	5,409.9
Total	14,366.1	16,871.7	16,264.8	15,073.1	18,377.7
Government	4,126.9	5,505.9	4,823.3	3,009.5	6,433.1
Private	10,239.2	11,365.8	11,441.5	12,063.6	11,944.6
Major items					
Unspecified items	4,984.2	5,749.2	6,480.6	7,194.4	7,706.5
Machinery and transport equipment	3,597.4	4,655.8	3,289.4	2,631.4	4,000.9
Base metals and manufactures	1,498.6	1,933.5	1,722.8	1,437.9	1,386.1
Electrical machinery	1,202.8	1,692.0	1,578.3	1,122.7	1,109.2
Crude oil	n/a	225.3	554.6	95.7	1,555.5
Edible vegetable oils	805.5	670.0	477.6	475.4	550.9
Pharmaceuticals	185.9	242.2	302.5	413.1	402.2
Paper and paper board	202.4	300.8	343.7	344.4	452.7
Fertilizer	357.4	152.1	329.0	254.6	140.8
Cement	502.6	393.3	252.9	187.2	179.7

Source: Central Statistical Organization, Selected Monthly Economic Indicators, various issues, Statistical Yearbook 2001, Yangon.

Notes
a Preliminary.
b Includes border trade, synthetic fibres and refined mineral oil.

candidates were defeated. Myanmar has been ostracized internationally since that date, with sanctions imposed by the United States and the European Union. Myanmar's main trading partners today are Japan and China. Despite the sanctions, the country was admitted to the Association of South East Asian Nations (ASEAN) in 1997. The decision to admit Myanmar was controversial. It was hoped within the region that this gesture of international engagement might encourage economic and political reform within Myanmar. To date, the reality has been disappointing and both economic and civil life remain repressed. Significant economic and political reforms were reportedly conditions for the resumption of international assistance to Myanmar, which, except for that received from Japan and China, has been suspended for several years. But the required reforms have not been forthcoming.

Myanmar apparently derives some economic benefit from its participation in AFTA, but the volumes of trade occurring under this agreement are quite small, partly because of restrictions on the commodities that can be traded under the agreement. More recently, it has been proposed that a new Free Trade Agreement (FTA) be formed from a wider grouping of countries in the Bay of Bengal region. The grouping is called Bangladesh, India, Myanmar, Sri Lanka and Thailand Economic Cooperation (BIMSTEC). An FTA is particular form of a Preferential Trading Agreement (PTA) in which all internal tariffs within the grouping are zero, but in which the various members do not necessarily share a common external tariff (which would make it a Customs Union). Figure 8.2 summarizes the definitions of the various forms of Preferential Trading Agreements.

The BIMSTEC grouping was formed in 1997 and grew out of an earlier grouping which had not included Myanmar. The grouping did not immediately form a PTA but emphasized sectoral cooperation and an economic forum enabling business groups to interact with government officials and academics. That is, it was initially a "talk shop." Myanmar was added to the grouping in 1998 and Nepal was given observer status in 1999. The intention to extend BIMSTEC to FTA was announced in 2000.

For many countries, dissatisfaction with the slowness of the multilateral liberalization process under the WTO has provoked an interest in regional PTAs, like AFTA and the BIMSTEC FTA proposal. But for Myanmar there are additional motives. First, due to sanctions, Myanmar has no prospect of admission to the WTO and regional PTAs have seemed the only available alternative. The fear is that by not joining some form of regional trading arrangement Myanmar may be left out of opportunities to benefit from expanded trade. If near-neighbours were to join discriminatory trading arrangements not including Myanmar, then even trade with these near-neighbours could become much more difficult. Second, also due to the sanctions, the government is anxious to receive any international recognition that it can. Acceptance into a regional PTA offers some such political acceptance.

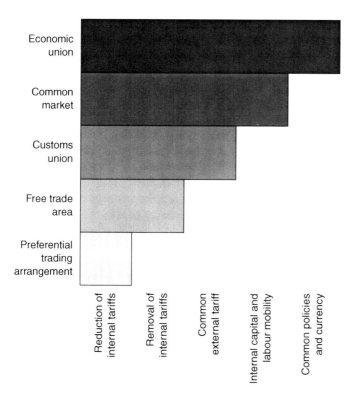

Figure 8.2 The taxonomy of economic integration.

The BIMSTEC initiative came from the three most developed members of the five countries. The two least developed members, Bangladesh and Myanmar, expressed reservations and declared their wish to study the matter. Tourism was identified as a priority sector for BIMSTEC coopera-tion and 2001 was identified as Visit BIMSTEC Year." Importantly, a trans-regional highway, linking India, Bangladesh, Myanmar and Thai-land, was identified as a priority area and negotiations have progressed towards its construction.

The question remains whether Myanmar would derive any economic benefit from joining such a trade-based grouping. An enormous liter-ature, building on Viner's classic 1950 study, has analysed this issue. This literature emphasizes the point that the trade creating (welfare enhanc-ing) effects of the PTA must be set against the trade diverting (welfare reducing) effects. The magnitudes of the trade diversion and trade creation effects depend on several key features. The economic literature has emphasized the nature of the partners that join the PTA. Krueger (1999) and Lawrence (1996a) have argued that the net benefits are great-est when factor endowments, including both physical and human factor endowments, are dissimilar because this implies that the member countries will be natural trading partners. Krueger (1999), Bhagwati and Panagiriya (1996) and Panagariya (2004) point out that the fact that countries are neighbours does not necessarily mean that they are natural trading partners.

For example, these authors argue that in the case of the North American Free Trade Agreement (NAFTA), the USA is a natural trading partner for both Mexico and Canada, but that the reverse does not apply. Mexico is not a natural trading partner for the USA, but Canada is. Moreover, Canada and Mexico are not natural trading partners for each other. Lawrence (1996b) emphasizes that the evidence does not support the notion that geographical proximity alone makes countries natural trading partners. A more important issue is the complementarity of their trade.

Drawing on the contributions of Wonnacott and Lutz (1989), Summers (1991), Krugman (1993) and De Melo *et al.* (1993), the largest net gains to members of a PTA will arise when four conditions are met: (i) initial tariffs are high; (ii) external tariffs are not raised after the formation of the PTA; (iii) pre-PTA trade among the PTA members is large; and (iv) trade complementarity exists among members. The BIMSTEC PTA proposal meets condition (i) and apparently meets condition (ii). But does it meet conditions (iii) and (iv)?

Myanmar's total legal exports are a little under one half as large as those of Bangladesh. Thailand is a large trading partner, in 2002 representing about one quarter of Myanmar's total legal exports. These exports grew rapidly since 1999 and the main reason was the export of gas to Thailand via a newly constructed pipeline. Exports to other BIMSTEC partner countries are small, with the partial exception of India. Trade with Sri Lanka is very small. Myanmar has bilateral trade surpluses with each of the BIMSTEC partner countries. The structure of Myanmar's foreign trade is summarized in Tables 8.10 to 8.17. From Table 8.10, agricultural goods and light manufactured goods have dominated Myanmar exports, but the gas exports to Thailand, mentioned above, have now become important as well. It has been claimed that informal trade is important for Myanmar, but these data do not include estimates of the magnitudes involved. In short, pre-PTA trade between Myanmar and the other PTA members is not large.

Tables 8.13 to 8.15 present calculations of the Intensity, Complementarity and Bias Indices described by Drysdale and Garnaut (1994). Intensity simply measures the extent to which countries trade more or less with each other than with the rest of the world in general. Complementarity refers to the degree to which one country's export structure matches another country's import structure. Bias measures whether issues other than complementarity are responsible for the intensity of trade between two countries. By construction of the indices, for any pair of countries, Intensity is equal to Complementarity multiplied by Bias. Because the cal-

Table 8.10 Myanmar: direction of trade, 1990 to 2002 (US$ millions)

	1990	1991	1992	1993	1994	1995	1996	1997	1998	1999	2000	2001	2002
Exports to:													
Bangladesh	0.59	0.12	0.56	6.02	6.85	4.24	3.19	2.41	11.08	12.53	20.03	17.92	18.02
India	44.20	46.56	94.60	106.40	109.40	145.80	134.80	168.60	169.40	156.50	162.80	179.10	194.40
Sri Lanka	12.54	0.14	2.96	6.37	0.91	0.91	10.90	5.45	0.91	0.76	1.09	1.14	1.24
Thailand	48.88	0.00	0.00	0.00	28.77	36.53	0.00	0.00	0.00	102.50	232.90	735.40	831.10
Malaysia	8.64	15.63	17.05	52.43	24.98	37.55	36.34	51.04	52.13	52.17	63.22	71.08	68.71
Pakistan	3.75	5.03	29.46	23.70	10.68	27.82	14.64	13.27	10.46	7.19	18.74	15.87	13.21
United States	9.35	26.63	37.81	45.54	66.00	79.00	105.60	112.10	158.90	222.10	442.70	456.10	345.30
EU 15	28.05	37.22	41.97	63.04	67.62	71.70	101.80	141.70	159.10	209.20	325.90	400.20	363.90
World	405.70	510.10	662.00	842.90	915.00	1,160.00	1,154.00	1,104.00	1,113.00	1,365.00	1,963.00	2,617.00	2,599.00
Imports from:													
Bangladesh	0.96	0.26	2.61	13.93	7.53	2.05	1.05	0.42	0.42	1.38	0.77	0.74	0.94
India	1.44	4.23	4.62	15.93	26.35	23.36	50.47	50.15	38.39	36.41	52.85	58.35	63.32
Sri Lanka	0.00	0.00	0.00	0.00	0.00	0.00	1.10	0.00	0.59	0.36	0.49	0.65	0.71
Thailand	19.78	4.19	0.00	0.00	0.00	0.00	0.00	0.00	0.00	435.20	554.60	390.50	355.80
Malaysia	31.62	73.72	98.60	114.20	243.50	252.20	242.70	407.50	322.50	257.70	254.10	216.70	270.10
Pakistan	1.08	2.26	1.85	2.76	5.50	3.06	2.45	9.20	3.60	2.20	4.16	3.59	4.53
United States	19.29	26.18	4.51	13.64	12.21	17.71	35.20	22.00	35.20	13.31	18.81	12.65	11.55
EU 15	103.60	108.70	78.26	119.40	130.50	172.90	212.00	196.90	136.90	134.20	114.50	80.94	93.78
World	667.80	1,067.00	1,045.00	1,280.00	1,538.00	2,340.00	2,674.00	2,856.00	2,351.00	2,517.00	3,018.00	2,649.00	2,748.00

Source: Author's calculations from United Nations Trade data, IEDB data base, Australian National University

Table 8.11 Myanmar: export structure by commodity group, 1990 to 2000 (US$ millions)

	0 Food and live animals	1 Beverages and tobacco	2 Crude materials excluding fuels	3 Mineral fuels etc.	4 Animal, vegetable oil, fats	5 Chemicals	6 Basic manufactured goods	7 Machines, transport equipment	8 Miscellaneous manufactured goods	9 Goods not classified by kind
1990	154.9	0.4	341.4	3.0	0.1	8.2	72.1	9.2	15.6	3.5
1991	188.9	6.6	218.0	1.1	0.0	3.5	16.8	0.3	28.8	0.0
1992	204.1	0.0	190.6	1.3	–	0.2	21.9	1.3	19.5	–
1993	282.2	0.0	480.2	11.7	0.0	2.0	104.7	9.8	59.1	2.9
1994	315.6	0.1	497.4	2.1	0.3	6.1	81.4	16.8	87.6	2.4
1995	451.7	0.7	605.8	2.3	0.4	13.3	82.2	9.8	124.3	1.9
1996	343.9	0.9	293.8	2.6	0.1	5.1	85.6	11.0	183.0	3.5
1997	425.9	5.9	373.9	2.3	1.0	1.8	69.9	11.5	247.1	3.8
1998	350.9	0.6	325.2	0.5	0.7	1.4	59.5	7.0	309.4	3.9
1999	260.1	1.1	430.2	2.2	0.2	2.5	123.6	13.3	439.4	4.3
2000	287.2	2.1	345.9	119.3	0.0	1.6	103.5	16.4	837.5	7.2

Source: Author's calculations from United Nations Conference on Trade and Development, *United Nations Trade Data* (various issues), Geneva: UNCTAD. Australian National University, International and Economic Database (IEDB), Australia, ANU.

Table 8.12 Myanmar: import structure by commodity group, 1990 to 2000

	0	1	2	3	4	5	6	7	8	9
	Food and live animals	Beverages and tobacco	Crude materials excluding fuels	Mineral fuels etc.	Animal, vegetable oil, fats	Chemicals	Basic manufactured goods	Machines, transport equipment	Miscellaneous manufactured goods	Goods not classified by kind
1990	26.9	36.8	14.0	65.5	55.2	81.3	233.6	309.9	54.2	12.4
1991	44.4	4.1	5.8	40.9	61.3	83.2	216.0	320.2	64.7	5.2
1992	24.1	2.6	3.7	13.9	63.9	90.3	144.3	241.3	33.9	0.5
1993	44.1	136.8	12.5	87.9	76.4	136.0	320.7	394.9	83.2	13.3
1994	72.8	176.3	13.8	88.2	116.1	152.2	335.1	527.5	113.5	8.8
1995	116.0	208.5	20.1	96.8	210.5	234.6	530.1	779.8	200.4	31.7
1996	80.9	198.3	15.9	134.1	135.7	204.4	529.7	872.0	146.2	16.7
1997	117.6	148.1	10.7	218.0	166.4	272.4	770.7	956.5	175.4	114.8
1998	85.5	82.1	11.2	189.0	154.3	200.7	636.4	906.4	131.2	42.6
1999	114.4	61.6	12.5	272.4	108.0	245.9	642.0	608.4	174.9	23.8
2000	144.8	63.7	14.6	382.6	81.1	271.6	797.3	673.7	209.8	16.9

Source: Author's calculations from United Nations trade data, IEDB data base, Australian National University.

Table 8.13 BIMSTEC countries: Intensity index (1998 to 2000)

Exporter	Importer						
	Bangladesh	India	Myanmar	Sri Lanka	Thailand	EU 15	USA
Bangladesh	–	1.18	–	0.32	0.77	1.26	2.15
India	14.16	–	1.35	9.56	1.41	0.70	1.28
Myanmar	–	11.98	–	0.24	12.30	0.51	1.24
Sri Lanka	0.78	0.88	0.06	–	1.45	0.84	2.31
Thailand	2.80	0.94	16.26	2.82	–	0.45	1.17
EU 15	0.18	0.44	0.08	0.36	0.18	1.02	0.30
USA	0.33	0.59	0.05	0.26	0.76	0.48	–

culation of the Complementarity and Bias Indices requires commodity level data, the analysis has been performed at the three-digit ISIC level, and then aggregated to give the results summarized in Tables 8.14 and 8.15. The data relate to the total trade for the years 1998, 1999 and 2000. The calculations are performed for the total of these three years to minimize the effect of random year to year fluctuations. The year 2000 is currently the most recent for which usable trade data at the commodity level are available.

Table 8.13 shows that Myanmar exports intensively to India and Thailand, but not to either Bangladesh or Sri Lanka. Moreover, the high Intensity Index does not arise from Complementarity between Myanmar's exports and Indian or Thai imports (Table 8.14), but rather from high values of the Bias Index (Table 8.15), presumably reflecting proximity and historical linkages. Myanmar's exports are not complementary with the imports of any of the BIMSTEC partner countries.

Based on this analysis, it is concluded that Myanmar may gain from joining a BIMSTEC FTA, but that the net gains would be quite small. A strong trade-based case for joining such an FTA does not exist. There are two aspects to this point. The first aspect is the relatively small levels of intra-regional trade between Myanmar and the other BIMSTEC

Table 8.14 BIMSTEC countries: Complementarity index (1998 to 2000)

Exporter	Importer						
	Bangladesh	India	Myanmar	Sri Lanka	Thailand	EU 15	USA
Bangladesh	–	0.49	–	0.66	0.36	1.01	1.45
India	2.39	–	0.99	2.09	0.91	1.03	0.99
Myanmar	–	0.91	–	0.28	0.69	0.96	0.99
Sri Lanka	0.63	0.75	0.35	–	0.33	1.00	1.27
Thailand	1.72	0.65	0.81	1.15	–	0.96	1.00
EU 15	1.02	0.82	1.06	1.06	0.90	1.12	1.01
USA	0.81	0.73	0.67	0.91	1.01	1.00	–

Table 8.15 BIMSTEC countries: Bias index (1998 to 2000)

Exporter	Importer						
	Bangladesh	India	Myanmar	Sri Lanka	Thailand	EU 15	USA
Bangladesh	–	2.43	–	0.48	2.12	1.24	1.49
India	5.93	–	1.36	4.57	1.55	0.68	1.29
Myanmar	–	13.18	–	0.83	17.94	0.53	1.25
Sri Lanka	1.24	1.18	0.16	–	4.42	0.84	1.82
Thailand	1.62	1.45	20.08	2.45	–	0.46	1.17
EU 15	0.17	0.54	0.08	0.35	0.20	0.91	0.30
USA	0.41	0.82	0.08	0.28	0.75	0.48	–

Source: Tables 8.13–8.15, author's calculations from United Nations Trade Data; IEDB data base, Australian National University.

countries.[5] This point suggests that although these trade volumes would almost certainly increase under an FTA, they may not increase sufficiently to make the BIMSTEC FTA economically significant. The second aspect is that the pattern of trade between Myanmar and the other BIMSTEC countries, does not suggest that they are natural trading partners. The implication is that the trade-creating effects which generate net benefits may be small.

The strongest case for an FTA involving Myanmar would be with the USA and the European Union. Of course, these opportunities are not currently available, but a BIMSTEC FTA would not be a good substitute. There may be strong political reasons for forming an FTA among these countries, but the evidence indicates that if Myanmar were to join a BIMSTEC FTA, large trade-related gains should not be expected.

Several qualifications to these results are necessary. First, the analysis presented in this study uses past data to project about the gains that may arise in the future. This procedure has clear dangers, and often misses important developments. Second, a BIMSTEC FTA could have non-trade economic benefits important effects, including the provision of regional public goods. The construction, management and maintenance of a highway connecting India, Bangladesh, Myanmar and Thailand is a prominent example. It would be possible to achieve these benefits through BIMSTEC-based regional cooperation which does not include an FTA, but the possibility cannot be dismissed that a trade grouping would facilitate this form of regional cooperation. If so, there could be benefits from a BIMSTEC FTA which go beyond the small net benefits which would apparently derive from the trade dimension alone.

The third qualification is that the analysis of this paper has been based on existing trade flows. Ideally it would be based on the trade flows that would exist under liberalized trade between all the countries concerned (not just the proposed members of the FTA). The difference between the two derives from the existing structure of tariffs and NTBs affecting trade.

If trade were liberalized, the levels would be higher and the structure would be different. A study of the structure of trade barriers (tariffs and NTBs) among the BIMSTEC countries could be useful in this respect. Nevertheless, taking account of this point would seem unlikely to reverse the overall conclusion that the BIMSTEC countries are, in general, not natural trading partners, because such an outcome would require that the existing structure of protection dramatically reduced trade *among* the BIMSTEC countries, relative to their trade with other countries.

The fourth qualification is that the analysis here (based on the three-digit ISIC classification) disregards trade *within* these commodity categories. This phenomenon, known as intra-industry trade, is potentially important no matter how fine the level of commodity classification that is used. For example, trade among countries in brands of commodities increases the volumes of trade flows relative to the levels that would otherwise be predicted. Finally, the analysis above has focused on trade in goods and has not accounted for trade in services or investment. These issues would also be important under a BIMSTEC FTA.

The decision as to whether Myanmar should join a regional FTA based on the BIMSTEC grouping presumably will not be based on trade issues alone. If it was, the case for joining such an FTA would not be strong. Political concerns would presumably be more important, along with the establishment of a platform for regional cooperation in a range of areas, of which trade is only one. This has been the experience of AFTA.

Agricultural policy and performance

Agricultural growth has been relatively stagnant since 1995 and yields have been static. There are two ways output could be increased: by cultivating existing farming lands more intensively, or by opening new lands to cultivation. Elsewhere in Asia, the green revolution"made the first of these approaches possible. It required that new agricultural technologies were available and that farmers had the economic incentives to apply them. In Myanmar, neither condition applies. New technologies have not been adapted to local conditions because domestic agricultural research and extension capabilities are almost non-existent. More important, the prices of agricultural commodities and the markets for the inputs required for agricultural expansion are suppressed to such an extent that farmers lack incentives to expand production.

The government's response to static yields in agriculture has been surprising. Rather than encouraging the more intensive cultivation of existing cropped areas, by addressing the causes of poor performance, the government has instead given high weight to expanding the areas under cultivation by granting large tracts of uncultivated land to local entrepreneurs"and offering preferential conditions for production on these large farms. It is argued in this paper that this approach is economically wasteful and environmentally dangerous and that it threatens to exacerbate the already serious problem of rural poverty. We discuss first the disappointing performance of agriculture in Myanmar, then the policy environment that has brought this about, and finally the reforms that seem most urgently required.

Performance

Since the disastrous year of 1988/89, agricultural output has mirrored the overall performance of the economy, but its worsening performance since the early 1990s has been significant. Nevertheless, Table 8.16 shows that since 1999 paddy production has grown significantly. As noted above, rice exports have also grown. Despite this, in 2001, real agricultural output per head of population remained below its level in 1985.

About 25 per cent of Myanmar's total land mass is arable. Roughly half of the arable land, 23 million acres, is cultivated, mostly by farm families holding small plots of land. The average size of a farm holding is around 5.6 acres. About 86 per cent of Myanmar's farms are less than ten acres in size and they account for 58 per cent of the total cultivated area. Farms over 50 acres comprise less than 1 per cent of the total number and they account for only about 3 per cent of total cultivated land (Table 8.17). Beyond these cultivated lands, a further 20 million arable acres are classified as ČultivaВle waste land." The government views this land as an abundant resource, available for agricultural exploitation. Much of this land is already under environmental pressure related to population growth,

Table 8.16 Myanmar: output of key crops, 1996/97 to 2000/01 ('000 tons unless otherwise stated)

	1996/97	1997/98	1998/99	1999/2000	2000/01[a]
Paddy	17,397.0	16,391.2	16,807.8	19,808.0	20,986.9
Sugarcane	3,978.7	5,055.9	5,343.9	5,363.2	5,800.5
Pulses, green gram	327.9	441.6	456.9	470.9	511.0
Pulses, black gram	323.2	413.0	437.1	420.7	523.3
Peanut	550.5	531.3	552.9	623.8	719.5
Maize	281.4	303.4	297.9	343.6	358.9
Cotton (long staple)	135.8	141.5	135.1	146.3	123.0
Rubber	25.6	26.6	22.6	26.2	35.1
Memorandum items					
Net area sown ('000 ha)	9,277.0	9,277.8	9,672.4	10,135.0	10,467.1
Irrigated	1,556.4	1,591.6	1,692.4	1,841.3	1,910.1
% of total area sown	16.8	17.2	17.5	18.2	18.2

Source: Central Statistical Organization, Statistical Yearbook 2001, Yangon.

Note
a Provisional.

Table 8.17 Myanmar: distribution of cultivated land holding sizes, 1997/98

Size of holdings	Number of holdings	%	Total acres	%
Under 5 acres	2,804,000	62	6,719,400	27
5 and under 10 acres	1,139,400	25	8,133,500	32
10 and under 20	493,400	11	6,852,200	27
20 and under 50	101,000	2	2,783,800	11
50 and under 100	1,900	0	121,500	0
100 acres and over	1,100	0	599,200	2
Total	4,540,800	100	25,209,600	100

Source: Ministry of Agriculture, Land Records and Settlement Department, Yangon (unpublished).

increased fuelwood cutting, land clearing for cultivation and unofficial logging. As of June 1999, 1.1 million acres had been granted to the private sector for establishment of large scale farming and much more was planned. It is not yet clear to what extent, if any, the expansion of output since 1999 is attributable to the government's large scale farming initiative.

By Southeast Asian standards, Myanmar's growth in total agricultural output per head of population has been low since the mid-1980s (Table 8.18). Paddy yields are also low, especially considering Myanmar's natural advantages as a rice producer. Once the largest exporter of rice in Southeast Asia, Myanmar is now a minor participant in the international rice market. With some exceptions, such as pulse and bean production for export, the gains in agricultural performance achieved during the first half of the 1990s have not been sustained. In the case of rice, these earlier gains derived primarily from expansion of the effective area planted, through double cropping, rather than from increased yields per crop planted.

Table 8.18 Southeast Asia: average annual growth of agricultural output and yields, 1974–84 and 1985–96

Country	Average annual growth rate of agricultural output per capita (%)		Paddy yields tons/acre
	1974–84	*1985–96*	*1994–96*
Indonesia	2.2	1.6	1.78
Malaysia	1.0	1.3	1.25
Philippines	0.7	0.6	1.00
Thailand	1.8	0.7	0.86
Vietnam	2.8	2.4	1.28
Myanmar	2.8	0.7	1.07

Source: Calculated from FAO, Production Yearbooks (1985, 1996) Rome: FAO.

Poverty

Between April 1996 and January 1997 the United Nations Development Programme financed a representative survey of 20,000 households in 23 townships across Myanmar (Shaffer 1999). The results of this survey, known as the Human Development Baseline Survey (HDBS) included an estimate that 77 per cent of rural households are directly engaged in agricultural production as their main source of income. Although 70 per cent of Myanmar's poor households are located in rural areas, only 56 per cent of poor rural households are directly engaged in agricultural production. Clearly, rural poverty and farming are not synonymous. The HDBS estimated that 35 per cent of rural households were landless, 40 per cent owned no livestock and 24 per cent owned neither land nor livestock. Moreover, many households who do own land are poor. Although the minimum size of plot required for reasonable subsistence varies across agro-climatic zones, five acres is considered a good guide, given current levels of productivity. The HDBS found that of the 4.7 million households who owned land, over 60 per cent owned less than five acres. The 1993 Agricultural Census estimated that 45 per cent of all land-owning households employed workers, and had an average farm size of eight acres. The 55 per cent of farms which did not employ workers averaged 3.7 acres in size. For the landless rural poor, off-farm employment and petty trading supplement the seasonal availability of agricultural employment, the latter accounting for just over 60 per cent of their total incomes.

Policy

Myanmar's socialist agricultural programme operated from 1962 until its demise in 1988. It consisted of taxation and suppression of the agricultural sector by means of compulsory government procurement of agricultural products at a fraction of market prices, severe restrictions on domestic trade and restrictions on farmers' choice of crops. Government agencies monopolized processing, domestic marketing and international trade in agricultural products. Private export of agricultural commodities was prohibited. By the early 1980s the official price of paddy, which farmers were paid for rice procured by the government, was less than one quarter of the unofficial market price. Agricultural output collapsed after 1986, falling by 6 per cent in 1987/88 and by 13 per cent in 1988/89.

In the late 1980s important market reforms were introduced. Controls over domestic trade in rice and other key commodities were abolished and private trading was permitted. Private exports of some commodities, not including rice, was also permitted. Production and export of beans and pulses was privatized, resulting in the export boom described above. Farmers were able to make cropping choices relatively freely, except that the government continued to encourage production of the five pillar crops", rice, beans, pulses, sugar and cotton. Fertilizer importation was decontrolled and the government ceased to monopolize its distribution. Domestic production of fertilizer remains a public sector monopoly, however, with large, antiquated plants delivering poor quality supplies at high cost. Fertilizer subsidies were abolished. These subsidies were intended to encourage fertilizer use by reducing its price to the farmer in an environment where the farm gate prices of rice and other commodities were suppressed. The fertilizer subsidies were thus intended as a form of price compensation (Larkin and San Thein 1999). But although the fertilizer subsidies have now been abandoned, the suppression of commodity prices continues. Fertilizer use remains low, not because of non-availability of supplies but because of lack of demand, reflecting output prices.

Official statements continue to emphasize the urgency of raising agricultural output and in the allocation of public capital expenditures, agriculture and agriculture-related expenditures have received high priority. Public capital expenditures in agriculture increased during the late 1990s. Large, capital-intensive public works, such as irrigation facilities and rural roads and bridges were relatively well funded, especially in the rice-growing areas.

The theme of this discussion is that poor performance of agriculture has derived from the inadequate incentive structure facing the farmer. There are two types of taxes implicitly levelled on rice production, both of which reduce incentives for farmers to produce rice. The first is an implicit rice export tax, which arises from the difference between domestic rice prices and f.o.b. export prices. The second is an implicit tax on land used for rice cultivation, which arises from the difference between market prices and the procurement price at which the government's rice trading company compulsorily acquires rice from farmers. These policies are remnants of the earlier socialist programme. Both have the effect of suppressing agricultural output prices, thereby taxing agricultural producers for the benefit of urban consumers and the government itself.

Rice exports are a legal monopoly of Myanmar Agricultural Produce Trading (MAPT), a government-owned enterprise under the control of the Ministry of Commerce. In 1999 Myanmar's rice exports received f.o.b. prices of between US$200 and 220 per metric ton. These are relatively low average prices, compared with exports from neighbouring countries, such as Thailand, reflecting the generally low quality of rice available for export from Myanmar. To see the degree of taxation of rice exports implicit in the rice export monopoly, it is necessary to compare the above f.o.b. prices with domestic prices of rice of similar quality.

Domestic farm gate prices of export quality rice currently average around Kt500 per basket of paddy. Around 80 baskets of paddy produce one metric ton of milled rice, so this farm gate price is equivalent to Kt40,000 per metric ton. MAPT report that transport, milling and handling costs for delivery to the port are equivalent to Kt4,400 per metric ton, bringing the domestic price, landed at the port and comparable to the f.o.b. prices cited above, of Kt44,400 per metric ton. At the 1999 market exchange rate of Kt340 = US$1, this converts to f.o.b. prices of US$130.60 per metric ton. The implicit rate of export tax, using the export price as the base, is thus 35 per cent. At US$210 a farm gate price of Kt500 implies a rate of export tax of 38 per cent and at US$220 the implicit tax is 41 per cent.

MAPT procures paddy from farmers in quantities which are compulsory for the farmers concerned. The procurement quotas are fixed per acre and reflect land quality. This procurement system is made administratively feasible by the detailed land records maintained by the Land Records and Settlement Department of the Ministry of Agriculture. The rice obtained in this manner is used as the supply delivered to civil servants and other fixed income groups at subsidized prices and is also the stock used for export. In crop year 1998/99, the price at which the procurement took place averaged Kt320 per basket of paddy. This was the same procurement price used in the previous crop year and will be retained for the following crop year. With inflation at 30 per cent, it is obvious that the real value of the procurement price is declining rapidly and the gap between this price and the market price is widening.

At farm gate prices of Kt500 per basket, the procurement price is equivalent to a tax of 36 per cent of the market farm gate price. However, since the quantity of rice required to be delivered at these (below market) prices is fixed per unit of paddy land, the system is equivalent to a land tax. Overall, the quantity of paddy procured in this manner (two million metric tons) is around 10 per cent of the total crop. As a proportion of total production, procurement quotas are close to 20 per cent of output in highly fertile areas and much lower in upland areas.

The effect of this procurement system is to tax land used for rice production relative to land used for other purposes. The system has a perverse effect on the quality of rice available for export and for distribution to civil servants. Because the procurement price is so low, farmers have an obvious incentive to supply their worst rice to the procurement agency, subject to meeting the minimum requirements as to quantity and quality which are demanded of them. But because MAPT is the sole exporter, this rice becomes the stock available for export, with obvious consequences for the prices subsequently received from foreign purchasers.

The present rice procurement system provides the rice used for export and for civil service distribution, but since it is acquired compulsorily at substantially less than market prices, it gives farmers an incentive to supply their lowest quality rice. This rice then becomes the stock available for export. This system could be replaced with direct purchase of rice by MAPT at market prices at the wholesale level, combined with an explicit land tax system levied in cash, rather than kind, as at present. The rate of tax per acre would depend on the quality of land (as is the case with the present procurement quotas) and could be progressive with respect to farm size. That is, the rate of tax per acre could be lower for small-sized farms than for larger farms.

Recent changes to rice export policy

In April 2003 the government announced a major revision to the rice export policy described above, to be implemented in 2004. Under this scheme, compulsory rice procurement would be abolished. Private agents would be allowed to export rice, provided their proposals to export are approved by a government committee set up to oversee rice exports. There would be a 10 per cent rice export tax, which is the same rate applied to other export categories. In addition, the government would retain one half of the remaining 90 per cent of the foreign exchange receipts from exporting. This retention of 45 per cent of the export proceeds would be intended to compensate the government for its 'investment'in the cost of exporting. The latter means that the government will reimburse the exporter (in local currency) for half of all costs of getting the rice to the f.o.b. stage, including purchase of the rice, transport, milling and storage.

If the 50 per cent reimbursement of all costs was actually carried out, without cost to the exporter, the rate of export tax would be just 10 per cent, well below the present rate. But if the reimbursement does not actually happen, which seems possible, the rate of export tax would be 55 per cent, above the present rate. It remains to be seen how the policy will actually operate. Two features of the scheme seem clear. First, the fact that a government-appointed committee must approve all applications for export, means there is ample scope for rent seeking. Second, the policy could prove to be far from facilitating the liberalization of exports, because the government is still intervening through the mechanisms described above. Dispensing with both the 50 per cent foreign exchange retention (after payment of the 10 per cent explicit export tax), and also the supposed 50 per cent subsidy to rice exporting, would be a genuine liberalization.

Land reclamation schemes

The government has decided to develop large tracts of land, to be farmed by private, national entrepreneurs. Of the total land area of Myanmar, a total of 45 million acres are considered potentially cultivable. Of these, 23 million acres are presently cultivated, leaving a further 22 million acres of currently 'vacant'land. A high proportion of this land is considered potentially eligible for the reclamation programme, which began in late 1998. The land concerned includes wetlands, coastal land and dry zone land not presently under cultivation. In late 1999, around 1.1 million acres had been allocated to around 82 business groups. The average size

of these holdings is thus 13,400 acres, but aside from a few very large holdings, the largest of which is 72,000 acres, most are around 3,000 to 5,000
acres. The objective of the project is to expand agricultural production,
both for domestic consumption and for export.

The government provides assistance for these projects in the following
ways.

- The land itself is made available in a 30 year lease, provided free of
  charge, under the condition that the land be developed for agricultural production within three years.
- The public works required for flood control, drainage and irrigation
  are provided to the project area free of charge.
- Government agencies assist in supplying the heavy earth-moving
  machinery used to create the level fields to be used for paddy production. They do this under contract with the developer, but at subsidized rates.
- The government assists in providing technical assistance in developing the project, free of charge.
- Local private banks are encouraged to provide loans to the projects
  on a preferential basis.
- Fuel required for project construction and land preparation is provided at the government price of Kt160 per gallon, compared with the
  current market rate of Kt320 per gallon.
- Project investors may export 50 per cent of the rice they produce and
  are exempted from the rice procurement system operated by the
  government agency, Myanmar Agricultural Produce Trading (MAPT).
- Preferential provision of telephone services, including cellular phones
  and land-based phone lines.
- Provision of security services to protect project staff and equipment,
  free of charge.
- Permission to import equipment, including water pumps, tractors,
  bulldozers and excavators, duty free and without limit, and without
  the need to demonstrate foreign exchange earnings through
  approved channels, which applies to other importers.

Warr (2002) describes one such large reclamation scheme, which
involves draining a wetlands area for intensive irrigated production.
Large-scale capital works are required for drainage, flood control and irrigation for the project. Warr argues that in purely economic terms the
social costs of the project exceed its social value in that the combined
social opportunity cost of the publicly supplied or subsidized inputs used
by the project exceeds the value of the reclaimed land þroduced", even if
it is assumed that the land would have had zero social value in the absence
of the project. In addition, the social implications of the project are potentially significant. Local communities lose access to the wetlands being

drained. In place of these wetlands, very large, capital intensive agricultural enterprises are created which are more typical of Latin America than Asia. The long-term social and environmental consequences of these developments could be more costly than the purely economic considerations summarized above.

Land reclamation schemes are also under way in upland and coastal areas. The business groups given access to the land are required to "develop" the sites within three years as a condition for the grant of the land. In the case of upland areas this means clearing the entire area and establishing crop cultivation on at least part of it within this period. The potential for avoidable ecological damage caused by this haste is obvious, not least the danger of land degradation in fragile upland areas. There is also the potential for enduring social conflict between the local groups now denied access to these lands and the business groups being established on large agricultural estates.

In summary, the land reclamation scheme is unnecessarily costly. It is financially attractive to the business groups participating in it because of provision by the public sector of inputs priced below their social opportunity costs, including the land itself. Moreover, the scheme is likely to have unfavourable and significant social and environmental effects. The additional food supplies this scheme may deliver would be more efficiently obtained by improving productivity on land already in intensive cultivation. As described above, this requires improving the price incentives facing farmers and improving the supply of crucial inputs.

Conclusion

Myanmar remains economically backward and impoverished. Official data from the current government of Myanmar suggest that the country is growing rapidly, at over 10 per cent per annum in real terms, but other indicators contradict this claim. The growth rate of investment and the share of investment in GDP are too low for such a rapidly growing economy. A comprehensive opening of the economy to international trading and investment opportunities would improve economic opportunity and reduce poverty simultaneously. Preferential Trading Agreements currently under discussion promise small economic gains, but they are not the answer to Myanmar's economic problems. The continued repression of agriculture, including the taxation of rice exports, impedes economic progress and increases poverty. By pursuing a policy regime which impedes international trade and investment, Myanmar's government has denied its citizens the achievement of better growth and equity outcomes.

Notes

1 The official change of name occurred in 1989. Because many observers reject the legitimacy of the country's military government, which implemented the name change, the name "Burma" continues to be widely used. "Myanmar" is used here merely because it is the official name used by such agencies as the United Nations.
2 The official exchange rate is a mechanism for stripping them of any foreign exchange earnings they generate.
3 A Deputy Minister in the Ministry of National Planning and Economic Development (Brigadier-General Zaw Tun) was reportedly dismissed in 2001 for stating that the official GDP growth data were not reliable (Institute of Southeast Asian Studies 2002).
4 The governing group was renamed the State Peace and Development Council (SPDC) in 1997.
5 An exception to this point is the level of Myanmar's exports to Thailand, which have grown rapidly in recent years, due mainly to natural gas exports. However, the level of these gas exports may not be affected by a PTA.

9 Global integration, growth and equity in Tajikistan

Kishor Sharma

Introduction

The Republic of Tajikistan was little known to the rest of the world until the early 1990s.[1] It was only after the collapse of the FSU in the late 1980s that it became known to the international community. While break up from the FSU enabled Tajikistan to be known as an independent state, it had to pay higher price for this. For example, its institutions and administrative structure collapsed, production fell significantly and international trade transactions were disrupted. To address these Tajikistan had no option but to introduce reforms in its economic, social and institutional fronts. Reform so far has gone through three distinct phases. The first stage of reform (1992–95) focused on the creation of institutions and the legal framework for the operation of the private sector, abolition of the monopoly of state trading enterprises, reform in the agriculture sector and privatization of small-scale enterprises. In the second stage (1996–99) attention was paid towards liberalization of prices, adoption of IMF programmes and privatization of large-scale enterprises. The third phase (2000–05) focuses on reform in the banking sector as well as infrastructure and the telecommunications sector.

While these reforms have made Tajikistan one of the most liberal regimes in the region, its transition to the market economy has been painful.[2] The extensive focus paid on improving current account deficit and controlling inflationary pressure has significantly reduced its investment in infrastructure, health and education. Also, progress towards developing institutions and its administrative structure has been very slow and Tajikistan has not yet recovered most of its lost output. The purpose of this chapter is to assess the growth and equity implications of reform in Tajikistan.

Attempts towards global integration[3]

Tajikistan has a moderately restricted trade regime in the region (see Table 7.1 in Chapter 7). It has very low tariffs and it does not apply non-tariff measures to restrict imports. However, there remain several procedural barriers. These include requirements to secure several documents for customs clearance from different departments and time consuming customs formalities. Import permission is not required (except for medical drugs, narcotics, weapons and fertilizers) and there are no import quotas (except for tobacco and alcohol products). Tajikistan has made significant progress in reducing import tariffs. During 1999 to 2002, import tariffs fell by 60 per cent. In May 2002, import tariffs were unified at 5 per cent, with a few exceptions. According to the IMF, Tajikistan has moderate trade restrictions, scoring five out of ten. Tajikistan does not have export restrictions nor does it encourage exports through export-processing zones (EPZs). There are no taxes or charges on exporters, except for a 0.15 per cent customs service fee. All exporters are to be registered at the Ministry of State, Revenues and Duties (MSRD) to be entitled for VAT refunds under the duty drawback scheme. Under Articles 58 to 67 of the Customs Code, VAT collected on imported inputs used by exporters are to be refunded once the evidence of exports is presented within two years at the MSRD.

Reform in the foreign exchange regime

Tajikistan had a tight exchange control regime until the end of 1999. Apart from the foreign exchange surrender requirements, the government introduced the foreign exchange duty on remittances in 1992. The foreign exchange surrender requirements acted as a tax on exporters because they had to sell their foreign exchange earnings at lower rates, which prompted under-invoicing of exports, while the foreign exchange duty encouraged unofficial inflows of foreign exchange. Both undermined the future of the banking system. In 1996, the government abolished the foreign exchange surrender requirements and adopted a unified exchange rate regime. In the same year, the local currency was made fully convertible to all current account transactions. In early 2000, the foreign exchange duty was abolished. Tajikistan has not yet signed up to IMF article VIII. Although, local currency (somoni) is fully convertible, traders tend to keep their earnings in US$.

Privatization of public enterprises

The Republic of Tajikistan has privatized a large number of public enterprises, deregulated business activities and partially removed water and energy subsidies to increase competition and reduce budget deficit. However, public sector control remains significant in aluminium production as well as electricity and railways. Likewise, the liquor and cigarettes industries are still owned by the government.

Most small enterprises, which were previously run by the government, were privatized by 2000. Privatization of medium and large enterprises has already begun and about 52 per cent of such enterprises were privatized by 2002. In 1995, the monopoly of state trading corporations in the importation and distribution of agricultural inputs was abolished and the licensing requirement for agriculture trade was eliminated. Deregulation of agriculture input and output markets, together with the privatization of land and the deregulation of grain and bread prices, significantly boosted agricultural production, particularly of wheat and cotton, leading to an increase in exports. While most manufacturing industries have been privatized, in the absence of finance for modernization, their production and exports remain very low.

Reform in foreign investment policy

Tajikistan has a liberal foreign investment policy, which allows foreign investors to purchase land and mines. Also, there are no restrictions as to the share of foreign holdings and foreign investment is allowed in most sectors. Foreign investors are permitted to repatriate 100 per cent of profits. There are no local content and technology transfer requirements. Foreign Investment Law (Article 18) provides tax holidays for foreign investment, which vary from two to five years, depending on the amount of investment. For example, foreign investment between US$100,000 to US$500,000 is exempt from profit tax for two years, while foreign investment of over US$5 million is exempt from tax for five years.

These reforms have enabled Tajikistan to apply for the membership of the World Trade Organization (WTO).

Why is WTO accession important for Tajikistan?

A resource deficit country like Tajikistan should strive to create an appropriate business environment to develop the private sector's confidence and attract foreign investment. WTO membership is an important step towards this direction, which can bring several benefits along with its membership (Drabek and Laird, 1997). First, WTO membership improves domestic institutions and policies, leading to an improvement in Tajikistan's image as a credible nation for trade and investment. Second, WTO membership improves market access because about 90 per cent of the world market exists among the WTO members. Being a member, Tajikistan will have unconditional market access on most-favoured nation (MFN) basis. Third, membership of WTO provides access to a powerful dispute settlement mechanism, which is otherwise difficult to access. Fourth, Tajikistan is a resource deficient country and needs to attract private sector investment. The membership of WTO helps develop investors' confidence and attract much needed development assistance. However, it should be noted that this does not automatically happen without good governance and efficient infrastructure and institutions.

Hence, Tajikistan should strive to develop these. The actual benefits to Tajikistan from WTO membership will come in the long run when it attracts private sector investment including foreign investment in hydro-electricity, garments, carpets and processing of agriculture.

Being a non-market economy for 70 years, Tajikistan mainly relied on state trading corporations and public enterprises. It neglected the role that the private sector can play in economic growth, and made no effort to create an appropriate legal environment for private sector development. However, to gain WTO membership, this has to be changed. In the process of WTO accession, Tajikistan will have to develop efficient institutions and an appropriate legal environment, which will help the country to grow and integrate into the world trading system. Tajikistan is an easy target for anti-dumping measures because some countries can still regard it as non-market economy due to its long association with the FSU. This increases uncertainty and discourages the development of potential export-oriented industries, namely processed fruits, textiles and carpets. By joining WTO, this can be avoided because it will have access to a powerful dispute settlement mechanism. Also, being a WTO member, it will have a transparent pricing policy, reducing the chances of anti-dumping action against its exports (Michalopoulos, 1998). This should result in better export performance.[4]

Accession negotiation strategies for Tajikistan

Although Tajikistan has one of the lowest average tariffs in the region, it should not bind tariffs at higher levels than the existing levels as this can delay the accession negotiation process. Also, once it commits to bind tariffs at higher levels it is difficult to lower them because of the pressure from domestic lobby groups. In the past, countries that have tried to bind their tariffs at much higher levels than the applied ones to improve their future bargaining power, have encountered serious difficulties in the accession negotiations. This strategy delays accession because of the suspicion it creates (Michalopoulos, 1998). Binding tariffs higher than the current levels would be a mistake because vested groups would start lobbying for more protection, which is not in the best interests of the country. Also, higher tariffs can lead to corruption and rent seeking behaviour when customs organization is inefficient, leading to distortion in resource allocation.

As discussed before, there are several procedural barriers with regard to exports and imports. It is very likely that, at the accession negotiations, Tajikistan will be asked to reduce these procedural barriers and follow standard procedures in line with a market economy. Hence, Tajikistan should start refining and reforming these barriers. Tajikistan should commit further liberalization in services, including telecommunications, electricity, railways and banking. Since export insurance and export financing are crucial to facilitate Tajikistan's trade, liberalization of services should be at the top of the negotiation agenda.

These strategies will not only expedite the accession negotiations, but also give a greater degree of certainty to investors, including foreign investors. This will allow resource allocation in line with the nation's comparative advantage. If Tajikistan fails to make commitments to liberalize service sectors, and privatize utility-providing enterprises, it will not be able to attract efficiency-enhancing foreign investment, which is crucial for sustaining growth. The experience from other developing countries suggests that trade liberalization alone, in the absence of reforms in services, basic utilities and labour markets, does not bring significant gains to the country.

Being a less developed country, Tajikistan will get more time to implement WTO rules regarding agriculture subsidies (LDCs are given eight years to phase out export subsidies), as well as the implementation of agreements under the trade-related intellectual property rights (TRIPs) and sanitary and phytosanitary standards (SAPs). Although it can make its own decision in binding tariffs and the extent of liberalization in the services sector, it is advisable that it does not increase the tariff protection and continues with the privatization of SOEs and opens up the service sector.

While Tajikistan has taken steps towards creating an appropriate legal environment for private sector development by introducing the free tradability of land rights, bankruptcy laws, competition laws and mortgage laws, it lacks appropriate institutions and legal expertise to implement these legislations. At the accession negotiations, it will have to demonstrate that the appropriate institutions and legal expertise are in place. Tajikistan should also show its commitment to develop legislations to implement agreements on TRIPs and SAPs.[5]

Structure of the economy and its performance

Growth and structure of the economy

Tajikistan arrested declining growth in real GDP from mid-1996. In fact during the period 1998–2001 growth rate of GDP almost doubled from 5.3 per cent to 10 per cent. Despite this Tajikistan is the poorest country in the region in terms of per capita income. The Tajik economy relies on agriculture, which contributes about one-quarter to GDP and two-thirds to employment. The industry sector, which includes mining and energy, contributes about 19 per cent to GDP (in 2001), while the share of the service sector, which includes trade, transport and communication and finance, is 13 per cent. Since 2001, there has been a rise in other activities, for example, supplies, procurement, material sectors and non-material services. Its share in GDP has almost doubled during 1992 to 2001 (from 19.5

per cent in 1992 to 34 per cent by 2001, see Table 9.1). This dramatic rise in the share of other activities partly explains why the GDP shares of agriculture, industry and services have fallen in 2001. Table 9.1 presents Tajikistan's basic economic indicators.

Within the agriculture sector, cotton, wheat and potatoes are most important commodities, contributing to over 90 per cent of the sector's output. Although privatization of farms has significantly increased their production since the mid-1990s, the agriculture production index (base year 1989–91 = 100) shows that the sector has not yet recovered from the disintegration (Table 9.2). By 2002, it had recovered only 54 per cent of the lost output (1989–91 = 100). Like the agriculture sector, the industry and manufacturing sectors have also suffered due to poor governance, lack of private sector investment and disruption in international trade transactions caused by transit problems in neighbouring countries. Despite an abundant supply of water resources, Tajikistan relies on imports of electricity from neighbouring countries. Clearly, reforms introduced since 1992 have failed to attract resources in the areas of its comparative advantage.

The Tajik economy has suffered significantly due to the civil war that lasted for five years (1992–97) and claimed about 50,000 human lives. Many technocrats and entrepreneurs left the country during the war and the physical infrastructure which was badly damaged has not yet been rebuilt due to the lack of resources. Also, there is a lack of a transport network between the rural and urban areas, which has significantly discouraged production and processing of agricultural output.

Macroeconomic performance

Table 9.3 presents the macroeconomic performance of Tajikistan from 1990–2001 and compares its performance with other CIS countries. Until the mid-1990s, it suffered significantly partly due to the disintegration from the FSU, which caused the loss in subsidies and traditional market, and partly due to the civil war as mentioned above. It was only after 1998

Table 9.1 Basic economic indicators

	1992	1994	1996	1998	2000	2001
Growth in real GDP	−29.0	−18.9	−4.4	5.3	8.3	10.0
GDP (million somoni)	–	–	308.5	1,025.2	1,806.7	2,512.1
GDP per capita in US$	51.5	140.7	174.1	213.3	157.0	–
Share of agriculture in GDP (%)	27.0	19.0	36.0	25.1	27.0	22.0
Share of industry in GDP (%)	36.3	22.0	25.7	20.1	23.9	18.7
Share of service in GDP (%)	7.7	15.4	18.6	26.2	23.2	13.0
Share of others in GDP (%)	19.5	12.7	9.5	17.1	14.3	34.0

Sources: ADB (2002a) and EBRD (1999), 'Transition Report 1999 Ten Years of Transition'.

Table 9.2 Key production indices of Tajikistan

Item	1991	1992	1993	1994	1995	1996	1997	1998	1999	2000	2001	2002
Population (million: as of July 1)	5.46	5.57	5.64	5.75	5.84	5.93	6.02*	6.11*	6.20*	6.29*	6.31	6.44*
GDP at current market prices	–	–	–	–	69.8	308.5	518.4	1,025.2	1,344.9	1,806.8	2,528.8	3,345.6*
Labour force (thousand: calendar year)												
Employed	–	1,915	1,876	1,886	1,891	1,777	1,842	1,855	1,780*	1,794*	1,872	–
Agriculture	1,970	1,908	1,854	1,854	1,853	1,731	1,791	1,796	1,726*	1,745*	1,829	–
Mining	881	892	949	1,002	1,095	1,026	1,145	1,080	1,118*	1,120*	1,218	–
Manufacturing	405	382	335	315	264	249	216	200	174*	170*	162	–
Others	683	634	570	538	494	456	430	516	434*	455*	500	–
Unemployed	–	7	22	32	38	46	51	59	54*	49*	43	47
Unemployment rate (%)	–	0.4	1.2	1.7	2.0	2.6	2.8	3.3	3.0*	2.7*	2.5	2.6
Production (thousand metric tons: calendar year)												
Agriculture, crop year												
1 Seed cotton	826	515	524	531	412	210	175	183	169	180	453	516
2 Wheat	153	156	159	182	174	548	559	500	483	550	489	701
3 Potatoes	181	167	147	134	112	108	128	175	240	303	308	357
4 Cotton (lint)	247	174	180	167	130	120	104	108	103	107	123	–
5 Grapes	121	100	88	80	96	122	127	46	54	110	110	81
6 Rice	26	20	23	20	24	21	44	40	47	82	40	50
7 Barley	51	39	30	25	22	17	23	26	25	19	16	36
8 Maize	60	32	34	18	19	90	30	36	36	38	34	55
Mining												
1 Hard coal	313	214	174	106	34	14	9	8	9	9	10	27
2 Crude petroleum	100	57	49	32	24	26	26	19	19	18	16	16
3 Natural gas (Mn cu. m.)	93	72	49	33	39	47	42	32	36	40	52	33
Manufacturing												
1 Cement	1,013	447	262	178	78	49	36	18	33	55	69	89
2 Wheat flour	756	628	667	360	304	271	322	417	341	307	315	293
3 Aluminium	380	345	252	237	237	198	189	196	229	269	289	–

Production indexes period averages

Agriculture (1989–91 = 100)	–	75.8	71.5	69.3	60.4	51.8	50.2	48.4	47.4	54.3	51.4	54
Industry (1990 = 100)	96.0	73.0	67.0	50.0	43.0	33.0	32.0	–	–	–	82.3	–
Manufacturing (1990 = 100)	96.0	73.0	66.0	40.0	41.0	29.8	26.6	28.1	31.7	–	41.3	–
Energy (annual values)												
Crude petroleum ('000 m. t.)												
Production	99	57	39	33	26	26	26	19	19	18	16	16
Exports	–	–	–	–	–	–	–	–	–	–	3	–
Imports	–	–	–	–	–	–	–	–	–	–	–	–
Consumption	–	–	–	–	–	–	–	–	–	–	–	–
Coal ('000 m.t.)												
Production	313	214	174	106	34	20	17	19	19	22	24	36
Exports	274	186	80	42	–	14	219	–	60	–	–	–
Imports	649	422	33	14	–	–	–	–	–	–	5	–
Consumption	688	450	127	78	–	–	–	–	–	–	1	–
Natural gas (Mn cu. m.)												
Production	93	72	49	33	39	47	42	32	36	40	52	33
Exports	–	–	–	–	–	–	–	–	–	–	–	–
Imports	2	1	1	1	1	1	2	1	1	1	565	486
Consumption	–	–	–	–	–	–	–	–	–	–	–	–
Electricity (mn kWh)												
Production	17,600	16,800	17,700	17,000	14,800	14,980	14,005	14,422	15,797	14,247	14,382	15,244
Exports	5,400	5,600	6,400	5,800	4,200	4,890	4,247	3,724	3,831	3,909	4,047	3,874
Imports	6,900	6,400	5,200	4,900	4,900	3,978	4,345	3,969	3,641	5,242	5,396	4,659
Consumption	19,100	17,600	16,500	16,100	15,500	14,068	14,103	14,667	15,607	15,580	15,731	16,029

Source: Asian Development Bank (2002c and 2003).

Note
*ADB internal estimates.

Table 9.3 Tajikistan in a regional context: key macroeconomic indicators

	1990	1992	1994	1996	1998	2000	2001
Growth in real GDP							
Kazakhstan	−0.4	−2.9	−12.6	0.5	−2.5	9.8	13.2
Kyrgyz	0.3	−19.0	−20.0	7.1	1.8	5.4	5.3
Tajikistan	−1.6	−29.0	−18.9	−4.4	5.3	8.3	10.0
Turkmenistan	2.0	−5.3	−18.8	−8.0	4.2	17.6	20.5
Uzbekistan	1.6	−11.1	−4.2	1.6	3.3	49.6	53.8
Inflation (change in CPI in %)							
Kazakhstan	104.6	2,984.1	1,160.0	28.6	8.3	13.2	8.4
Kyrgyz	170.0*	1,259.0	95.7	35.0	10.4	18.7	6.9
Tajikistan	204.0*	1,364.0	1.1	40.1	–	32.9	38.5
Turkmenistan	155.0*	644.0	1,328.0	446.0	–	7.4	6.0
Uzbekistan	169.0	910.0	885.0	64.0	9.5	3.2	2.0
Central government balance (% of GDP)							
Kazakhstan	1.4	−7.3	−7.5	−4.2	−3.9	−0.1	−0.6
Kyrgyz	0.3	−17.4	−11.6	−9.5	−4.6	−10.0	−4.0
Tajikistan	−16.4*	−30.5	−5.4	−5.8	−2.9	−0.4	−0.2
Turkmenistan	1.2	13.2	−1.4	−0.2	−2.6	−0.3	−0.9
Uzbekistan	−1.1	−18.4	−6.1	−7.3	–	–	–
Current account balance (% of GDP)							
Kazakhstan	–	−31.5	−7.7	−3.6	−5.6	−4.1	−4.6
Kyrgyz	–	−1.8	−11.3	−23.6	−16.7	−5.6	−0.7
Tajikistan	–	18.4	−21.0	−7.3	−10.8	−5.9	−7.7
Turkmenistan	–	14.1	3.8	2.2	−45.8	−13.0	–
Uzbekistan	–	−11.9	2.1	−8.6	−1.7	–	–

Sources: EBRD (1999); ADB (2002a) and ADB (2002b).

Note
* 1991.

that Tajikistan achieved a positive growth in GDP. Like other CIS countries, Tajikistan experienced hyperinflation in the immediate independence years. Inflation rose from 204 per cent in 1991 to 1,364 per cent by 1992, but was brought down to 38.5 per cent by 2001 mainly due to tight monetary and fiscal measures pursued since the mid-1990s. Tajikistan still has the highest inflation among the Central Asian countries, which appears to be mainly due to supply-side rigidities, including poor internal transport and lack of finance for production activities.

By early 2000, Tajikistan significantly controlled the central government budget deficit mainly attributed to price liberalization and privatization of state owned enterprises (SOEs). By 2001, budget deficit was brought down to 0.2 per cent of GDP from just over 16 per cent in 1991. The current account deficit, however, remains very high (7.7 per cent GDP in 2001).

Despite huge demand for investment, particularly in the infrastructure sector, gross fixed capital formation has significantly fallen. It fell from 22.3 per cent of GDP in 1990 to about 11.6 per cent by 2001– a decline of about 50 per cent (Table 9.4). Per capita FDI remains extremely low despite liberalization in investment policy since the mid-1990s, while the external debt percentage of GDP has increased from 111.6 per cent in the 1990s to 158 per cent by early 2000.

Trade performance and prospects

Tajikistan is highly dependent on foreign trade as reflected by the higher shares of exports and imports in GDP. After an initial decline, both exports and imports rose sharply from the mid-1990s, but this did not last long mainly due the 1997 Russian financial crisis. Exports rose from US$456 million in 1993 to US$839 million in 1995 then declined to US$652 million by 2001. A similar pattern was also observed in imports, which fell from US$880 million in 1995 to US$688 million in 2001 (Table 9.5).

Despite fluctuations in exports, strong commodity prices contributed to an improvement in Tajikistan's terms of trade during 1993 to 2001 (except for 1997, see Table 9.5). During the period under review,

Table 9.4 Key economic indicators

	1990	2001
Gross fixed capital formation % of GDP	22.30[a]	11.58[b]
Exports of goods and services % of GDP	79.1	85.10[b]
Per capita FDI (US$)	1.54[c]	1.59
External debt % of GDP	73.30[c]	97
External debt % of export	111.6[c]	158.20[d]

Sources: ADB (2002a) and EBRD (1999).

Notes
a 1996.
b 2000.
c 1993.
d 1994.

Table 9.5 Performance of foreign trade

	1993	1995	1997	1998	1999	2000	2001
Merchandise exports (million US$)	456	839	746	597	689	784	652
Merchandise imports (million US$)	660	880	750	711	663	675	688
Unit value index for exports	100	182	154	163	169	180	143
Unit value index for Imports	100	158	164	158	162	175	104
Terms of trade (1993 = 100)	100	115	94	103	104	103	138
Trade balance % GDP[a]	(29.4)	(7.8)	0.4	(8.6)	2.4	11.3	(3.4)
Exports % of GDP[a]	65.7	161.2	67.1	45.2	63.4	79.1	61.7
Imports % of GDP[a]	95.1	169.1	67.4	53.9	61.0	68.1	65.1

Source: ADB (2002a).

Note
a GDP data for 1993 to 1998 are taken from EBRD (2000).

Tajikistan received higher prices for its exports than it paid for imports (except for 1997). During the 1993 to 2001 period, taking 1993 as a base year, the unit value of Tajikistan's exports increased by 43 per cent, while that of imports increased by 4 per cent, contributing to an improvement in terms of trade by 38 per cent. The improvement in terms of trade helped improve the current account deficit from 18 per cent of GDP in 1992 to about 8 per cent by 2001.

Tajikistan's exports are dominated by two major commodities, namely cotton and aluminium, which together account for over 70 per cent share in export earnings. The third major export item is hydro-electricity whose share in the total exports has been fluctuating partly due to inefficiency in the electricity agency, which is run by the state.

Over 90 per cent of Tajikistan's imports are dominated by electricity, aluminium oxide, oil products and natural gas. It also relies on imports of grain and flour. However, their shares in the country's total imports have fallen in recent years mainly because of an increase in wheat production. Wheat production increased due to deregulation of agricultural input and output markets in the late 1990s. Tajikistan also imports electricity despite a huge potential in electricity generation as the generation of power is seasonal and the domestic grid network is not linked between the northern and southern regions of the country. While Russia and the FSU countries of Central Asia, as a group, remain major destinations for its exports (together a 45 per cent share in total exports in 2000), it has successfully penetrated the Dutch, Iranian, Swiss and Asian markets in recent years (Table 9.6). The Netherlands is a key market for its aluminium and Switzerland is a major market for cotton. Its exports to the FSU countries of Central Asia have dramatically fallen from 33 per cent in 1996 to 15 per cent by 2000. Russia and the FSU countries of Central Asia, as a group, remain major sources of Tajikistan's imports. Their combined share in Tajikistan's total imports rose from 57 per cent in 1996 to 83 per cent in 2000.

Despite abundant supplies of cotton and cheap labour, Tajikistan has only been able to process about 10 per cent of its cotton into various types of textile products and carpets. There is a tremendous scope for garments and carpet production in the country, and this is an industry in which world trade is growing rapidly. Tajikistan is also endowed with precious stones, such as rubies and emeralds that can be processed into jewellery for export markets. It has not yet fully exploited its water resources mainly due to a monopoly of the state in generating and distributing hydro-electricity. Deregulation of electricity generation and distribution will help attract foreign investment and increase its production and exports of hydro-electricity. Tajikistan has the potential to export its hydro-electricity not only to the Central Asian countries but also to China.

Tajikistan's development in the long run depends on the performance

Table 9.6 FDI in Tajikistan and direction of foreign trade

Item	1991	1992	1993	1994	1995	1996	1997	1998	1999	2000	2001	2002
FDI, net	–	8	9	12	20	25	30	24	21	19	9.5	36
External trade (US$ million: calendar year)												
Exports, f.o.b.	–	185	456	559	839	770	746	597	689	784	652	737
Imports, c.i.f.	–	240	660	707	880	668	750	711	663	675	688	721
Trade balance	–	–55	–204	–148	–41	102	–4	–114	26	109	–36	16
Direction of trade (US$ million: calendar year)												
Total exports	–	29.3	349.8	491.9	748.6	771.5	803.4	596.6	688.7	935.0	651.6	536.6
1 Netherlands	–	–	1.1	147.6	255.2	218.0	229.4	221.4	222.3	211.3	194.4	2.8
2 Uzbekistan	–	–	20.3	22.7	132.0	190.7	172.5	125.7	181.0	236.3	87.2	94.7
3 Russia	–	–	62.5	46.2	95.3	79.0	63.5	47.8	115.1	215.7	104.7	64.4
4 Switzerland	–	0.4	5.8	44.9	37.2	83.5	140.7	94.9	75.1	108.5	52.2	54.1
5 Kazakhstan	–	–	16.3	10.1	7.0	24.3	10.0	10.0	3.6	3.6	–	–
6 Korea, Republic of	–	–	0.9	2.9	9.3	24.9	3.2	0.2	7.4	14.5	–	–
7 Iran	–	–	–	1.4	0.7	1.7	3.5	13.6	13.5	13.5	29.9	24.8
8 Italy	–	6.8	2.5	0.4	2.4	6.6	7.8	9.8	5.1	11.6	5.8	18.9
9 Belgium	–	–	–	–	–	–	14.7	12.7	7.0	6.4	6.0	5.0
10 United Kingdom	–	–	119.9	30.3	20.7	15.2	6.5	5.1	5.5	7.1	–	–
Total imports	–	72.9	532.1	547.0	809.9	668.1	750.3	711.0	663.1	800.9	687.5	704.5
1 Uzbekistan	–	–	65.4	83.2	251.4	198.9	261.6	227.3	264.4	301.6	150.7	163.6
2 Switzerland	–	0.1	4.3	100.4	51.7	99.8	185.1	157.9	25.1	31.7	2.1	2.1
3 Russia	–	–	83.8	60.7	136.0	74.4	115.1	102.2	92.4	61.5	129.4	88.0
4 Kazakhstan	–	–	65.5	32.8	26.5	52.4	42.0	51.9	78.8	105.7	89.1	96.7
5 United Kingdom	–	–	16.4	68.0	161.2	78.3	10.1	3.8	70.5	93.2	2.5	1.2
6 Ukraine	–	–	4.4	13.6	2.2	19.2	20.7	16.6	37.7	58.7	63.6	69.0
7 Turkmenistan	–	–	26.0	39.4	57.4	26.3	29.7	31.3	15.2	15.2	62.3	67.6
8 United States	–	9.7	8.7	31.9	25.3	16.0	3.2	32.8	1.7	15.7	–	–
9 Iran	–	–	–	0.1	0.7	10.5	12.0	11.3	10.4	10.4	10.0	10.6
10 Azerbaijan	–	–	1.1	0.2	1.2	0.0	3.2	1.8	15.6	29.4	33.5	36.4

Source: FDI data comes from EBRD (2000) except for 2001 and 2002 which are taken from ADB (2003). Other data come from Asian Development Bank (2002c and 2003).

of agricultural exports, given that the sector employs about 64 per cent of the labour force and contributes about one-quarter to GDP. However, due to the poor transport network within the country, processing and marketing of fruits has been restricted. As a result, despite abundant supplies of fruits, Tajikistan relies on imports of fruits and juices from Russia. Improvements in the internal transport network and some assistance in packaging will significantly reduce its reliance on imports of juice. In fact, with an improvement in internal and external transport networks it could be an exporter of juices and dry fruits. Given the land-locked position and the weak physical infrastructure, Tajikistan's integration into the world trading system largely relies on cooperation with its neighbours in the areas of hydro-electricity, transport and transit. Simplification of cross-border procedures could significantly improve its trade performance.

Poverty and inequity in post-independence Tajikistan

Among the CIS countries, Tajikistan has suffered the most since independence partly due to the loss in subsidies and traditional markets, and partly due to the five-year civil war which left the country's finances and physical infrastructure badly damaged. The latter has not yet been repaired and in the absence of a reliable road network between rural and urban areas, the rural population has a very limited choice in disposing of their output. Not only is the road infrastructure in a bad shape, but also the rail network which transports about 95 per cent of the country's exports and imports, needs urgent upgrading and maintenance. However, due to the lack of resources it has not been maintained and repaired. Besides poor state of infrastructure, the enforcement of laws has been very weak and the country's human rights records have been very poor (Table 9.7). In 2001, Tajikistan ranked below the tenth percentile in all key governance measures except 'voice and accountability' in which it ranked in the 27th percentile (Gleason, 2003).

The poor physical infrastructure, on the one hand, and lack of law and order on the other has significantly distorted the business climate for private sector development. As a result, despite significant openness in recent years, foreign direct investment (FDI) remains very low in the country (Table 9.6). While Tajikistan has attracted some FDI in the post-independence period, they have mainly gone into the capital-intensive mining sector, motivated by lucrative tax concessions for such activities under the foreign investment policy. It has failed to attract FDI (and local investment) in labour-intensive processing of cotton and textiles and carpet production as well as the processing of agricultural products. As a result the unemployment rate remains as high as 30 per cent although official figures suggest about 5 per cent unemployment in the country.

Table 9.7 World Bank Institute governance indicators for Tajikistan

Governance indicator	Year	Percentile rank (0–100) in %	Estimate (−2.5 to +2.5)	Standard deviation	Number of surveys/polls
Voice and accountability	2000/01	27.6	−0.69	0.19	3
Political stability/no violence	2000/01	3.1	−1.77	0.42	2
Government effectiveness	2000/01	7.5	−1.31	0.28	3
Regulatory quality	2000/01	5.9	−1.46	0.38	3
Rule of law	2000/01	4.7	−1.25	0.22	4
Control of corruption	2000/01	9.3	−1.08	0.24	3

Source: Kaufmann *et al.* 2002 quoted in Gleason (2003).

Rising unemployment has not only increased poverty but has also increasingly contributed to crime and violence. Poverty is very high and rising. As shown in Table 9.8, the percentage of people living below the poverty line has increased from 59 per cent in 1988 (before independence) to 83 per cent in 1999 (post-independence). Not only is poverty high but also inequality, as measured by the Gini coefficient. In terms of HDI, it was ranked in 112th place in 2000. The lower level of HDI is a reflection of the lower level of investment in health and education and this has been falling significantly (Table 9.9). Investment in health and education as a per cent of GDP has fallen from over 17 per cent of GDP in the early 1990s to 3 per cent by 1999. Clearly, poverty and inequality has increased significantly in the post-independence period.

A key challenge Tajikistan faces today is how to reduce growing poverty and inequality. To address this, it needs to develop efficient institutions and the infrastructure needed to facilitate private sector development. Being a land-locked country, Tajikistan relies on the territories of its neighbours for international trade transactions. Currently, gaining access to international markets is costly and time consuming because of the visa requirements, transit permit system and cross-border formalities. This has discouraged investment in export-oriented activities. In this context, Tajikistan should view regional cooperation as a means of achieving political and economic stability, as well as a forum to resolve issues relating to cross-border movements of goods and people.

Conclusion

Tajikistan adopted outward-looking strategies after its independence from the FSU in early 1990. It has significantly lowered tariffs, removed quantitative restrictions, liberalized foreign investment and exchange rate regimes, and privatized public enterprises. It has even applied for WTO membership, which is viewed as an important step for several reasons. First, membership of the WTO can create an image for Tajikistan as a credible nation for trade and investment, which will help attract foreign investment, which is badly needed. Second, as the WTO members cover 90 per cent of the world market, membership can significantly improve market access to Tajik products. Third, WTO membership can provide a powerful dispute settlement mechanism, which is otherwise not available. Although these are potential benefits of WTO membership, they can only be realized by creating an appropriate business climate. However, transit problems in neighbouring countries, a poor transport road network within the country and lack of maintenance of the rail network have significantly distorted the business climate in the country. The enforcement of rules of law, protection of private property and political stability also seems to be a problem. Liberalization *per se* in the absence of

Table 9.8 Poverty, inequality and human development in Tajikistan

% of population below the national poverty line*		% of population below $2.15 per capita per day	Income ratio of highest 20% to lowest 20%	Gini coefficient	Human Development Index			Rank in 2000
1988	1999	1999	1998	1998	1980	1990	2000	
59	83	68	5.0	0.35	na	0.74	0.667	112

Source: IMF and World Bank (2002).

Note
* The national poverty line is defined as percentage of population earning a per capita income lower than the minimum consumption basket. For 1988, a per capita income of 75 roubles per month was used as the conventional poverty line.

Table 9.9 Non-monetary indicators of poverty and inequality in Tajikistan

	1991	1992	1993	1994	1995	1996	1997	1998	1999
Expenditure on health and education (% of GDP)	17.4	11.7	8.5	14.5	3.6	3.5	3.4	3.3	3.1
Mortality rate (per 1,000 male adult)	n.a.	n.a.	n.a.	n.a.	n.a.	n.a.	234.0	233.0	n.a.
Basic school enrolment (%)	96.7	92.5	87.1	87.0	86.6	85.1	84.9	87.8	
Earning inequality (Gini coefficient)	Check in 2001/2								

Source: EBRD (1999)

appropriate institutions and infrastructure has failed to achieve the expected gains in Tajikistan, leading to a painful transition to the market economy.

Acknowledgement

I thank Richard Pomfret for useful suggestions. Data presented in this chapter were collected while I was working on a related project for the African Development Bank. I thank the Bank for financial assistance.

Notes

1 Tajikistan declared its independence from the Soviet Union on 9 September 1991. It is a land-locked country and borders with Afghanistan in the south (1,030 km), People's Republic of China in the east (430 km), Kyrgyz Republic in the north (590 km) and Uzbekistan in the west (950 km). Tajikistan occupies 134,000 square km and is a mountainous country. High mountains cover about 93 per cent of the landscape.

2 About 80 per cent of Tajik people live below the official poverty line and over 30 per cent of young people are unemployed and/or underemployed, although official statistics suggest that unemployment is below 5 per cent. According to the World Bank (2003), Tajikistan's per capita income has declined by 85 per cent since independence. It fell from US$1,050 in 1990 to US$150 by 2000. In the same period pensioners' income dropped from US$70 to US$2.

3 This section draws heavily on Sharma (2004).

4 Note that the WTO dispute settlement mechanism is time consuming because both parties involved in a trade dispute will have to produce enough evidence to justify their positions. By the time a decision is made, enough damage can be done to a poor country involved in the dispute.

5 There is a strong feeling among intellectuals in developing countries that incorporating TRIPs into the WTO rule was a big mistake, which serves the interest of rich countries but not poor ones.

Part IV

Latin American experience

10 Trade liberalization, inequality and poverty in Brazil

Afonso Ferreira and Antonio Aguirre

A relatively large number of empirical studies evaluating the impacts of the Brazilian trade liberalization of the 1990s are already available. This chapter presents a detailed review of this literature and highlights the main conclusions that can be derived from it, relative to the effects of those reforms on GDP growth, employment, income distribution and poverty. By way of introduction, we consider some data relating to Brazilian trade reforms.

Table 10.1 reports the protection structure in Brazil. The average nominal tariff on the Brazilian imports was reduced from 54.9 percent, in 1987, to 13.4 percent, in 1998. Tariff dispersion was also reduced, with the standard deviation of the nominal tariff structure falling from 21.3 percent to 6.6 percent. Effective tariff fell substantially, with the average effective tariff being cut from 67.8 percent to 16.2 percent and the standard deviation was falling from 53.8 percent to 21.3 percent, in the same period. The average tariff was raised again between 1995 and 1998, a response to the overvaluation of the domestic currency, but, even in that period of abundant trade and current account deficits, the movement towards a more open trade regime was essentially preserved.

Non-tariff barriers such as the "Annex C", a list of around 1,300 products which could not be imported, import licenses, special import

Table 10.1 Nominal and effective tariffs (percent)

	Nominal tariffs			Effective tariffs		
	1987	*1994*	*1998*	*1987*	*1994*	*1998*
Simple average	57.5	11.2	15.5	77.1	13.6	20.2
Weighted average*	54.9	10.2	13.4	67.8	12.3	16.2
Standard deviation	21.3	5.9	6.6	53.8	8.4	21.3
Maximum	102.7	23.5	38.1	308.1	27.7	129.2
Minimum	15.6	0.0	0.0	8.3	−4.9	−2.2

Source: Kume *et al.* (2003).

Note
* Value added weighted average.

programs etc. were also eliminated in the early 1990s.[1] As shown in Appendix 10.1, this reduction of tariff and non-tariff barriers led to an increase in import penetration into Brazilian industry from 7.0 percent in 1990–93, to 10.8 percent in 1994–98 and 14.2 percent in 1999–2001 (Ribeiro and Pourchet, 2002). Table 10.3 shows yearly estimates of the GDP growth rate, the rate of unemployment, income distribution and the poverty rate before (1984–92) and after trade liberalization (1993–2002). GDP growth rates rose and the unemployment rate fell for a short period immediately after the trade reforms. Since 1998, however, the expansion of GDP decelerated to only 1.37 percent per year, a figure close to population growth, while the unemployment rate rose to 8 percent. In spite of its dismal performance in the period 1998–2003, the growth figures for the Brazilian economy in the 1990s are more encouraging than those for the 1980s, (Table 10.3). In particular, GDP per capita and labor productivity, which fell in the 1980s, again attained positive, even if low, rates of growth in the 1990s. The Gini coefficient for the distribution of personal income has displayed a remarkable stability in Brazil, remaining, virtually unchanged at 0.60 since the late 1970s (Table 10.2). The poverty rate presented a once and for all sharp decrease in the mid-1990s, falling from more than 40 percent in the first half of that decade to about 33 percent in the second.

The precise contribution of trade reforms to the good performance of the Brazilian economy in the period 1993–97 and to its dismal perform-

Table 10.2 GDP growth, unemployment, income inequality and poverty

Year	GDP growth rate	Unemployment rate	Gini index	Poverty rate
1984	5.40	8.15	0.59	50.4
1985	7.85	5.90	0.60	43.6
1986	7.49	4.00	0.59	28.2
1987	3.53	4.08	0.60	40.9
1988	−0.06	4.18	0.62	45.3
1989	3.16	3.64	0.64	42.9
1990	−4.35	4.65	0.62	43.8
1991	1.03	5.24	–	–
1992	−0.54	6.14	0.58	40.8
1993	4.92	5.75	0.60	41.7
1994	5.85	5.44	–	–
1995	4.22	4.96	0.60	33.9
1996	2.66	5.81	0.60	33.5
1997	3.27	6.14	0.60	33.9
1998	0.13	8.34	0.60	32.8
1999	0.79	8.25	0.60	34.1
2000	4.36	7.84	–	–
2001	1.31	6.83	–	33.6
2002	1.93	7.88	–	–
2003	−0.23	–	–	–

Source: IPEA DATA available online at www.ipeadata.gov.br.

Table 10.3 GDP per capita and labor productivity, annual rates of growth (per cent), 1970–2000

	GDP per capita	*Labor productivity*
1979/80	6.00	4.70
1980/91	−0.40	−0.92
1991/2000	1.16	1.80

Source: Bonelli (2002).

ance since 1998 cannot be easily ascertained and nothing of this sort will be attempted here. However, enough is known about the impacts of the reforms to make it possible to put together a quite comprehensive and relatively accurate picture of their effects on the most relevant dimensions of the Brazilian economy. This is the aim of this chapter.

Impacts of Brazilian trade liberalization

Effects on efficiency

In the international literature, few studies have been able to present evidence, at the micro-level, of a relation between trade reforms and an acceleration of productivity growth. The Brazilian trade liberalization of the 1990s was at first seen as a remarkable exception in this context, a view only recently challenged by the use of new, better quality data, extending to other sectors of the economy beyond manufacturing.

Hay (2001) uses panel data for the period 1986–94, from the Pesquisa Industrial Annual (PIA), an industrial survey covering 349 firms, conducted by Instituto Brasileiro de Geografia e Estatistica (IBGE), the national statistics office, to assess the impact of trade liberalization on the performance of large manufacturing firms in Brazil. He estimates an equation for net sales per worker, in which this variable, taken as a proxy for labor productivity, is assumed to depend on the capital–labor ratio, the level of employment, protection, the real exchange rate and its own value in the previous year. The inclusion of the level of employment in the regression equation allows for the possibility of scale effects. The real exchange rate is included in the regression because, in principle, whereas devaluation protects domestic industry (increases import prices), appreciation exposes domestic firms to import competition, requiring them to become more efficient to survive (Hay, 2001).

The results obtained suggest that total factor productivity was stable in the period 1986–88, fell in 1989 and especially in 1990 and recovered strongly in 1993–94, increasing by more than 55 percent from the low of 1990 to the high of 1994. The regression coefficient on the protection variable is negative and significant. Given the magnitude of this coefficient, the reduction in the average effective tariff between 1990 and 1994 may have led to an increase in efficiency of about 11 percent. The exercise also suggests a minor role for the real exchange rate, with a devaluation of 10 percent reducing efficiency by 2 percent.

The large efficiency gains observed between 1990 and 1994, according to Hay (2001), were a joint product of the recovery after the 1990–91 recessions and of trade liberalization. Admitting that it is not possible to distinguish these influences quantitatively, he suggests, however, that both had large effects. Ferreira and Rossi (2001) report that labor productivity, measured as output per total labor force employed in production, increased in 16 industries comprising 92 percent of total industrial production in Brazil, at average annual rates of 0.6 percent in the period 1985–89, 5.9 percent in 1990–93 and 7.4 percent in the 1994–97 period. Total factor productivity (TFP) *declined* at an average annual rate of 1 percent from 1985 to 1989, in those 16 industries. However, from 1990 to 1993, this trend was reversed, with TFP *increasing* at an average annual rate of 2 percent. Finally, between 1994 and 1997, annual TFP average growth reached 4.3 percent, with eight industrial sectors presenting rates of growth above 5 percent.

Using panel techniques, Ferreira and Rossi (2001) identify a negative relationship between labor and total factor productivity, on the one hand, and the level of nominal and effective protection, on the other. Their results imply that the reduction in effective protection, between 1987 and 1997, led on average to an absolute increase of three to four percentage points in labor productivity and TFP annual growth rates. In several additional exercises, the authors show that these results are robust to changes in data definitions, control variables and estimation methods and they do not depend on any restrictive assumptions. They conclude that trade reform was an important determinant of industrial performance. Increased protection was associated with lower industry growth rates of TFP and labor productivity (Ferreira and Rossi 2001).

Also using data from IBGE's Pesquisa Industrial Annual (PIA), Muendler (2001) examines the evolution of total factor productivity in manufacturing firms, between 1986 and 1998, seeking to quantify the relative importance of three channels through which trade liberalization may have affected productivity: (i) greater access to imported inputs and capital goods; (ii) increase in competitive pressure; and (iii) exclusion of less efficient firms from the market and the resulting increase in the market share of the more efficient surviving firms. More intensive use of better quality imported inputs (channel (i)) was not found to have a significant impact on TFP, while even relatively small tariff reductions (channel (ii)) appeared to have a strong effect. The reduced probability of survival of less efficient producers (channel (iii)) also contributed to improve the measured productivity performance of the industrial firms in the PIA sample after trade liberalization.

Bonelli (2002) offers a more nuanced view of the effects of trade liberalization on productivity growth than the one that can be found in Hay

(2001), Ferreira and Rossi (2001) and Muendler (2001). According to Bonelli (2002), the three aforementioned studies use physical output, not value added, their productivity estimated are overstated after trade reforms, when imports of raw materials, parts and components etc. are replaced by domestically produced inputs. To avoid this problem, he uses data from the Brazilian National Accounts on real value added per occupied person in 42 sectors that cover the whole economy (not only the industrial sector, as done in the three previous studies). His main results are: (i) total average labor productivity grew at 1.5 percent yearly between 1990 and 2000; (ii) there was a significant dispersion of sectoral productivity growth rates around the simple (unweighted) average rate of growth of 3.5 percent;[2] (iii) of the 17 sectors with above average (higher than 3.5 percent) productivity growth, 15 are in manufacturing; (iv) of the six sectors with negative productivity growth, four are related to services (commerce, services to firms, services to families and private non-profit services).

Using regression analysis, Bonelli (2002) found no overall association between productivity growth in the 31 sectors producing tradable goods and indicators of trade liberalization and/or import penetration ratios, a surprising result in view of the findings reported in the previous literature. Conducting an informal analysis of the data, the author suggests that productivity growth was the response to increased import competition in only a limited number of sectors – in general, those sectors that displayed high import penetration rates, even before the trade reforms were enacted.

Effects on employment

The impact of Brazilian trade liberalization on the level of employment has been examined by, among others, Barros and Corseuil (2001), Moreira and Najberg (1997) and more recently by Maia (2003). Following a methodology first adopted by Greenhalg *et al.* (1998) in their UK study, Maia (2003) identifies sources of a shift in total employment in the Brazilian economy between 1985 and 1995. A total of 53.5 million workers were employed in the Brazilian economy in 1985. The proportion of unskilled workers (i.e. workers with up to 11 years of schooling) in the labor force was 93 percent. According to this author's estimates, the increase in final consumption, during the period 1985–95, led to the creation of 12.9 million job posts (24.1 percent of total employment in 1985). The increase in imports, during the same period, eliminated almost two million jobs (3.7 percent of total employment in 1985), while technological change resulted in a loss of another 3.8 million jobs (Table 10.4). Although the total job losses associated with the increase in imports are only half those caused by technological change, it should be considered that changes in technology may have been motivated to a large extent by trade liberalization itself.

Table 10.4 Sources of change in total employment, 1985–95

	Unskilled labor	Skilled labor	Total	Percent of 1985 employment
Final consumption	11,876,478	1,018,780	12,895,258	24.1
Exports	278,812	60,175	338,987	0.6
Imports	−1,842,004	−141,816	−1,983,820	−3.7
Technological change	−4,398,445	596,342	−3,802,103	−7.1
Total	5,914,841	1,533,481	7,448,322	13.9

Source: Maia (2003).

Maia (2003) also shows how final consumption, trade flows and technological change affected the employment of skilled and unskilled labor. Changes in technology led to significant job losses for unskilled workers (4.4 million job posts) but gains for skilled workers (approximately 0.6 million new jobs created between 1985 and 1995). The increase in imports, in turn, led to 1.8 million low skill job losses. Compared with those figures, the impact of the increase in exports appears to be minor. Based on these figures, Arbache (2002) argues that the increase in the unemployment rate, the expansion of the informal labor market and the steep fall in the participation rate of less educated workers, observed in the 1990s, were due not only to short-term macroeconomic imbalances but also to technological change and international trade.[3]

Menezes Filho and Rodrigues (2001) also use Pesquisa Nacional por Amostra de Domicilios (PNAD) data to examine the connection between the recent increase in the utilization of skilled labor (defined as workers with at least 11 years of schooling)[4] and measures of technology, physical capital and trade liberalization in the Brazilian economy. Between 1981 and 1997, skilled labor increased its share in labor force (from 16.3 percent to 27.1 percent) and wage bill (from 38.8 percent to 53.28 percent). A similar trend was observed in virtually all activities (agriculture, industry, construction, services and government). This shift towards a more intensive use of skilled labor was more pronounced in the 1990s, after trade liberalization, than in the 1980s (the average annual rates of change in the shares of the labor force and the wage bill corresponding to skilled labor tended to be higher in the former than in the latter decade). In general, during the 1980s, utilization of both skilled and unskilled labor increased, with the use of skilled labor expanding at higher rates. During the 1990s, a small increase was observed in the utilization of skilled labor, while the use of unskilled labor declined in absolute terms.

An increase in the supply of skilled labor certainly contributed to these changes, but adopting a procedure first proposed by Autor *et al.* (1997) and Menezes Filho and Rodrigues (2001) also identify a clear trend towards an increase in the relative demand for skilled labor, during the period 1981–97. These authors decompose the change in the utilization of skilled labor into two effects: (a) *substitution effect*, corresponding to the change in the factor mix (skilled/unskilled labor ratio) adopted by firms, keeping constant the allocation of factors among sectors (intra-industry changes); and (b) *scale effect*, corresponding to the change in the allocation of factors among sectors, keeping constant the factor mix adopted by firms (inter-industry changes). They find that the substitution effect (intra-industry changes) accounts for 105 percent of the increase in the utilization of skilled labor in manufacturing in the period 1981–97. The scale effect is negligible (−5 percent), a result which again contradicts the Hecksher–Ohlin (H–O) model prediction of large inter-industry changes in the allocation of factors following trade liberalization. Moreover, in the period 1992–97, *after* trade liberalization, this small-scale effect is positive, implying that factors were moving towards (and not away from) industries which are intensive in skilled labor.[5]

Three explanations for the recent increase in the demand for skilled labor in the Brazilian economy are explored:

i   skilled labor biased technological progress;
ii complementarily between physical capital and skilled labor;
iii adoption of new production methods requiring a greater use of skilled labor, as a result of the increase in competition brought about by trade liberalization.

The econometric model estimated by Menezes Filho and Rodrigues (2001) gives some support for hypotheses (i) and (ii) suggesting that an increase in demand for skilled labor may be related to a technological bias and to the fact that physical capital and skilled labor are complementary in production. The effect of the reduction in nominal and effective protection on the relative demand for skilled labor is stronger in the period 1990–93, but the econometric results concerning the protection variables are not robust.

Effects on wages

Green *et al.* (2001) and Arbache *et al.* (2004) both use PNAD data to examine the impact of Brazilian trade liberalization on wages. Their database relates to the employed individuals in the PNAD samples earning a positive wage and aged between 18 and 65, during the period 1981–99. They show that, in the pre-liberalization period (1981–90), workers in the traded goods sector were paid on average 7.6 percent less than similar workers in the non-traded goods sector (the controls adopted in this exercise were gender, experience, educational attainment and possession of a work card). Post-liberalization wages (the period 1992–99), fell 8.1 percent in the non-traded sector and 15.9 percent in the traded sector, after controlling for the increase in education levels and changes in the other factors just mentioned. The wage disadvantage of those working in the traded sector, therefore, widened from 7.6 percent to 15.4 percent.[6]

Arbache *et al.* (2004) suggest that increased competition in product and labor markets, following trade reform, may have led to a reduction of rents and of the bargaining power of unions and, thus, to a reduction of wages, in the traded sector. Privatizations and deregulation, on the other hand, may have had a depressive effect on wages in both sectors. In spite of the fall in sectoral conditional wages, i.e. in the wages paid to workers with the same gender, level of education, experience etc., the average economy-wide wage level barely changed over this 20 year period – measured at September 1998 prices, the average real hourly wage was R$2.81 in 1981 and R$2.83 in 1999. This is explained by an increase in the employment share of the non-traded sector, where wages are higher.

Arbache *et al.* (2004) also show that, taking the wage of illiterate workers as the basis for comparison, the returns to all levels of education fell in the period 1992–99 with respect to the 1980s, due to greater supply of more educated workers. The marginal returns to education, which are calculated by comparing the log wage of each education level with that of the education level immediately below it, were also lower in the 1990s than in the 1980s, except for college-educated workers for whom the marginal return increased. The onset of this upward trend of the marginal return to college education coincides with the period of trade liberalization. Since the share of college graduates in the work force increases over this period, the rise in the college premium is ascribed to an increase in the demand for highly skilled workers, again probably due to skill-biased technological change associated with the trade reform. The reduction in the relative wages of workers with primary and secondary education, on the other hand, is seen as a result of the increase in the relative supply of this type of labor, suggesting that the technological innovations associated with trade reforms in Brazil were not biased towards the use of intermediate-level skills.

Green *et al.* (2001) note that the rise in the college wage premium has not led to a significant rise in overall wage inequality. They show that there was a small rise in inequality up to the mid-1980s and a small subsequent fall, predating trade liberalization. In the trade liberalization period, inequality leveled off. At the end of the period, the Mean Log Deviation (MLD) of wages stood at 0.54, the same as at the beginning. The same picture of stability emerges from the estimation of Theil and Gini indices. This stability of wage inequality, in spite of the increase in the college premium, according to Green *et al.* (2001), may be explained by (i) the fact that college educated workers constitute only a small portion of the workforce (8 percent in 1999); and (ii) the rise in the wages of illiterates relative to the wages of all other workers.

Pavcnik *et al* (2002) investigate whether it is possible to reconcile the above-mentioned changes in the returns to education in Brazil (increased

marginal returns to skilled workers) with the Hecksher–Ohlin/
Stolper–Samuelson (H–O/S–S) framework. They use labor market data
from the Monthly Employment Survey – PME, conducted by IBGE in the
six largest Brazilian metropolitan areas. Their data refer to workers and
self-employed people, affiliated with 20 manufacturing industries, who
worked more than 25 hours per week in the period 1987–98. According to
Pavcnik *et al.* (2002), an increase in the skill premium would be consistent
with the H–O/S–S model if:

i   The largest tariff reductions and, thus, the largest reductions in
    prices, occurred in unskilled labor-intensive industries.
ii As a result of the tariff induced declines in relative prices, the
    unskilled labor intensive sectors also experienced a contraction in
    their employment share.
iii The share of skilled labor in industry employment declined, with
    firms substituting away from skilled workers because of the increase in
    the skill premium.

Regarding the first prediction of the H–O/S–S framework, Pavcnik *et
al.* (2002) show that, in the Brazilian case, the largest tariff cuts occurred,
in fact, in the unskilled labor-intensive sectors. With respect to the second
prediction, although no general association between employment contrac-
tions and tariff reductions could be found, an increase in the industry
import penetration was associated with a contraction in the industry's
employment share. Furthermore, tariff reductions had a larger impact on
the employment share in industries with higher import penetration.
Finally, the third prediction is clearly rejected by the data – only two of the
20 manufacturing sectors under analysis experienced a decrease in the
employment share of skilled workers. Given that the evidence does not
validate this prediction, the increase in the economy-wide skill premium
cannot be ascribed to H–O/S–S effects.

The empirical evidence is, however, consistent with skill-biased technological change. According to Pavcnik *et al.* (2002), firms might adopt skill-
biased technology in response to intensified competition from abroad or
because lower barriers to trade make the importation of technology and
capital equipment cheaper. In the Brazilian case, the share of skilled
workers in an industry's employment is not related to tariffs or the export
to output ratio. It is, however, positively associated with import penetration. Increased exposure to trade led to an increase in the demand for
skilled labor via skill-biased technological change and to a higher skill
premium. Trade liberalization may, thus, have had an indirect effect on
the rise of the skill premium.

Pavcnik *et al.* (2002) did not find significant changes in industry wage
premiums between 1987 and 1998, a result supported by Green *et al.*
(2001), and found no relationship between tariffs or import penetration

and inter-industry wage differentials. They conclude that trade liberalization did not affect the inter-industry wage structure and did not lead to a rise in wage inequality, despite the increase in skill premium, possibly because, owing to the large size of the Brazilian economy, import penetration continues to be relatively low, even after the significant tariff reductions of the 1990s.

Effects on profits and mark ups

Hay (2001) estimates an equation for the market shares of the 349 manufacturing firms in the PIA's sample already mentioned above. The explanatory variables are the firm's own costs, the rate of effective protection in the firm's sector and the real exchange rate. As expected, protection has a large impact on market shares: the net effect of a 1 percent fall in protection is a loss of 1.8 percent in market share. Given the reduction in average protection between 1990 and 1994, an average loss of 30 percent in market share for the domestic manufacturing firms was predicted by the estimated regression. Although considering this effect "implausibly large", Hay (2001) concludes that, in the end, trade liberalization did have a dramatic effect on the market share of domestic firms.

Hay (2001) also estimates a profit equation in which a firm's profits are specified as a function of the average efficiency of domestic firms in the respective industrial sector, of the relative efficiency of the firm, measured as the difference between firm efficiency and sectoral average efficiency, and of measures of protection. The results derived from this exercise suggest that:

i   There was a substantial fall in profits following the 1990–91 recession and trade liberalization.
ii This fall in profits was offset, to a large extent, by the improved efficiency of domestic producers. A 1 percent fall in protection had a direct 0.7 percent *negative* effect on profits due to import competition; it also had an indirect 0.6 percent *positive* effect on profits due to increased efficiency; the net effect of the reduction in protection on profits was therefore a small decrease of 0.1 percent.

Similar results were also obtained by Ferreira and Guillén (2001) who, adopting a methodology proposed by Hall (1988) and Harrison (1994), estimated the mark up for 16 industrial sectors in Brazil, testing the hypothesis that trade liberalization was associated with a reduction in the market power of domestic firms and, thus, with a reduction in mark ups. A *reduction* in the mark up after trade liberalization in Brazil is detected in only one sector – pharmaceutical and veterinarian products. Two additional exercises identified *increases* in the mark up in the food and plastic materials sectors, after trade liberalization. The results obtained suggest that most of the industries that entered the study are competitive. In the great majority of the industries where some degree of market power was detected, no significant changes in market power occurred after trade liberalization.

Effects on income distribution and poverty

The benefits of productivity increases can be passed on to consumers (buyers) in the form of lower prices, to workers in the form of higher wages, or can be appropriated by firms via increased profit margins. Bonelli (2002) separates the log change in labor productivity, in the period 1990–2000, into log changes in sectoral mark ups, real wages and relative prices. Since at least part of the productivity gains of the 1990s were associated with trade reforms, the results of such an exercise shed some light on how the benefits of trade liberalization were distributed among consumers, workers and firms.

According to Bonelli (2002), since "gainers" and "losers" differed from sector to sector, no general distributional pattern can be discerned. Consumers were the main beneficiaries of productivity growth in 11 sectors and firms and workers benefited more in nine and six sectors respectively. In another ten sectors, the productivity gains were shared more or less equally by more than one type of agent, while in the remaining six sectors productivity decreased in the 1990s. Therefore, "the benefits of productivity growth were spread over the agents in the economy, if not evenly, at least in a not too much concentrated fashion" (Bonelli, 2002: 24).

Also with respect to the distributional impacts of the 1990s reforms, Barros and Corseuil (2001) use a computable general equilibrium (CGE) model to estimate the effect of trade and foreign direct investment (FDI) liberalization on the Brazilian income distribution. Their research strategy consists in asking what the Brazilian income distribution would have been in 1996 if the barriers to trade and FDI which existed in 1990 had not been removed between 1990 and 1996 – i.e. they simulate the effects of a reversal of the 1990s Brazilian liberalization. The transmission mechanism from trade and FDI barriers to the distribution of income is modeled as follows.

i   Given a rise in import tariffs, the level and composition of labor demand will change as domestic consumers and firms shift their expenditures away from imported goods and towards domestically produced goods.

ii   The rise in import tariffs will also affect government revenues, which may increase or decrease, depending on how strong is the impact of the increase in import prices on the domestic demand of imported goods. As a result, either government expenditures or government savings will change, leading to changes in the level and composition of aggregate demand and thus in the level and composition of labor demand.

iii   Since barriers to capital flows reduce the amount of resources available to finance government expenditure or savings, they also affect the level and composition of aggregate demand and consequently of labor demand.

iv   Finally, the changes in labor demand resulting from (i), (ii) and (iii) affect labor income and therefore the overall distribution of income (since 85 percent of household earnings in Brazil correspond to labor income, changes in the distribution of income are determined to a large extent by changes in labor income).

Simulations of the CGE model suggest that the labor market is not significantly affected by changes in import tariffs, while increased restrictions to FDI lead to a generalized contraction in labor demand, with unemployment increasing and wages decreasing for both skilled and unskilled labor. Because the labor market is not significantly affected by these shocks, poverty indices and the Gini and Theil indices of income inequality also do not change much. When only tariff shocks are considered, the magnitude of the estimated changes in those indices is negligible. When increased barriers to FDI are also assumed, a slight deterioration of poverty and inequality indices is observed. The results suggest that the 1990s trade liberalization had no effect on the Brazilian income distribution and poverty and that the FDI liberalization had a very limited beneficial effect.

What, then, is the explanation for a fall in poverty rate (from more than 40 percent of the population in the first half of the 1990s to around 33 percent in the second half of that decade)? Reimer (2002) lists, among others, the following potential linkages between changes in trade policy and poverty: (i) changes in the price and availability of goods; (ii) changes in factor prices, income and employment; (iii) changes in government transfers as a result of changes in revenue from trade taxes; and (iv) changes in the incentives for investment and innovation, which affect the long-term rate of GDP growth. Of these, "the factor price, income and employment link may have the greatest relative importance of all the links between trade and poverty" (Reimer, 2002: 4).

The literature relating to the impacts of the 1990s reforms on employment, wages, prices of goods and productivity, the linkages between trade and poverty listed above, does not suggest a major role for trade liberalization in the reduction of poverty observed in Brazil in the mid-1990s. Neri and Considera (1996) ascribe this reduction of the poverty rate to (i) the government's decision to increase the minimum wage in 1995, (ii) to the high rates of GDP growth in 1994/95 and (iii) to the substantial fall in the inflationary tax that resulted from the end of hyperinflation.

Conclusion

The Brazilian experience in the post-reform period suggests a minimum impact on productivity growth. There has been an increase in the ratio of skilled to unskilled labor trade liberalization. This was due, in part, to the increase in the relative supply of skilled labor, but the evidence suggests that demand factors – in particular, skill-biased technological change, possibly related to the effects of trade liberalization itself – were also at play. Average conditional wages, after controlling for factors such as gender, experience, education attainment and possession of a work card, fell both in the traded and non-traded goods sectors (by more in the former than in the latter), in the period after trade liberalization. Average unconditional wages remained virtually unchanged due to improvements in education and changes in the structure of employment (increase in the employment share of the non-traded sector, which pays relatively higher wages in Brazil).

Available evidence suggests that the marginal returns to education also declined in the 1990s, except for college graduates for whom the marginal return increased, another indication of skill-biased technological change. The rise in the college premium has not led, however, to a significant increase in wage inequality because college educated workers constitute only a small portion of the workforce and because the wages of illiterates have increased relative to the wages of all other workers. Profits and mark ups apparently have not been significantly affected by trade liberalization, possibly because the negative effect of import competition on profits has been to a large extent compensated by gains in productivity. It is not possible to ascertain a general pattern in the distribution of the productivity gains of the 1990s among firms, workers and consumers. The benefits of productivity growth have not been distributed in a concentrated fashion and gainers and losers differed from sector to sector.

The aggregate impacts of the Brazilian trade reforms of the 1990s were apparently minor – certainly much weaker than predicted and probably still believed both by supporters and opponents of reforms. New data suggest that trade reforms have not been linked to productivity growth as strongly as initially thought, GDP growth has not accelerated after the reforms were implemented, while the indices measuring inequality in the distribution of total income and wage income have remained virtually unchanged. The reforms, on the other hand, have certainly had important effects on some sectors of the economy, specific groups of workers and firms. Relevant sector effects and minor aggregate effects can occur simultaneously, if, as in the case of Brazil, the traded goods sector is relatively small. In general, the observed sectoral effects contradict the predictions of the standard H–O/S–S model for an unskilled labor-abundant economy like Brazil. These discrepancies are probably due to the fact that import penetration has induced firms to adopt skill biased technological innovations.

Appendix

Table A10.1 Import penetration coefficients (percent)

Sectors	1990–93	1994–98	1999–2001
Mineral extraction	*13.0*	*11.9*	*21.8*
Oil and coal	*42.4*	*38.3*	*23.2*
Manufacturing	*5.8*	*10.2*	*13.8*
Non-metal minerals	1.3	2.4	2.8
Steel	2.3	2.8	3.7
Non-ferrous metals	8.0	11.0	14.5
Other metal products	1.7	4.1	5.7
Machinery	12.8	21.9	24.4
Electric material	10.7	17.5	28.7
Electronic equipment	19.6	31.1	60.5
Vehicles	4.3	14.8	15.6
Parts and other vehicles	13.3	20.0	37.6
Wood and furniture	0.5	1.7	2.4
Cellulose, paper etc.	2.6	5.9	5.8
Rubber products	5.4	10.2	13.4
Chemicals	11.8	14.8	17.2
Petroleum refinery	5.5	9.5	11.3
Pharmaceuticals and perfumes	8.9	14.1	21.9
Plastics	2.7	6.3	9.6
Textiles	4.3	9.9	10.3
Clothing (apparel)	0.6	2.7	2.9
Footwear and leather products	5.9	9.3	16.0
Dairy products	2.6	5.5	5.7
Miscellaneous	16.2	25.4	31.3
Total	7.0	10.8	14.2

Source: Ribeiro and Pourchet (2002).

Notes

1 Since the main facts relative to this trade liberalization episode are well known, in order to save space, we have avoided a detailed description here. For brief accounts about this subject see Hay (2001) and Pavcnik *et al.* (2002).
2 The fact that the simple average (3.5 percent) is much higher than the weighted average (1.5 percent) implies that productivity growth was concentrated in sectors that have relatively low employment levels.
3 The proportion of workers holding a work card, an indicator of the relative size of the formal labor market, fell from 52 percent, in the early 1980s, to only 40 percent, in the late 1990s. The participation rate of workers with up to four years of schooling decreased by 21 percent, between 1991 and 2002, whereas for workers with 12 or more years of schooling it decreased by only 5 percent (Arbache, 2002).

4 High school graduates are classified as skilled workers by Menezes Filho and Rodrigues (2001) and as unskilled workers by Maia (2003).
5 The latter evidence, however, can be reconciled with the H–O model, if the largest tariff reductions occurred in the unskilled labor-intensive sectors, a point made by Pavcnik *et al.* (2002) and discussed in the next section.
6 The wage differential between non-traded and traded goods sectors is partially explained by the fact that the non-traded sector includes the public sector, which pays relatively high wages in Brazil.

11 Reform, growth and poverty in Bolivia

Lykke E. Andersen, Osvaldo Nina and
Dirk Willem te Velde

After several decades of "state-capitalism" characterized by import substitution policies, Bolivia implemented in 1985 a New Economic Policy (NEP) following neo-liberal ideas of free trade, privatization, and liberalization of capital flows. The NEP started with a very effective stabilization package that stopped record level hyperinflation (almost 25,000 percent per year), liberalized prices, exchange rates and interest rates, abolished export and import controls, and reduced the public sector deficit.[1] The NEP was later complemented by structural reforms, consisting of privatization, pension reform, decentralization, and education reform.[2] It was hoped that the opening up of the economy would attract foreign direct investment (FDI) which in turn would help modernize Bolivian industry, improve productivity, increase exports, stimulate growth, and reduce poverty. In this chapter we will investigate to what extent this actually happened. As part of an outward-mental strategy, the NEP quickly simplified the previously very complex tariff regime introducing a single import tariff of 20 percent for all goods. By 1990, this tariff was further reduced to 10 percent, and later the tariff on capital goods was reduced to 5 percent. Simultaneously, there were various efforts to promote and diversify exports. In 1987, the National Institute for Exports was created, and various tax incentives were offered to exporting enterprises (Antelo and Jemio, 2000: 42). Although Bolivia was hailed as an early and profound reformer (Lora, 2001), the shift to a more open economy actually had little effect on trade. If anything, it appears that exports as a percentage of GDP fell after the implementation of trade liberalization policies (Figure 11.1).

In order to improve access to export markets, Bolivia signed several regional trade agreements and improved on already existing agreements. During the 1990s, Bolivia signed several partial integration agreements through the Latin American Integration Association (LAIA): Peru (1992), Chile (1993) and MERCOSUR (1997), and a free trade agreement with Mexico (1995). Moreover, Bolivia is a beneficiary country of the Andean Trade Preference Act (1991) from the United States and the Andean Generalized System of Preferences (1990) from the European Union. Both agreements granted preferential tariffs as support for the Andean Community's

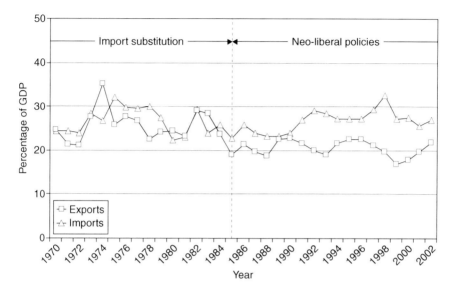

Figure 11.1 Bolivian exports and imports (official) (source: World Bank (2002)).

war on drugs, under the principle of shared responsibility. Recently, Bolivia signed a partial integration agreement with Cuba (2000) and is a beneficiary country of the Andean Trade Promotion and Drug Eradication (ATPDEA). This chapter aims to examine the effects of outward-oriented strategy on trade and foreign investment and through these on poverty in Bolivia.

Trade performance

The disappointing export performance since 1985 could potentially be due to falling export prices, so it is important to have a look at the evolution of prices for our main export goods. Between 1980 and 2002, Bolivia's main export good has been natural gas with a contribution of US$4.8 billion. Natural gas does not have a world market price, but is determined by long-term contracts in bilateral negotiations between the seller and a very limited number of buyers.

Figure 11.2 shows the evolution of the price that Bolivia has been able to charge for its natural gas from its two international buyers, Argentina and Brazil. During the last 30 years, that price has varied by more than a factor of 17, from a low of US$0.28 per thousand cubic feet in 1972 to a high of US$4.81 in 1983 and 1984. Before the first oil crisis, the price was even lower. Between 1962 and 1967, the price was fixed at just US$0.08 per thousand cubic feet.

The price has dropped dramatically since 1985, clearly contributing to a worsening in the terms of trade. However, the current price levels do

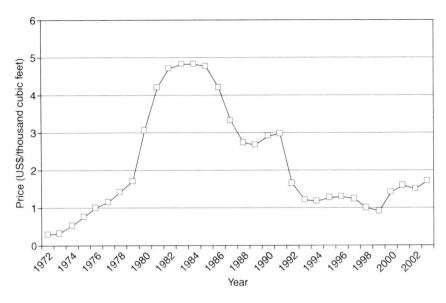

Figure 11.2 Price of Bolivian natural gas, 1972–2003 (source: YPFB, Bolivia).

not appear low, neither in a long-term perspective nor in comparison to alternative energy sources. It is not clear, either, that high prices would be beneficial for Bolivia. The high prices during the early 1980s coincide with the worst recession in recent history, and the relatively favorable prices by the beginning of the present century also coincide with a recession period (see Figure 11.6 below).

Bolivia's main export metals are tin, zinc, gold, and silver with exports of US$3.0 billion, 2.4 billion, 1.2 billion and 1.2 billion, respectively between 1980 and 2002. Figure 11.3 shows price indices for these four commodities, with 1985 US$ current prices set to 100. The prices of tin and silver have been relatively low since 1985, which helps explain part of the poor export performance. On the other hand, the prices of zinc and gold have been relatively high. There was also a period between 1979 and 1984 where all prices were highly favorable, but exports nevertheless were not particularly high, and the whole economy was in deep recession with per capita GDP growth between −2 percent and −6 percent (see Figure 11.6 below).

The last very important export product, soya, with accumulated exports of US$2.3 billion just between 1990 and 2002, has experienced relatively stable prices, with the high prices in 1998 being only 30 percent higher than the low prices in 2001.

The poor export performance since 1985 can only partly be attributed to unfavorable export prices, and the prices only appear low in comparison to the unusually high prices experienced in the early 1980s. In 2003,

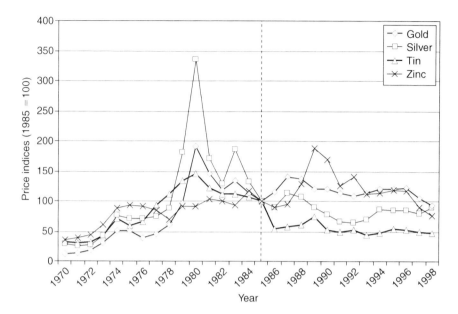

Figure 11.3 Export price indices (source: International Financial Statistics, IMF (2000), Washington DC).

export prices were considered quite favorable, but exports were still insufficient for creating economic growth (e.g. Fundación Milenio, 2004).

It would seem, at a first glance that the basic premises of the NEP have failed. Privatization and trade liberalization did *not* stimulate more exports, and exports could thus not help generate faster growth and more rapid poverty reduction. However, this is too superficial a conclusion, because much more important than the total volume of exports is the composition and quality of exports, and this has changed substantially since the period of import substitution.

Figure 11.4 shows that in 1980, mining products (mainly tin and silver) comprised almost two thirds of the total value of exports, and hydrocarbons contributed almost one quarter. These two groups together are called traditional export goods in Bolivia, because they historically have accounted for almost all of the country's exports. In 1980, only 14 percent of exports were non-traditional, including mainly sugar, coffee, and some wood products.

By 2002, the picture had changed substantially. Mining only accounted for around one quarter of exports, while non-traditional exports have become almost as important as traditional exports. Soya and soya derivatives accounted for half of all non-traditional exports, but jewellery and other products with higher value added have also become significant.

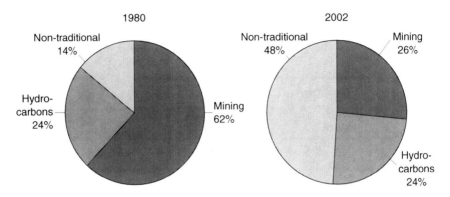

Figure 11.4 Change in the composition of Bolivian exports, 1980–2002 (source National Statistical Institute (various issues), Bolivia).

The change in the composition of exports may not have much effect on the overall GDP growth rate. However, it could still have substantial impacts on the distribution of income, and thus on poverty, since the persons involved in the production of non-traditional export products are completely different from the ones working in the mining and hydrocarbon sectors. Hence, our focus in this chapter is on the impacts of changes in the composition of exports on the distribution of income and poverty. We will also explore to what extent FDI has played a role in changing the composition of Bolivian exports.

Privatization and FDI in Bolivia

For most of the 1990s, the Bolivian economy experienced a sharp increase in the levels of FDI. Although the stock of FDI is one of the smallest in Latin America, it represented the largest average annual ratio of FDI to GDP (Table 11.1). During the period 1990–2000, most FDI into Bolivia came from the USA (39 percent), Europe (28 percent), and South America (27 percent). FDI from the neighboring countries Argentina (11 percent), Brazil (7 percent), and Chile (5 percent) is also important. Over the same period, the hydrocarbons sector attracted around 40 percent of total FDI inflows, while the services sectors attracted 26 percent (mostly finance, construction, and transport), utilities and telecommunication 17 percent, manufacturing 9 percent, and mining 7 percent.

Figure 11.5 shows that the interest of foreign investors in Bolivia accelerated in the second half of the 1990s, when the Second Generation Structural Reforms (SGSR) improved the economic policy framework. The new set of reforms constituted a deepening of the original First Generation Structural Reforms (FGSR), launched at the same time as the stabilization program in 1985. The reforms established a favorable regulatory

Table 11.1 Net inflows of FDI, 1990–2000

Region or country	Accumulated flows		Annual average	
	(US$ m)	*Share (%)*	*(US$ m)*	*(% of GDP)*
Latin American and Caribbean	453,558	100.0	41,233	–
South America	328,012	72.3	29,819	–
Argentina	79,795	17.6	7,254	2.7
Bolivia	4,730	1.0	430	5.6
Brazil	137,494	30.3	12,499	1.9
Chile	36,308	8.0	3,301	5.2
Colombia	20,406	4.5	1,855	2.2
Ecuador	5,264	1.2	479	2.9
Paraguay	1,491	0.3	136	1.7
Peru	16,016	3.5	1,456	2.8
Uruguay	1,374	0.3	125	0.6
Venezuela	25,134	5.5	2,285	2.7

Source: World Bank (2002c).

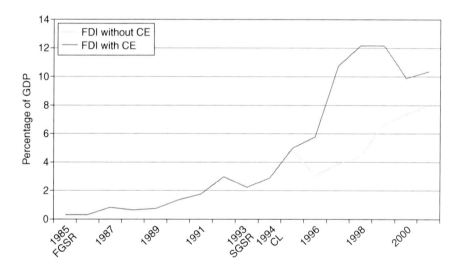

Figure 11.5 FDI inflows in Bolivia (in percent of GDP) (source: Central Bank and Ministry of Foreign Trade and Investment of Bolivia, official records).

framework for FDI by relaxing rules regarding market entry and foreign ownership and improving the treatment accorded to foreign firms and the functioning of markets.

An inappropriate policy framework can in part explain the slow growth of FDI in the early 1990s. The FGSR, which included goods markets deregulation, and reforms in fiscal, trade, and financial factors, appear not to have been focused on the location decisions of foreign investors. Moreover, political instability and the uncertainty regarding the success of the stabilization program constrained both foreign and domestic investment. Although clear rules for foreign investment were already set out in the early 1990s, mainly through the Investment Law (1990) and the Privatization Law (1992), foreign investors did not really become interested until strategic state monopolies were opened up to private investors.

The Capitalization Law (CL) was launched in 1994 and is considered the centerpiece of the SGSR. It established the economic and legal conditions for capitalizing (Bolivian term for privatizing) large state-owned companies and promoting foreign capital inflows. Under the capitalization process, the six principal state-owned enterprises, YPFB (oil and gas), ENDE (electricity), ENFE (railways), ENTEL (telecommunications), LAB (aviation), and EMV (mining and smelting), were put up for sale by international tender and the winning bidders gained management control and a 50 percent stake in the enterprise, while the government retained the remaining 50 percent share. In addition, unlike traditional privatization schemes where funds are transferred to the government, capitalization required the successful bidder to invest the money in the company itself over a stated period, effectively securing fixed capital investment.

The process has had a considerable impact on FDI because it has promoted the creation of firms backed by foreign capital or capitalized enterprises (CEs) and produced investment commitments worth around US$1.7 billion in the period since 1995. In addition, the policy framework has given enterprises the opportunity to access abundant natural resources, such as hydrocarbons and water, and control of companies with monopoly power, such as electricity and telecommunications.

Capitalized enterprises were responsible for almost 40 percent of all inflows to Bolivia in the period 1995–2001. While the investment boom in the CEs is now coming to an end, FDI in other sectors shows a continued upward trend, partly encouraged by the liberal investment climate demonstrated by the capitalization process. However, the end of the wave of capitalizations coincided with a worldwide economic crisis as well as increased political and economic instability in Bolivia, all of which deterred FDI inflows.

Growth, poverty and inequality

Economic growth in Bolivia has been very erratic and insufficient for reducing the very high poverty rates observed, especially in rural areas.

Figure 11.6 shows annual per capita GDP growth rates between 1966 and 2002. The average growth rate is zero, implying that the level of productivity in Bolivia is now precisely the same as it was in the mid-1960s. It does appear, however, that the volatility of growth has fallen after the introduction of the NEP in 1985, and average per capita GDP growth has

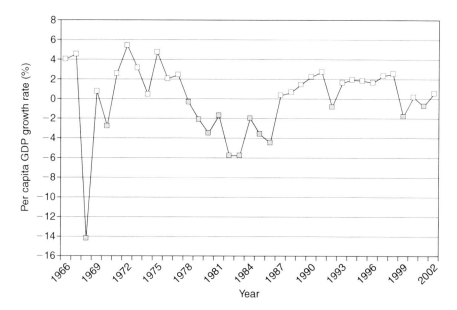

Figure 11.6 Per capita GDP growth in Bolivia, 1966–2002 (source: World Bank (2002)).

also been positive since 1985 (averaging 0.7 percent per year between 1986 and 2002).

Despite the lack of productivity growth, there has been some progress in poverty reduction. Especially non-monetary indicators of well-being show significant improvements between 1976 and 2001. According to the census of 1976, 85.5 percent of the populations were suffering from unsatisfied basic needs (UBN). By 2001, this share had fallen to 58.6 percent, reflecting massive public investment in basic services, such as water, sanitation, and education (Table 11.2).

The share of people who do not have even their basic needs satisfied is still much too high, however, and the regional disparities are getting more and more pronounced. Table 11.2 shows that the regions that were initially less poor have shown sharper reductions in poverty than the initially poorest regions, implying that regional inequality is widening. Potosí continues to be the poorest department in the country, with 79.7 percent of its population with unsatisfied basic needs, showing hardly any progress since 1992 (80.5 percent). Santa Cruz, on the other hand, had the lowest level of unsatisfied basic needs in 1976 and showed the biggest reduction in poverty between 1976 and 2001 (41.2 percentage points).

Much of the improvement in non-monetary poverty indicators has been possible due to generous foreign aid (averaging 10 percent of GDP since 1985). Although people have access to education, water, sanitation, and

Table 11.2 Population with unsatisfied basic needs (UBN), 1976–2001

Region	Census (%)			Average annual change	
	1976	*1992*	*2001*	*1976–2001*	*1992–2001*
Chuquisaca	90.5	79.8	70.1	−0.82	−1.05
La Paz	83.2	71.1	66.2	−0.68	−0.53
Cochabamba	85.1	71.1	55.0	−1.21	−1.74
Oruro	84.5	70.2	67.8	−0.67	−0.26
Potosí	92.8	80.5	79.7	−0.53	−0.09
Tarija	87.0	69.2	50.8	−1.45	−1.99
Santa Cruz	79.2	60.5	38.0	−1.65	−2.43
Beni	91.4	81.0	76.0	−0.62	−0.54
Pando	96.4	83.8	72.4	−0.96	−1.23
Bolivia	*85.5*	*70.9*	*58.6*	*−1.08*	*−1.33*

Source: INE-UDAPE (2002).

health services, their income earning capacity has barely increased, and monetary poverty has thus remained stubbornly high. The data on income poverty is very limited, due to a lack of national household surveys before 1997. However Klasen and Thiele (2004) have recently made a fair attempt at estimating national poverty rates back to 1989 using a new methodology combining urban income surveys with national health surveys. Although the estimations are still preliminary, the basic trends are likely to be correct. Their results show substantial reductions in income poverty in urban areas during the 1990s, but there appears to be a partial reversal during 2000–02. In rural areas, there was a moderate reduction in poverty during the second half of the 1990s, but an almost complete reversal during the first years of this decade (Figure 11.7). Thus, these 13 years of structural and social reforms supported by a massive influx of foreign aid and foreign direct investment, have barely made a dent in rural poverty. It appears that the rural part of the country is insulated from the rest of the Bolivian economy, unable to benefit from any trickle-down effects there might be from reform-induced growth.

It is interesting to notice that the relatively good year in terms of poverty (1999) coincides with a record *low* level of exports (17 percent of GDP, see Figure 11.1), whereas the relatively bad years (1989 and 2002) coincide with relatively high levels of exports, at least by post-1985 standards (22 percent of GDP). These casual observations make it unlikely that even a thorough empirical analysis could demonstrate that overall exports would have a significant beneficial impact on poverty in Bolivia.

Klasen and Thiele (2004) also provide estimates of the evolution of inequality between 1989 and 2002 using the same methodology of combining national health surveys with urban income surveys. The results indicate that overall inequality is approximately the same in 2002 as it was in 1989 (Gini coefficient around 55) but with a dip in 1999 corresponding

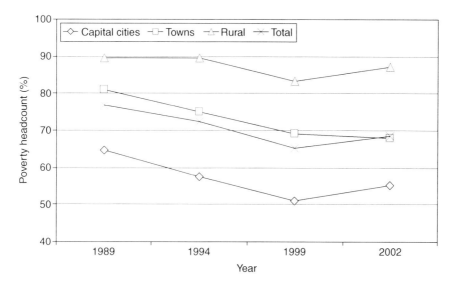

Figure 11.7 Evolution of monetary poverty in Bolivia, 1989–2002 (source: Klasen and Thiele (2004)).

Note: 1989 and 1994 poverty are estimated using National Health Surveys in addition to urban household surveys.

to the lower poverty that year, and with substantial differences between rural and urban areas (see Figure 11.8). Whereas inequality in the capital cities seems to have increased dramatically between 1994 and 2002, rural and provincial poverty seem to have fallen. It thus appears that the fate of the urban population, including the urban poor, has been closely linked to macro developments and has recently led to a significant deterioration in poverty and inequality. In contrast, the much poorer rural population have been more detached from improvements and deteriorations in the overall economic environment and their poverty trends have followed a different logic.

Impact of trade and FDI policies on the economy

FDI and growth

FDI is generally believed to promote economic growth in the recipient country by increasing total investment and improving efficiency through the introduction of new technology and better management practices. In developing countries, the empirical evidence shows a positive relationship between FDI and growth, but there is no agreement on whether FDI leads to growth or vice versa. Cross-section evidence supports the hypothesis that FDI requires preconditions to promote growth. For example,

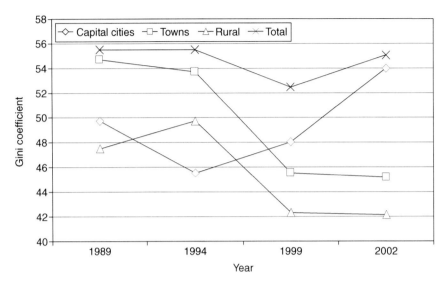

Figure 11.8 Evolution of inequality in Bolivia, 1989–2002 (source: Klasen and
         Thiele (2004)).

Note: 1989 and 1994 numbers are estimated using National Health Surveys in addition to
urban household surveys.

Borensztein *et al.* (1998) point out that FDI has a positive effect on growth
when the country has a minimum threshold stock of human capital; and
Alfaro *et al.* (2002) find that FDI promotes growth in economies with sufficiently developed financial markets.

While international evidence for these complementary effects is relatively
strong, the empirical findings from Bolivia are weak. Table 11.3 shows that
neither education nor financial market development interact significantly
with FDI in their effect on growth. Trade, on the other hand, does seem to
have a complementary effect on FDI: only when the ratio of trade to GDP is
more than 52 percent. This suggests that policies that promote exports (e.g.
reducing the fixed costs of exporting by supporting transport infrastructure
and distribution networks) would improve the impact of FDI. When interac-
tions are omitted, FDI is not significantly correlated with growth.

The lack of complementary effects between FDI and education and FDI
and financial market development indicates that the contribution of FDI
to economic growth may have been limited by local conditions. A low level
of human capital limits the capacity to absorb new technology and apply
modern management techniques, while underdeveloped financial
markets limit the economy's ability to exploit potential FDI spillovers,
because, in order to take full advantage of new knowledge, firms will
generally have to do some restructuring, which will require financing
(Alfaro *et al.*, 2002). The commercial banking system in Bolivia is charac-

Table 11.3 The effect of FDI on per capita GDP growth: Bolivia (1970–2000)

Independent Variable	(1)	(2)
Constant	−0.51*	−0.40*
	(0.13)	(0.05)
Freedom index[a]** (1-SPEI)[b]	0.0047**	0.0036***
	(0.0021)	(0.0018)
Log (government spending/GDP)	−0.22*	−0.20*
	(0.04)	(0.02)
Education[c]	0.12	
	(0.17)	
Private sector credit/GDP	−0.01	
	(0.05)	
Trade/GDP		−0.03
		(0.05)
FDI/GDP (lag 1)	0.94	−1.36**
	(0.67)	(0.66)
FDI/GDP (lag 1)* Education	−1.99	
	(1.40)	
FDI/GDP (lag 1)* Private sector credit/GDP	0.06	
	(1.34)	
FDI/GDP (lag 1)* Trade/GDP		2.66***
		(1.38)
R^2	0.78	0.77
R^2 – adjusted	0.71	0.72
Durbin Watson	2.24	2.09
Number of observations	30	30

Notes

All the variables were found to be non-stationary, I(1), and the residuals from the regressions turned out to be I(0). The standard error is given in parentheses and the asterisks indicate level of significance at *1%, **5%, and ***10%.

a State of Freedom by Freedom House: Those with ratings averaging 1–2.5 are generally considered "Free," 3–5.5 "Partly Free," and 5.5–7 "Not Free."

b Structural Policy Efficiency Index (SPEI) (Lora, 2001): where 0 corresponds to the worst reading for any year and 1 to the best.

c Secondary Gross Enrollment.

terized by very high real interest rates, short-term loans, and requires 200 percent collateral security.

The economy's ability to exploit potential FDI spillovers may also depend on its sectoral distribution. Table 11.4 shows that the most important destination of FDI has been capital-intensive and skill-intensive sectors, like hydrocarbons, telecommunications, and electricity. While the hydrocarbons sector did experience the introduction of new processes, advanced technologies, managerial skills, employee training, international production networks, and access to markets, it created relatively few linkages with the local economy and thus fewer possibilities for significant spillovers. Similarly, FDI has contributed to the modernization of telecommunications and electricity services, but the linkages with local suppliers are weak. As more than half of all FDI over the period 1996–2001 was

Table 11.4 FDI and export compositions by sector (%) (accumulated stock: 1996–2001)

Sector	FDI share	Export share
Primary	*35.5*	*42.6*
Hydrocarbons	34.1	11.6
Mining	1.3	20.3
Agriculture	0.1	10.7
Manufacturing	*8.0*	*57.4*
Food products and beverages	3.3	22.8
Refined petroleum products	2.1	0.9
Non-metallic mineral products	0.8	0.2
Furniture and jewelry	0.7	6.4
Basic metals	0.3	15.7
Chemicals and chemical products	0.3	0.7
Paper and paper products	0.2	0.2
Other manufacturing	0.2	10.4
Service	*56.1*	*0.0*
Telecommunications	14.1	–
Construction	10.2	–
Electricity	7.3	–
Transport via pipeline (natural gas)	5.3	–
Financial intermediation	4.7	–
Transport	3.3	–
Other services	11.3	–
Total (US$ m)	4,965	7,090

Source: National Institute of Statistics of Bolivia.

directed into sectors with relatively few linkages, there may be fewer benefits of FDI to Bolivia than was expected by looking at the experiences of FDI in many East Asian countries where spillovers and linkage creation often related to manufacturing sectors such as electronics, automobile, and garments and textiles. In Bolivia, only 8 percent of FDI went into manufacturing during 1996–2001, thus limiting the possibilities for reaping the advantages of potential spillovers.

On the basis of the results of a survey conducted with executives of foreign companies in Bolivia, Nina and Rojas (2001) find that access to natural resources and regional markets was among the main motivations for FDI. Recently, FDI in natural gas has helped gas to become the main export, accounting for 20 percent of total exports in 2002. However, Andersen and Faris (2002) argue that the effects of a substantial increase in natural gas exports due to capitalization may lead to a temporary (but not permanent) increase in GDP growth during the few years of rapidly expanding export volumes.

Since FDI does not automatically lead to growth, public policies may be required to attract FDI and create an enabling environment to benefit from it. Vidaurre (2002) points out that the government needs to pay attention to additional factors that influence investors' location decisions. He suggests a range of business facilitation measures that seek to reduce costs through a combination of improvements in communications infrastructure and the creation of larger markets. He also mentions that the manufacturing sector would benefit from a clear investment policy, since technology diffusion is not an automatic consequence of the presence of some knowledge stock.

One of the channels through which FDI can enhance economic growth in host countries is by increasing total investment. FDI can crowd in or crowd out domestic investment. However, on average, Bosworth and Collins (1999) find that an increase of a dollar in FDI is associated with an increase in total domestic investment by an average of 80 cents in developing countries. In Bolivia, evidence suggests that only half of FDI translates into an increase in total domestic investment (Figure 11.9), although this increases to a one-for-one increase in total domestic FDI investment through the capitalization process. In the remaining sectors, the impact of FDI on total domestic investment has been very low, and it has encouraged little if any complementary local investment.

FDI through capitalization may also have reduced the need for local public investment and this may have enabled a reallocation of public investment from the productive to the social sector. This reallocation can partly compensate for the lack of spillovers, as it allows the government to invest directly in people, including those outside the foreign companies. However, the role of government should extend beyond reallocating public funds. For instance, privatized natural monopolies, such as water and electricity, require strict regulation to protect consumers.

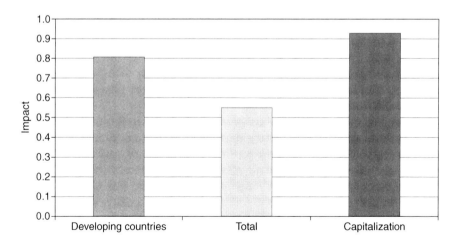

Figure 11.9 The impact of $1 of FDI on total domestic investment (sources: developing countries: Bosworth and Collins (1999), period 1979–95. Bolivia: own estimations, period 1976–2000).

FDI, inequality and poverty

The effects of FDI on income inequality can be analyzed through its effects on wage inequality and non-wage inequality. According to te Velde (2002), the effects of FDI on wage inequality can be analyzed by looking at (i) composition effects (foreign firms may have different skill intensities from domestic firms), (ii) skill-specific technological change (FDI could induce faster productivity growth of labor in both foreign and domestic firms), (iii) skill-specific wage bargaining (skilled workers are usually in a stronger bargaining position than less skilled workers), and (iv) training and education (foreign firms generally undertake more training than local counterparts). The effects on non-wage income could be indirect, for instance through public policies or partnerships between foreign firms, governments, and local communities.

The empirical evidence shows that some Latin American countries have experienced an increase in wage inequality as a result of FDI. In the case of Bolivia, te Velde (2002) finds that FDI may have accounted for a significant part of the observed increase in urban wage inequality during 1987–97, with FDI correlated with lower real wages for skilled and unskilled workers. Recently, Vedia (2002) found that the capital-intensive sectors have significant positive correlations with the fifth quintile of urban income distribution. Furthermore, as Table 11.5 shows, the real wages of workers in the capital-intensive sectors have experienced a revival since 1996. Workers in these sectors tend to be the more educated workers. FDI is also concentrated in these sectors.

The results can in part be explained by the fact that FDI has gone into the skill-intensive sectors, thus creating a relative shortage of skilled labor. The TNCs have had to train their workers intensively, and subsequently pay them higher salaries to prevent their departure with their newly acquired knowledge. These findings are supported by Andersen and Faris (2002), who find that the expansion of the hydrocarbons sector mainly benefits the groups that initially earned the highest incomes, i.e. skilled workers. Similarly, Jemio and Wiebelt (2002) find that FDI worsens income distribution slightly.

There are valid reasons for concern about the deterioration in income distribution caused by FDI, particularly as there is no evidence of significant poverty reduction. The majority of poor people are working in agriculture, manufacturing, and other services, three sectors that have seen deteriorating or stagnant real wages. The dramatic fall in agricultural incomes during the period of the FDI boom is particularly worrying, as it inevitably contributes to a deepening of poverty and likely pushes many people into extreme poverty.

There are various public policies available that can help to improve the distributional effect of FDI. One is to use fiscal revenues for social investment (e.g. education) in order to develop the poorer segments of the economy.

Table 11.5 Employment, real income, and educated workers in Bolivia, 2000

Sector	Employment share	Educated workers[a]	Real wage[b] (Bs/month)	Annual growth (1996–2000)	
				Employment	Real wage
Agriculture	38.9	1.0	160	−2.0	−11.9
Hydrocarbons and mining	1.4	19.9	2,494	−4.7	28.3
Manufacturing	10.1	10.5	612	−1.4	−2.8
Electricity, water and gas	0.5	24.5	1,759	7.6	9.9
Construction	6.6	7.7	907	9.2	4.3
Transport and communications	4.3	19.3	1,160	1.5	−0.5
Financial intermediation	0.5	77.3	2,517	2.2	6.8
Other services	37.6	27.8	754	2.9	0.0
Total (persons)	3,637,048	509,187	–	–	–

Source: National Institute of Statistics.

Notes
a Workers with more than 13 years of education.
b June 1996 = 100.

Trade, inequality and poverty

While there appears to be little effect of trade openness on growth in Bolivia, trade is obviously necessary to service its debt and obtain essential investment goods that are not locally produced. It may also be the case that even though there is no relationship between aggregate trade, growth, and poverty in Bolivia, people working in specific export sectors do benefit from such exports in terms of higher salaries and less poverty. In order to test this hypothesis, we have identified the principal sector of work (down to four ISIC digits)[3] for each salaried person in the 2001 MECOVI household survey, and matched it with the value of exports in each of these sectors.

The Bolivian working population is distributed among more than 200 different sectors, but only a few of these are important in terms of export. Table 11.6 shows eight of the most important export sectors, accounting for close to 80 percent of all exports in 2001, together with the number of people employed in each sector and the average monthly income gained by those who work in the sector.[4] It is clear that the two main export sectors, soya and natural gas, are also the sectors that pay by far the highest salaries. The problem is that it is relatively few people who benefit from these high salaries, and the ones who do tend to be highly educated (in the case of the natural gas sector) or large landowners (in the case of soya production), so this kind of export would tend to worsen the income distribution.

Table 11.6 Main Bolivian export sectors, employment and exports in 2001

ISIC sector	Employment (1,000 persons)	Average salary (US$/month)	Exports (million US$)
1514 Manufacture of vegetable and animal oils and fat (soya)	3.7	510	317
1110 Extraction of crude oil and natural gas	6.0	495	285
1320 Mining of non-ferrous metal ores	35.0	137	185
2720 Manufacture of basic and non-ferrous metals	n.d.	n.d.	146
3691 Manufacture of jewellery and related articles	8.0	146	101
2010 Sawmilling and planing of wood	4.5	139	25
3610 Manufacture of furniture	40.8	131	23
1810 Manufacture of wearing apparel, except fur	54.5	95	15

Source: MECOVI (2001) and UN COMTRADE (2002).

Note
Employment numbers are estimated based on the MECOVI survey, which is not designed to be representative at the sectoral level. The numbers are therefore only rough approximations. In addition, the numbers only include persons who earn a positive income from the activity. Helping spouses and children who are not paid, are not included.

The remaining export sectors pay closer to the national average for salaried workers (US$135/month), with workers manufacturing jewellery doing slightly better (US$146/month) than average, and workers making clothes doing somewhat worse (US$95/month). Notice that the moderate poverty line is only about US$40/month, so the people working in these export sectors are in general well above the poverty line, and changes in their salaries would thus not directly affect the poverty headcount.

In order to test whether trade has a positive impact on salaries at the individual level, we run a regression with the logarithm of the monthly salary as the dependent variable and the log of sector exports and imports as explanatory variables. A number of control variables, such as education, age, gender, ethnicity, work sector, and location, are also included. The regression results are presented in Table 11.7.

Table 11.7 The effect of sector imports and exports on salaries (2001)

Independent variable: Log (income)	Coefficient	t-value
Constant	3.6551	20.78
Years of education	0.0566	19.27
Age	1.4326	14.55
Age squared	−0.1755	−11.82
Dummy for woman	−0.3967	−14.18
Dummy for indigenous	−0.1546	−6.48
Dummy for blue-collar worker	−0.3713	−5.03
Dummy for white-collar worker	−0.3522	−4.74
Dummy for self-employed	−0.8746	−12.01
Dummy for cooperative worker	−0.7255	−5.91
Dummy for work in family business	−0.6108	−6.48
Dummy for public sector	0.6557	6.20
Dummy for traditional agriculture	−0.3015	−5.51
Dummy for electricity sector	0.4263	3.69
Dummy for construction sector	0.4045	7.80
Dummy for commerce sector	0.4687	8.48
Dummy for hotel and restaurant sector	0.6709	8.72
Dummy for transportation sector	0.5254	9.02
Dummy for banking sector	1.0945	5.79
Dummy for highland residence	−0.3040	−10.46
Dummy for lowland residence	0.1545	5.49
Log (sectoral exports)	0.0301	4.09
Log (sectoral imports)	−0.0187	−2.51
R^2	0.3513	
Number of observations	8,014	

Source: Author's estimation based on MECOVI (2001) and trade data from UN COMTRADE (2002).

Note
t-values are based on robust standard errors as estimated by the Huber/White "sandwich" estimator.

The results show that the value of exports is indeed a positive and significant determinant of wages in the exporting sector. Holding everything else constant, persons working in sectors that export more would tend to earn higher monthly wages than persons working in tradable sectors with less export. However, the estimated elasticity of wages with respect to exports is quite low. If one sector has exports twice as high as another, the level of salaries would only be 3 percent higher. Assuming that this estimated difference in salaries is indeed due to exports (and not to some unobserved variable such as capital intensity) we can also conclude that, if, for example, exports of soya were to double, it would imply an increase in salaries of about 3 percent for the people who work in the soya sector.

Imports, on the other hand, tend to have a negative effect on salaries in the sectors that produce these goods locally, most likely because they compete with locally produced goods and push down prices and salaries. The problem is biggest in the sectors where there is a considerable local production, i.e. the manufacturing of food, drinks, and clothing, whereas the imports of capital goods have no such negative effect since there is virtually no local production to compete with. Needless to say, consumers might well have gained from imports.

The estimated coefficients on the control variables all have the expected signs. Holding all other characteristics constant, people with more education tend to earn higher salaries, people with more experience tend to earn more (until a certain point), women tend to earn about 40 percent less than men, indigenous people tend to earn about 15 percent less than non-indigenous people, people in the highlands earn about 46 percent less than people in the lowlands, and people in the public sector about 66 percent more than people in the private sector. Of the non-tradable sectors, the one that has the most attractive level of salaries is the banking sector, followed by hotel and restaurants, transportation, commerce, electricity, and construction. Far behind these comes traditional agriculture. The most attractive type of income earner is employer, followed by white-collar worker, blue-collar worker, family worker, and cooperative worker, while self-employed in the informal sector is the least attractive.

Persons who combine many of the characteristics with negative coefficients, for example indigenous women living in the rural highlands and working in subsistence agriculture from which there are no exports, have extremely low incomes and are thus extremely poor. Since they neither export nor import any goods there is little direct effect of trade on these unfortunate people. However, there may be indirect effects and medium- to long-term effects. It is possible that if some labor-intensive export sectors boomed, these sectors could attract previously self-employed people into blue- or white-collar positions, which could imply a substantial improvement for these persons in terms of income.

There has been a significant change in the composition of employment over the years (Table 11.8). The sectors that have lost most employment between 1992 and 2001 are clearly the agricultural sector, and most likely the traditional part of agriculture, without exports. This is a positive development, as extreme poverty tends to be concentrated in this sector. The mining sector has also lost a large number of jobs, which coincides with the fall in exports from that sector. This has likely contributed to an increase in poverty, as miners do not easily find alternative employment. The increase in hydrocarbon exports cannot be seen in the number of jobs in the hydrocarbon sector, as the capitalization process included a complete restructuring of the sector and a further intensification of capital instead of labor. The manufacturing sector created more than 100,000 new jobs between 1992 and 2001, likely affected by the substantial increase in non-traditional exports, but not by foreign direct investment, which was almost negligible in the manufacturing sector. Most job creation was found in the manufacturing of textiles, clothes, and leather products, followed by food products and furniture.

By far the biggest job generator between 1992 and 2001, however, was the service sector, largely unaffected by both exports and FDI. The hotel and restaurant business has created almost 280,000 jobs, which is a very positive development for several reasons. First, the sector employs a lot of unqualified labor and pays relatively well (compared to realistic alternatives for these workers). It is thus likely to have a beneficial effect on poverty. Second, it employs relatively higher numbers of women, offering a very desirable alternative to the informal and badly paid jobs in private residences. Third, to a large extent the sector services foreigners, which means that it generates foreign revenues, even if no goods leave the country. Fourth, there are many positive spillover effects to other sectors, as the sector uses mainly local inputs. This sector is likely to be responsible for a large part of the extra construction jobs and they may also have provided stimulation for several manufacturing subsectors (e.g. furniture, mattresses, and textiles). They may also help create a critical mass of tourist facilities, that can help stimulate the more lucrative parts of the tourism business than the young backpackers that currently tend to dominate the picture.

While there are many positive trends to be observed in the sector composition of jobs in Bolivia, it is not clear whether FDI and changes in trade patterns are among the drivers of those changes. An alternative way of analyzing the distributional impacts of exports from different sectors is presented in a recent study by Andersen and Evia (2003). It uses a highly disaggregated Computable General Equilibrium Model of the Bolivian economy to investigate the likely impacts of hypothetical, price-induced export booms in several different export sectors. The model operates with 13 different productive sectors and six different household types as well as a government sector and an entity called "Rest of the World." The flows in

Table 11.8 Occupied population by sector, 1992–2001

Sector	Census 1992	Census 2001	Difference 1998–2001	Average annual growth rate
Agriculture, hunting, fishing	*966,760*	*877,432*	*−89,328*	*−1.1*
Extraction of minerals and hydrocarbons	*51,291*	*37,863*	*−13,428*	*−3.3*
Mining	45,119	32,016	−13,103	−3.7
Hydrocarbons	6,172	5,847	−325	−0.6
Manufacturing industry	*218,553*	*330,871*	*112,318*	*4.7*
Food products and tobacco	48,669	75,016	26,347	4.9
Textiles, clothes and leather products	77,462	117,796	40,334	4.8
Wood products and paper	13,032	12,032	−1,000	−0.9
Editing and printing activities	7,377	11,308	3,931	4.9
Chemical products	4,517	5,537	1,020	2.3
Rubber and plastic products	1,547	3,115	1,568	8.1
Non-metallic mineral products	14,485	22,065	7,580	4.8
Metal products, except machinery and equipment	11,493	21,301	9,808	7.1
Machinery and equipment	3,975	4,760	785	2.0
Furniture and mattresses	35,996	57,941	21,945	5.4
Services	*1,194,883*	*1,749,890*	*555,007*	*4.3*
Electricity, gas, water	5,977	9,709	3,732	5.5
Construction	124,104	184,649	60,545	4.5
Commerce	204,039	483,328	279,289	10.1
Hotels and restaurants	24,855	125,312	100,457	19.7
Transport, storage, communication	114,078	167,214	53,136	4.3
Financial intermediation	9,305	15,131	5,826	5.6
Real estate, business and rental services	44,052	81,692	37,640	7.1
Public administration, defence, social security	57,855	73,654	15,799	2.7
Education	101,748	150,415	48,667	4.4
Health and social services	33,849	60,158	26,309	6.6
Community services	106,093	84,714	−21,379	−2.5
Domestic services	102,229	144,074	41,845	3.9
Services of foreign organizations	1,923	1,178	−745	−5.3
Not specified	*264,776*	*168,662*	*−96,114*	*−4.9*
Total	3,626,370	4,745,946	1,119,576	3.0

Source: National Statistical Institute, census tabulations.

the model are based on a social accounting matrix from 1997 that shows from which sectors each type of household earns its income and in which sectors they spend their money.[5] It also shows where the government gets its revenues from and how it spends these revenues. With such a model it is possible to experiment with the international trade variables and see who would be affected and how.

The results from the study indicate that there are three export sectors that have beneficial impacts on inequality and poverty, in the sense that exports from these sectors would tend to increase the income of the poorer population groups and reduce the Gini coefficient of inequality. One is "Modern Agriculture" whose expansion would tend to benefit especially rural unskilled workers, urban informal, and, to a smaller extent, employers. Another is "Consumer Goods"[6] which tend to benefit urban informal and rural smallholders, the two population groups that contain almost all urban and rural poor. The last export sector with such beneficial properties is the "Coca" sector, which provides dramatic benefits for rural unskilled workers and rural smallholders.

In sharp contrast to these three sectors stands the traditional export sector, namely "Mining." A boom in mining exports would tend to benefit the already richest population group, employers, and the relatively well-paid unskilled workers that work in the mines.[7] Rural workers and rural smallholders would suffer substantial reductions in their income, mainly due to the adverse effects on "Modern Agriculture" arising from the Dutch Disease that invariably would follow the mining boom. A natural gas boom would have little effect on household incomes and thus little effect on the income distribution. The only big effect is to be felt on government revenues, but even after all these revenues have been spent and invested, households are unlikely to be better off, unless the government dramatically changes their spending and investment patterns.

Conclusion

Bolivia introduced the New Economic Plan in 1985 in the hope that this would attract more foreign investment and foster trade, leading to faster growth and poverty reduction. Nearly two decades on, this plan seems to have failed to achieve many of its goals. Trade as a percent of GDP has not increased, though FDI has increased due to capitalization policy. GDP per capita has not increased when taken over the past four decades (though it must be noted that other politically unstable economies have seen GDP per capita fall), but there appears to be an upturn in GDP per capita over the latter half of the period.

Poverty has fallen in the 1990s particularly in regions that were already less poor, but there appears to have been some reversal in the most recent years. Inequality in capital cities increased dramatically. Thus, it seems that the increase in FDI and the continuation of existing exports have not been able to reduce (income) poverty and inequality significantly. For this, trade and FDI have not had a sufficient poverty focus. For example, FDI has not benefited export sectors (such as clothing and modern agriculture) that would help income opportunities for the poor.

Notes

1 For a complete description of the stabilization package, see Morales and Sachs (1990).
2 For a thorough review of structural reforms in Bolivia, see Antelo and Jemio (2000).
3 The International Standard Industrial Classification (ISIC) used by the United Nations.
4 Only people earning positive income are counted. Helping spouses and children who do not receive any salary are thus ignored.
5 The disaggregated Social Accounting Matrix was developed by a group of researchers at the Kiel Institute for World Economics. It is described in detail in Thiele and Piazolo (2002).
6 The "Consumer Goods" sector includes food, beverages, clothes, leather, wood, paper, wood products, and paper products.
7 Miners, as well as most other unskilled workers, earn about US$120–140/month and are thus located well above the moderate poverty line (US$60/month). The two large groups located below the poverty line are rural smallholders and self-employed urban informal.

12 Liberalisation, growth and welfare

The 'maquiliación' of the Mexican economy

Andrew Mold and Carlos A. Roza

[I]n every case where a poor country has significantly overcome its poverty this has been achieved while engaging in production for export markets and opening itself to the influx of foreign goods, investment and technology: that is, by participating in globalisation.

> Former Mexican President, Ernesto Zedillo,
> cited in Rodrik (2001: 57)

NAFTA means more and better paid employment for Mexicans. This is the essential thing, and it is so because more capital and investment will come, which means more opportunities here in our country for our citizens. Put simply, we can grow more rapidly and then concentrate our efforts more on those who have least.

> Former Mexican President Salinas de Gortaori,
> cited in Dussel Peter (2000: 46)

Arguments for free trade often appear most convincing to those who have no stake in their truth, but for the workers whose livelihood depends on the accuracy of the trickle-down models, the theories usually seem too flimsy to justify the risks.

> Moon (2000: 174)

One morning at the beginning of 2001, Mexico woke up to the disturbing news that the percentage of the population living in extreme poverty had increased by 4.5 per cent during the previous two years (INEGI, 2001). This announcement paradoxically coincided with the news that the economy had grown by 6.9 per cent in 2001. The question on many people's minds was 'how was this possible?'. This outcome was apparently incongruous with the idea that the 'outward-oriented' development model, which had been pursued aggressively by the Mexican administration since the beginning of the 1980s, would promote simultaneously both economic growth and welfare. Was the news simply a statistical blip in an otherwise promising panorama of underlying improvement? Or was something more profoundly amiss with the outward-oriented strategy?

This chapter attempts to demonstrate that while there has undoubtedly been important progress in particular dimensions of the Mexican economy, the disjuncture between export growth and welfare is symptomatic of some deep underlying problems with the strategy adopted. It is an (often overlooked) fact that, in absolute terms, the population living in extreme poverty has increased by 18.3 million over the same period. It is also highly significant that the pursuit of outward orientation has been accompanied by what we term the *maquiliación* of the whole Mexican economy – a hollowing-out of domestic industry and a sharply increased dependence on imported intermediate products. We argue that, although such tendencies have some positive aspects, they are essentially incompatible with the long-term development of the Mexican economy (i.e. increases the level of employment and real wages). The aims of the chapter are modest. We make no attempt to construct a theoretical model concerning the channels through which these changes have taken place. We limit the discussion to clarify the many contradictions which the current strategy has engendered.

Although we focus on the Mexican experience of trade liberalisation and export promotion, our analysis has implications for other countries which have followed a similar path, in the sense that Mexico represents one of the most dramatic and *a priori* favourable cases of reorientation of trade strategy. With the signing of the North American Free Trade Area (NAFTA) in 1991, the administration of Carlos Salinas de Gortari firmly locked Mexico into an outward-oriented strategy. Mexico is now the eleventh biggest trading nation of visibles in the world, ahead even of South Korea. Moreover, in adopting this strategy, Mexico has enjoyed some advantages that many other developing countries have lacked – principally, the large size of its domestic market and, above all, its proximity to the world's largest economy, the USA. In such a context, export growth from Mexico has been among the fastest in the world since the early 1980s. To some extent, therefore, it could be argued that the validity of the outward-oriented strategy stands or falls on the strength of the results produced in Mexico – nowhere could free traders conceive of a more favourable take-off point, and nowhere has that experience been so successful, if interpreted simply in terms of the promotion of a dynamic export sector. However, there is a widespread feeling of frustration, even among supporters of the strategy, regarding the failure of the new policies to produce the expected pay-off in terms of income growth and poverty reduction (Lustig, 2001; Tornell *et al.*, 2003).

In this chapter we first describe the achievements of the Mexican economy in terms of the dramatic increase in exports. We then consider how these developments have affected the structural characteristics of the Mexican economy, and analyse how these changes have influenced Mexico's growth performance. These achievements are then contrasted with the new model's performance in social terms – a lack of employment generation, low wages and negligible poverty reduction. Using an Error Correction Model, we then attempt to estimate empirically the long-term contribution of the export sector to economic growth in Mexico. Thereafter, a number of hypotheses are broached regarding the plausible linkages which explain the apparent divergence between export performance and general economic and social outcomes.

The positive results

Over the last two decades Mexico has succeeded like no other country in Latin America in achieving a structural shift in its economy and a rapid integration into the world economy (Table 12.1). Manufactured exports now contribute around 84 per cent of total exports in value terms, and oil has fallen to nine per cent of the total. Macroeconomic stability has also been achieved, with inflation falling from an average of 83.9 per cent for the period 1982–87 to 7 per cent in 2000–02. Foreign direct investment (FDI) inflows, expressed as a share of GDP, have increased nearly threefold. The change in strategy was a reaction to the debt crisis which struck the country in 1982, with the objective of restructuring the economy and allocating resources in line with international prices ('getting prices right'). A fundamental first step in this process was the dismantling of tariffs and restrictions on imports under the Immediate Programme of Economic Restructuring (*Programa Inmediato de Reorganización Económica* (PIRE)) at the start of the government of Miguel de la Madrid (1982–88). During this period, Mexico also entered into the GATT (1985), thereby giving an important signal regarding the seriousness of the reform

Table 12.1 Macroeconomic data, 1982–2002

	1982–87	1988–94	1995–99	2000–02
GDP per capita growth (annual %)	−2.2	1.6	1.3	0.9
Inflation, consumer prices (annual %)	83.7	30.8	24.5	7.0
Manufactures exports (% of merchandise exports)	28.0	58.2	81.4	84.3
Manufacturing, value added (% of GDP)	23.5	20.7	21.2	19.6
Oil exports (% of total)	61.3	24.0	9.3	9.0*
Current account balance (% of GDP)	0.9	−4.4	−2.0	−2.7
FDI, net inflows (% of GDP)	1.2	1.4	3.0	3.1
Total debt payments (% of GNI)	9.83	5.98	9.54	8.41
Registered unemployment	na	3.1	4.2	2.5
Remittances (US$ million)	1,146.7	2,699.0	4,859.7	8,427.4
Gross national savings (% of GDP)	23.1	18.2	21.3	19.4

Sources: World Bank, WDI online, available at www.publications.worldbank.org/register/WDI (accessed 8 August 2004); OECD online, available at www.oecd.org; INEGI (2001).

Notes
* Indicates figures up until 2001 only, na indicates not available.

process. Between 1985 and 1988, import licensing requirements were scaled back to about a quarter of their previous levels, reference prices were removed and tariff rates on most products substantially reduced. Between 1986 and 1988, average tariffs fell from 24 per cent to only 11 per cent. In 1989, Mexico also eased restrictions on the rights of foreigners to own assets in the country. Thus 'by 1989, Mexico was one of the most open economies in the developing world' (Revenga, 1997: 22).

It is therefore misleading, as some observers do, to portray Mexican trade liberalisation as principally the result of NAFTA. The process of liberalisation had already been pursued for some nine years when NAFTA came into force on 1 January 1994. Most analysts argue that the decision to enter into a free trade agreement with the USA was based not only on economic grounds, but also to ensure the irreversibility of the policy measures – to lock Mexico into a path of liberalisation and policy reform. That the resulting agreement has been full of tensions, misunderstandings and intentional blockages is well known – the United States has proved to be a difficult partner, and has conceded to Mexico far less than the Mexican administrations would have wished for. However, even in the dark period of the 'Tequila crisis' (the severe financial crisis which hit the Mexican economy the very year that NAFTA came into force – 1994), there has not been any question of withdrawing from NAFTA, and in this sense, the agreement has achieved its purpose from the Mexican side.

One policy which was key to this transformation process was the consolidation of the *maquila* industry, an investment attraction and export promotion scheme that offers benefits to qualified firms regarding import duties and other taxes. This policy actually predates the shift towards an outward-oriented strategy by 20 years, being originally established in the mid-1960s with the objective of mitigating the serious unemployment problem in the border areas with the United States (Buitelaar and Padilla Pérez, 2000). However, the maquila as a strategy for promoting exports came into its own under the new economic strategy. Employment in the maquila went from around 100,000 in 1980 to over a million by the end of the 1990s.

Between 1982 and 2000, Mexico almost tripled the degree of openness of its economy, expressed as total imports and exports as a percentage of GDP (from 21 per cent in 1982 to 59 per cent in 2000). At the same time, a remarkable inversion in the structural characteristics of exports occurred – oil falling from 78 to only 20 per cent of total exports in 2003.[1] During the government of Miguel de la Madrid, total exports (excluding oil) rose from US$6.3 billion in 1983 to US$13.9 billion in 1988, while under the administration of Salinas de Gortari (1988–94) they reached $53.4 billion by 1994. In total, that represents a growth of 750 per cent. In relative terms, manufacturing export growth (excluding the maquila) was even more dynamic, rising from US$4.6 billion in 1982 to US $24.1 billion at the end of the administration of Salinas. If we include oil and maquila industry exports, total exports in 2000 reached US$166.5 billion, making Mexico one of the ten most important exporters in the world. Only during the first three years of the Fox government have these trends reversed, with negative rates of growth for exports. To sum up, in terms of achieving its principal objectives of an increase in the volume and composition of exports, the success of the new developmental model has been truly impressive.

These structural changes have been accompanied by a sharp intensification of the links between the US economy and that of Mexico. The USA accounted for around 70 per cent of all exports at the beginning of the 1980s, but by the late 1990s accounted for almost 90 per cent. Mexico has also become increasingly dependent on FDI from the USA, on average accounting for two thirds of total inflows. Mexico has been drawn into the economic cycle of the US economy; whereas in the 1980s, economic performance was practically asymmetrical between the two countries, now the growth cycles have converged (Kose *et al.*, 2004; Garcés Díaz, 2003). While the increase in manufacturing exports has lowered the vulnerability of export revenue to changes in oil prices (OECD, 2004: 35), Mexico has replaced a sectoral dependence on a single commodity with one based on single market. An evaluation whether this strategy has been the correct one would have to revolve around the long-term prospects of the US economy, on which many analysts are quite pessimistic (Todd, 2002).

Liberalisation and structural change

In evaluating the impact of the new strategy on welfare, there are other important features of the new model to be taken into account. Foreign direct investment has played an increasingly important role in the dynamics of investment in Mexico. The FDI/GDP ratio rose from 1.2 per cent in the 1982–87 period to 3.1 per cent in 2000–02, and as a share of gross fixed capital formation, FDI increased fourfold, from 5 per cent between 1981 and 1985 to 20 per cent in 2001 (Table 12.1 and UNCTAD FDI database). Together with the indicators related to export performance, the figures on FDI inflows have been widely praised by the IFIs and the financial press. Nonetheless, some caveats are worthy of mention.

FDI is widely assumed to act as a catalyst for rapid export growth (e.g. OECD, 2002), and by 2000, nearly two thirds of Mexican exports came from foreign affiliates (Palma, 2003: 6). However, the presumption that increased FDI flows would lead to an improved trade *balance* for Mexico is not well-founded. For instance, the early surge in FDI into the Mexican automobile industry was accompanied by a steep rise in imports, especially in parts from the USA, so the sector experienced only small trade surpluses, and even deficits, up until 1994 (UNCTAD, 2002: 110). For the multinational sector as a whole, estimates of a negative trade balance of $6.9 billion rose in 1993 (up from $3 billion in 1990). If we also bear in mind the high rate of profit repatriation (see Palazuelos, 2001: 22), the overall contribution of multinationals to the balance of payments is massively negative. This point is relevant because Mexico suffers from an incipient balance of payments deficit, the root of the 1982 debt crisis and the 1994 Tequila crisis; these crises, and the responses to them, are the source of much of the deterioration in living standards witnessed in Mexico over the whole reform period. This puts into question the long-term sustainability of the export-oriented model – FDI has been associated with a much higher import intensity on the part of multinational corporations and, as we shall see later, this has been a *modus operandi* which has been generally copied by national manufacturing firms too. Thus, despite the extremely rapid growth of exports, this has been more than matched by import growth so there has been no sustained improvement in the trade balance (Figure 12.1).

A second caveat is that, although Mexico has achieved a remarkable success in promoting manufactured exports and foreign investment, this may have been at the expense of the domestic market. Value added in manufacturing as a share of total value added has decreased since the process of opening up began in the mid-1980s. As Table 12.2 shows, although Mexico's share of world manufactured exports has increased dramatically from 0.2 per cent in 1980 to 2.2 per cent in 1997, Mexico's

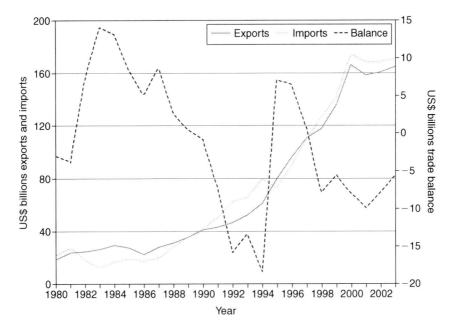

Figure 12.1 Exports, imports and trade balance, 1980–2003 (source: own elaboration, from World Bank, WDI online, available at: www.publications. worldbank.org/register/WDI (accessed 8 August 2004)).

Table 12.2 Share of world exports and value added of manufacturing in a selected group of newly industrialising economies, 1980 and 2002 (percentage shares)

Country	Share in world exports of manufacturing		Share in world manufacturing value added	
	1980	2002	1980	2002
Brazil	0.7	0.7	2.9	2.2
India	0.4	0.7*	1.1	1.1
Indonesia	0.1	0.6*	0.4	1.0
Mexico	*0.2*	*2.2**	*1.9*	*1.1*
Republic of Korea	1.4	3.1*	0.7	3.4
Taiwan	1.6	2.8*	0.6	1.4
Thailand	0.2	1.1	0.3	0.8
Turkey	0.1	1.2	0.4	0.6

Sources: UNCTAD (2002: 81) and UNIDO website, www.unido.org.

Note
* Indicates figures for 1997.

share of world value added in manufacturing has fallen, from 1.9 per cent to 1.2 per cent. It does not seem unreasonable to suggest that something might be amiss with a model of outward development which emphasises the growth of manufacturing exports but fails to increase the overall share of manufacturing in the economy.

A third point is the impact of the new strategy on the export structure of the economy. Although 78 per cent of exports in 1982 were accounted for by crude oil, there was a greater diversity in the relative contribution of the different manufacturing sectors. Now, outside the maquila sector, it could be argued that the subsequent export 'success' of Mexico has primarily been dependent upon the contribution of just a few sectors – in particular, metallic products, machinery and equipment, and its corresponding subsectors. By 2003, this one sector accounted for 64.4 per cent of manufacturing exports. This phenomenal growth in metallic products, machinery and equipment has been principally due to the dynamism of the auto industry in Mexico, with most exports destined for the North American market (UNCTAD, 2002: 136).[2] Chemicals and textiles each contribute another 7 per cent of manufacturing exports, again mostly to the USA. Mexico has become the second largest single exporter of apparel to the USA after China (Lopez-Cordóba and Moreira, 2003: 19). Thus, at present, just three sectors are responsible for 80 per cent of Mexican manufactured exports.

To summarise, NAFTA seems to have consolidated a trend that was already underway since the mid-1980s when liberalisation started. NAFTA has allowed Mexico to consolidate its position as a manufacturing goods exporter, but with an increasing dependence on the North American market which has been focused on a few specific industries. Given the vagaries of international markets and increasing competition from other newly industrialising countries like China and India, this could easily turn into a burden for the Mexican economy. There is evidence that this is already happening, particularly in sectors like textiles, where Mexican exporters will be exposed to the full force of competition from low-wage exporters like India, Bangladesh and China.[3]

One final and disturbing aspect of the new model is that there appears to be little relationship between the propensity to export and productivity rises. Rising productivity that leads to higher wages will expand domestic consumer demand, stimulating further production of goods and services and, hopefully, creating a virtuous circle of growth (Polaski, 2003: 11). A simple and suggestive analysis by Puyana and Romero (2001) of 49 manufacturing sectors over the period 1989–2000 reveals no association between higher productivity growth and the propensity to export. Rozo and Perez (2003) do not find strong evidence of a positive relationship between export-oriented manufacturing sectors, foreign direct investment and productivity. Indeed, in some sectors the estimated impact was negative. In more general terms, the economy has shown no productivity improvement over the last decade (see *Sistema de Cuentas Nacionales de México* (2003) vol. I, No. 94, pp. 183–4), a fairly damming indictment of a model sold precisely on its ability to bring about a more efficient allocation of resources. Moreover, the trend in manufacturing industry, where the bulk of the export growth has occurred, has actually been negative, with employees suffering real cuts in their wages.

The social impact

Against the backdrop of an exceedingly impressive export and foreign (though not domestic) investment performance, what has been the social outcome of the new model? The evidence regarding income per capita is not encouraging. Between the 1950s and the first debt crisis in 1982, growth rates were high and relatively stable; there were only three years during that entire 32 year period in which there was a decline in per capita income. However, the performance in the last 20 years has been markedly inferior, growth performance more volatile and per capita income remains very low. Even if some recovery in per capita GDP growth was registered for the period 1989–2000, compared with 1983–89, this was mainly due to a higher rate of participation of the labour force and was not propelled by productivity increases (Puyana and Romero, 2001).

The official data on poverty (see Cortés *et al.*, 2002), based on the national poverty line, give the impression that poverty has not worsened in relative terms over the last decade, fluctuating at around 44 per cent of the population (Table 12.3). However, the absolute number of persons below the poverty line did increase from 19.1 million to 23.8 million between 1992

Table 12.3 Percentage of people living in poverty, national poverty lines, 1992–2000

	1992	1994	1996	1998	2000
Households					
Line 1	17.4	16.1	28.8	26.8	18.6
Line 2	21.8	22.7	36.5	32.9	25.3
Line 3	44.1	46.8	60.8	55.6	45.9
Persons					
Line 1	22.5	21.1	37.1	33.9	24.2
Line 2	28.0	29.4	45.3	40.7	31.9
Line 3	52.6	55.6	69.6	63.9	53.7

Source: Cortés *et al.* 2002: 15.

Notes
Criteria of poverty as defined by the Comité Técnico para la Medición de la Pobreza.
Lines of poverty are monetary measures based exclusively on income or spending by households and/or persons.
Line 1: income is insufficient to acquire a basic food basket.
Line 2: income insufficient to acquire basic food basket plus health, clothes, shoes, housing, transportation and education.
Line 3: line 2 plus other non-food goods considered socially necessary.

and 2000 (Cortés *et al.*, 2002: 15). The most worrying aspect has been the way that the macroeconomic shocks have impacted upon the poorest sectors of the society – those living in extreme poverty, defined as individuals who do not even satisfy their basic food needs. The size of the fall in purchasing power in the aftermath of the Tequila crisis was dramatic, estimated at an average of 30 per cent in the years 1995–97 (Lustig, 2001: 102). As a consequence, whilst at the beginning of the decade, only 22.5 per cent of the population lived in extreme poverty, by the middle of the 1990s, that figure had reached 37.1 million people, equivalent to 28.8 per cent of total households. Although poverty subsequently fell in the last years of the decade it was still at a higher level than at the beginning of the decade.

Based on more recent survey data, the World Bank (2004a) reports some positive achievements over the last two years regarding poverty reduction, particularly in rural areas. However, bearing in mind the negative GDP per capita growth in 2001 and 2002 (Table 12.1), this improvement is hardly attributable to an improved economic performance. As the authors of the report concede, it is probably best explained in terms of higher remittances from Mexican migrants (which have almost quadrupled in value from $2.5 billion in 1990 to $9.8 billion in 2002, see Table 12.1), and better focused social policies.

Finally, there is also a growing regional divide in welfare. In 1980, for example, the per capita GDP of Chiapas was 75 per cent of the national average but by 1993 had fallen to 46 per cent of the national average (Campbell *et al.*, 1999: 140).

Econometric analysis of the contribution of the export sector

To investigate the relationship between export and income growth we opt for an econometric analysis in the form of an augmented Cobb-Douglas function (see Fosu, 2000; Medina-Smith, 2001). The model to be estimated is derived from the classical Cobb-Douglas production function, $Y = f[(L, K); X]$ where Y is real aggregate output, L and K denote labour and capital inputs respectively, and X is exports. Although X is not a proper argument of the production function, in that it is not an input in the neoclassical sense, it is intended to reflect international factors that may influence productivity but are not captured in L or K. Thus, X may be viewed as a systematic error term affecting Y, so that the conditional expection $E(X|L, K)$ is non-zero. Hence estimates of the impacts of L and K on Y may be biased or inconsistent unless the effects of X are controlled for.

The production function can be differentiated to be expressed in terms of growth rates and elasticities. For estimation purposes, the modified version is written as:

$$y = c + b_1 l + b_2 k + b_3 x + \epsilon \tag{1}$$

where y, l, k and x are the growth rates of Y, K, L and X respectively, and the $b_i (i = 1, 2, 3)$ are the respective coefficients to be estimated (interpreted as growth elasticities for L, K and X), c is the constant term, and ϵ is the stochastic perturbation. In principle, the model is easily estimated. However, as is frequent in time-series analysis, in practice there are considerable problems of non-stationarity with this type of estimation, which means that OLS could lead us to mistakenly accept spurious results. Preliminary tests using the Augmented Dickey-Fuller test for stationarity confirmed our suspicions that the series was non-stationary.

The annual data used in the analysis was taken from Penn World Tables (version 6.1), expressed in constant 1996 Mexican pesos, for the period 1950–2000. One serious limitation to the dataset was the lack of a homogeneous series for employment over the whole time period. The Mexican government has been supplying data on employment on a comprehensive basis only since 1995. Even when those data are available, the size of the informal sector and the very low level of social security payments means that official employment and unemployment figures need to be taken with a healthy degree of circumspection. As a consequence, as in Medina-Smith (2001), we were forced to use the population series available on Penn World Tables as a proxy for the level of employment. A dummy variable was included (DUM = zero before 1987, one thereafter) to account for the policy change towards an outward-oriented model initiated in 1985, but whose consequences were not really noticeable in terms of the elimination of tariffs until 1987 (Revenga, 1997).

Although co-integration tests reveal the existence of at least two co-integrating vectors,[4] we employ the error correction model (ECM) method that allows us to combine data in both levels and differences in the same equation. The results in Table 12.4 are at least consistent with our observations that the New Economic Model (NEM) has not been compatible with a rise in the growth rate of the economy – the dummy variable is negatively signed and highly significant. This implies that growth has slowed down in the years after the implementation of the NEM. The regression analysis suggests that, whereas investment has been a major determinant of income growth, neither the employment proxy nor the export variable are significant.

Aggregate production functions at an economy-wide level are of course extremely controversial instruments to use, with some authors claiming that, at that level of aggregation, variables are virtually meaningless (Fine, 2003). Whilst accepting in some degree these criticisms, our simple model yields at least indicative results to corroborate some important points:

1   Exports do not appear to have been a significant driving force for economic growth in Mexico over the last 50 years.
2   The dummy variable, representing the policy change in the mid-1980s towards an open model of development, has a negative and significant sign. This suggests that the policy change has coincided with a deterioration in the long-term growth performance of the Mexican economy.
3   It appears that it is investment which is the principal motor of growth in the Mexican economy. To the extent that the NEM has been associated with a relative fall in gross capital formation, the current model is not compatible with a high rate of income growth.

Table 12.4 ECM, Mexican aggregate production function, 1953–2000

Dependent variable	$\Delta(LnGDP)$
Included observations:	48 after adjusting endpoints
$\Delta(LnGDP(-1))$	0.028 [0.114]
$\Delta(LnGDP(-2))$	−0.078 [−0.313]
$\Delta(LnINVESTMENT(-1))$	0.111 [2.016]
$\Delta(LnINVESTMENT(-2))$	0.045 [0.898]
Constant	−1.144 [−1.915]
LnEXPORTS	0.027 [1.240]
LnPOPULATION	0.222 [1.432]
DUM	−0.093 [−2.831]
Adj. R-squared	0.198
F-statistic	2.450
Log likelihood	164.671
Log likelihood (d.f. adjusted)	154.705

Note
Figures in square brackets are t-statistics.

Explanations for the weak linkages

A number of possible explanations can be posited as to why the phenomenal export growth of the Mexican economy has not translated into faster economic growth or poverty reduction – rather it has coincided with a stagnation in average living standards and poverty levels. We highlight six different but interrelated explanations for the decoupling of export growth from income and welfare improvements. The first two could be considered more or less orthodox explanations related to processes of bilateral and multilateral liberalisation. The last four deal with structural issues associated with the change in the economic model.

Trade diversion

Many economists are sceptical about the advantages of regional integration schemes, seeing them as an impediment to the multilateral system, and claim that most processes of regional integration divert more trade from existing trading partners than they create with the associate members, thus risking welfare losses. Panagariya (2004) is one of the most vociferous critics in this context, and specifically cites the case of Mexico as an example of a country that chose and implemented preferential liberalisation but failed to achieve high rates of growth. NAFTA rules of origin in some sectors certainly have serious protective effects that shift trade and investment patterns from lower to higher cost sources. For instance, most clothing produced in Mexico gains tariff-free access to the North American markets only if inputs are almost all sourced in North America (World Bank, 2000: 76). Moreover, following the Tequila crisis, Mexico increased tariffs on non-NAFTA imports of clothing from 20 to 35 per cent in March 1995, just as it was reducing tariffs on NAFTA imports. Mexican imports from the rest of the world fell by 66 per cent between 1994 and 1996, while those from the United States increased by 47 per cent (World Bank, 2000: 42).

Whether the diversion of trade in itself is capable of explaining the fall in welfare observed above is a moot point. Trade diversion implies importing from a higher cost source instead of the lowest cost provider – in our case, imports from the US or Canada. The well-known Kemp-Wan theorem points out that if item-by-item trade flows with the rest of the world are no smaller after the formation of a regional free trade agreement than they were prior to it, then the agreement must have benefited the partner countries. Krueger (1999), using a combination of 'shift-share analysis' and a econometric gravity model, finds no evidence of significant trade diversion away from existing partners after the instigation of NAFTA. The author did however warn that the time passed since NAFTA had come into force was short, and thus her findings did not preclude significant trade diversion at a later date. A more general point is whether

NAFTA was a good agreement for Mexico. During the negotiations, it was clear that the Mexican administration aspired to achieve a lot more than was finally conceded by the US government. For example, Mexico obtained no benefits in terms of technology transfer (Rosenburg, 2002) and the rules of origin have been interpreted as excessively strict. The use of unfair trade practices by the United States related to antidumping and countervailing duties have also recently been singled out for criticism by the World Bank (2004c).

The impact of multilateral liberalisation

Although authors like Panagariya (2004) extol the virtues of multilateral versus regional integration, some Computable General Equilibrium studies suggest aggregate losses for particular developing countries due to the implementation of the Uruguay Round. For example, Brown *et al.* (2001) estimate losses for Mexico, primarily from the elimination of the Multi Fibre Agreement (MFA) and increased competition in agriculture. Relatively small gains in manufactured exports were deemed to be insufficient to offset these large losses. While these estimates are derived from model simulations, the losses correspond fairly well with the contemporary situation in Mexico, with a languishing agricultural sector and an increasingly vulnerable textile sector.

Segmentation of the Mexican export industry

An intrinsic part of Mexico's outward-oriented strategy has been its reliance on export-processing zones (EPZs). Neo-classical analysis suggests that EPZs have a negative welfare effect on the country: the creation of zones will increase inefficiency by distorting production away from its comparative advantage (Madini, 2000). Despite evidence that EPZs rarely achieve much integration with the local economy, they are usually defended on the grounds that they create employment and bring in much needed foreign exchange. A number of objections can be made to these arguments – the opportunity cost of resources dedicated to establishing the EPZs (in terms of infrastructure provision, tax breaks, etc.) may be excessively high; foreign exchange earnings are minimised because of the high import intensity of foreign firms; employment creation may be low, creating low-paid jobs in unstable circumstances and with high rates of turnover.

From the point of view of the interaction between poverty and trade, focusing too much attention on the maquila may not be merited – its contribution to total employment is little more than 3 per cent. However, from the point of view of its contribution to the trade balance, its role is fundamental, now accounting for a little under half of all exports. Indeed, if it were not for the net contribution to the balance of payments of maquila exports, the deficit in visibles would probably be unsustainable (Table 12.5). Moreover, the mere existence of the maquila has obliged the Mexican administration to replicate elsewhere the kind of incentive structure for export markets that are present in the maquila (Bouzas and Keifman, 2003: 162).

Unfortunately, in other spheres, the maquila policy has been far less successful, for a number of reasons. The most commented negative characteristic of the maquila is the low-level of local value added (Table 12.6). It is estimated that barely 1 per cent of the purchases of the maquila are

Table 12.5 Net trade balance, maquila and non-maquila, 1995–2003

Year	Exports		Imports		Balance ($m)		
	Total $m	Maquila (%)	Total $m	Maquila (%)	Total	Maquila	Non-maquila
1995	79.5	39.1	72.5	36.1	7.1	4.9	2.2
1996	96.0	38.5	89.5	34.1	6.5	6.4	0.1
1997	110.4	40.9	109.8	33.1	0.6	8.8	−8.2
1998	117.5	45.2	125.4	33.9	−7.9	10.5	−18.4
1999	136.4	46.8	142.0	35.5	−5.6	13.4	−19.0
2000	166.5	47.7	174.5	35.4	−8.0	17.8	−25.8
2001	158.4	48.5	168.4	35.2	−10.0	17.6	−29.2
2002	160.8	48.6	168.7	35.2	−7.9	18.8	−26.7
2003	164.9	47.0	170.5	34.6	−5.6	18.4	−24.0

Source: *INEGI*

Table 12.6 Overview of maquila industry, 1990–2003

Year	% value added	Employment	Change in employment	Productivity index	Salaries index
1990	19.7	451,169	–	100.0	100.0
1991	17.6	434,109	−3.8	97.9	99.1
1992	18.1	503,689	16.0	99.8	100.6
1993	16.9	526,351	4.5	100.0	100.2
1994	14.6	562,334	6.8	103.6	104.9
1995	13.2	621,930	10.6	104.0	96.7
1996	12.8	748,262	20.3	103.5	91.5
1997	12.3	903,736	20.8	97.5	93.2
1998	11.4	1,014,023	12.2	97.0	94.2
1999	10.7	1,143,499	12.8	96.7	95.0
2000	9.9	1,291,498	12.9	97.4	105.0
2001	9.5	1,202,954	−6.9	94.5	111.8
2002	8.4	1,087,746	−9.6	95.0	114.3

Source: own calculations from *INEGI* (2001).

Notes
Valued added is expressed as a percentage of the value of production. Salary figures are average yearly figures for workers, deflated by the consumer price index.

made locally. The booming export economy generates little demand for local industry, being highly dependent as it is on imported intermediate products, and hence little employment and investment outside of the maquiladora zone (Buitelaar and Padilla Pérez, 2000: 1636). Thus, because local value added is basically limited to the contribution of labour, this fall reflects the success that firms have had in constraining wages in the sector. Because of the massive presence of FDI in the maquila, it might be expected that wages in maquiladoras would be higher than in the rest of the manufacturing sector.[5] However, the Mexican case is atypical – maquila earnings are, on average, *less than two thirds of those paid in the rest of the manufacturing sector* and, in the particularly low wage industries like textiles (which is dominated by a female workforce), are considerably lower than this.

Productivity growth has also apparently been neglible over the last decade, while the share of skilled labour in the maquila has barely risen, from 6.6 per cent to 7.2 per cent in 1998 (and most of that in just one sector – the machinery sector). The technological diffusion that many expected from the maquila sector is not taking place, or at best a very slow pace (Sadni-Jallab and Blanco de Armas, 2004: 23). Thus, broadly speaking, the maquila corresponds with a 'Lewis-type' response to the market opportunities opened up by NAFTA, 'based on both an unlimited supply of cheap (and relatively unskilled labour) and on a large amount of "complementary investment" ... there has been neither productivity growth or wage growth associated with it' (Palma, 2003: 12; see also OECD, 2004: 29).

Labour market impact

Trade theory suggests that trade between two countries creates pressure for the convergence of factor prices between them, in our case the USA and Mexico. This was, of course, precisely what Mexican policymakers were hoping for by pursuing a policy of deeper integration with the USA. In principle, convergence of factor prices would be good for Mexican labour – wages, and the demand for unskilled labour, would rise. In practice, things have taken quite a different turn. Real wages for most Mexicans today are lower than when NAFTA took effect, mainly attributable to the peso crisis of 1994–95. Far from converging with US levels, as has been seen in countries like South Korea, real wages have fallen to as low as 11 per cent of US wages (Figure 12.2).

Investigating why this is so and what has been happening in the labour market is key to understanding the lack of linkage between trade performance, income growth and poverty reduction. Hanson (2003) provides an exhaustive review of the evidence on this point for Mexico. He notes that whereas trade liberalisation is supposed to contribute to raising demand for unskilled labour, given Mexico's presumed comparative advantage in

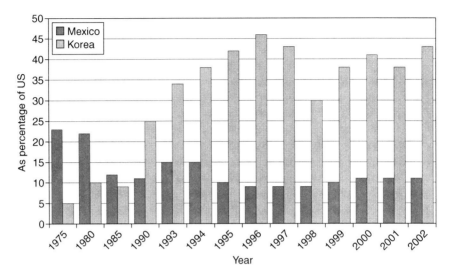

Figure 12.2 Hourly compensation costs for workers as a share of US average, South Korea and Mexico, 1975–2002 (source: US Bureau of Labor Statistics).

low-skill activities, in reality in Mexico the opposite seems to have occurred – there seems to have been a significant increase in the demand for skilled workers. This increase in the skill premia is reflected in figures on income distribution, which show a rise in inequality (partially offset by losses to the highest quintile due to exposure to the Tequila crisis). A number of possible explanations can be suggested. At the time when Mexico began to lower its trade barriers, labour-intensive sectors had the highest tariff barriers. Hanson and Harrison (1999) suggest that tariff reductions in Mexico due to NAFTA have been larger in more skill-intensive sectors, implying that the final stage of trade reform may halt the increase in skill premia. Paradoxically, therefore, they argue that tariff reductions have increased relative demand for skilled labour. It has also been argued that the large inflow of FDI has created another channel for increasing demand for skilled labour (Feenstra and Hanson, 1995; Revenga, 1997). The popular analogy that the wages of poor Latin Americans are set in Beijing, but those of rich Latin Americans are set in New York, would seem to be true in the case of Mexico.

Before accepting these arguments too readily, it is worth reflecting on the general plausibility. Palma (2003: 47) notes that the point at which Latin American income distribution differs from that in the rest of the world concerns the income-share of the top 10 per cent of the population. This would certainly appear to be true in the Mexican case – the marked increase in income inequality in Mexico during the 1980s reflected largely an increase in the income gap between the very rich and the rest (Corbacho and Schartz, 2002: 12). Moreover, this situation was not reversed in the 1990s – apart from a small reduction in the aftermath of the Tequila crisis, inequality continued to rise throughout the 1990s (Lustig, 2001: 89). In this context, workers – no matter how skilled they are – will hardly be found at the top end of the distribution of income. Thus it is not particularly credible that, by introducing new technologies which increases the demand for skilled labour, trade liberalisation has inadvertently increased wage dispersion and inequality. In all likelihood, the causes of the higher levels of inequality reside elsewhere.

Palma (2003: 48) suggests that it is the result of both radical institutional changes in the Mexican labour market and a drastic reduction in the bargaining power of the Mexican labour movement. The remuneration of workers has certainly been a decreasing component of GDP throughout the period of liberalisation. Labour surpluses and weak labour laws in Mexico preclude substantial upward pressure on wage rates for many years (Moon, 2000: 175). The large and burgeoning informal sector, estimated as contributing around a third of domestic GDP and almost half of total employment, must also contribute to the downward pressure on wages (OECD, 2004: 32–3). As noted earlier, during the NAFTA period, productivity growth has not translated into wage growth, as it did in earlier periods in Mexico. Liberalisation has been associated with an increase in Mexico's already high levels of inequality, something which makes the task of poverty reduction all the more difficult.

Impact on domestic consumption

An alternative line of analysis is to investigate the way that liberalisation has impacted on the different demand-side components of growth. UNCTAD (2004: 143) hypothesises that there is a weaker relationship between export expansion and private consumption growth per capita in countries, where export expansion predominates as the major demand-side component of economic growth, than in countries where there is a more balanced form of economic growth in which export expansion, domestic demand and import substitution all contribute. This hypothesis stems from the observation that there is no logical necessity, from an accounting point of view, for average private consumption per capita to be growing if economic growth is predominantly achieved through export expansion. Domestic demand expansion can of course be based on increases in investment, private or public consumption. Broadly speaking, however, average private consumption per capita is likely to rise in countries where domestic demand expansion makes a significant contribution to overall output growth. On reviewing the evidence for the 49 least developed countries, the authors of the UNCTAD report observe a fairly regular empirical regularity between trends in average consumption per capita and the incidence of poverty, and thus conclude that poverty reduction is likely to be more effective in economies in which domestic demand expansion is the most important contribution to growth.

This can be shown by a simple decomposition of the demand-side components of growth in GDP (Y) into domestic demand $(D = Y + M - X)$, total supply $(S = Y + M)$, total exports of goods and services (X), total imports of goods and services (M). Where α = GDP as share of total supply (Y/S), t = final year of period and $t - 1$ = initial year of period, the decomposition can be expressed:

$$(Y_t - Y_{t-1}) = \alpha_{t-1}(D_t - D_{t-1}) + (\alpha_t - \alpha_{t-1})S_t + \alpha_{t-1}(X_t - X_{t-1})$$

GDP	domestic	import	export
Increase	demand	substitution	effect
	contribution	contribution	contribution

For comparative purposes, this exercise was carried out for Mexico, Brazil and South Korea. To detect clearly any changes due to policy shifts, the computations were carried out for four periods of 11 years, between 1962 and 2002. Countries were classified according to the relative contributions of domestic demand (DD), import substitution (IS) and export effect (EE), labelled by whichever was the major demand-side determinant of economic growth. In DD1 countries, the export contribution is in excess of 20 per cent of GDP.

The results are in Table 12.7a–c. These show quite clearly the shift in the Mexican growth model. During the period between 1962 and 1982, domestic demand played the major role in economic growth. By the period 1982–92, although domestic demand was still the main demand-side component, exports were now contributing 41 per cent of growth. By 1992–2002, exports were the most important contributor to aggregate growth. The exaggerated dependence on demand from the export sector, and the fact that the productivity gains that exist are not being shared out in the form of wage rises, means that growth is having a minimal impact on consumption growth and, by implication, poverty reduction.[6] In the

Table 12.7a GDP growth decomposition Mexico, 1962–2002

	GDP increase (constant 1995 $ millions)	Domestic demand (DD) %	Import substitution %	Export effect (EE) %	Country classification (by type of real GDP growth)
1962–72	63,866	= 92.3	+ 2.5	+ 5.1	DD
1972–82	109,296	= 79.9	+ 2.8	+ 17.3	DD
1982–92	46,779	= 125.1	+ −66.1	+ 41.0	DD1
1992–2002	88,239	= 85.3	+ −84.8	+ 99.5	EE

Source: own elaboration based on World Bank WDI online, available at www.publications. worldbank.org/register/WDI (accessed 8 August 2004).

Table 12.7b GDP growth decomposition Korea, 1962–2002

	GDP increase (constant 1995 $ millions)		Domestic demand (DD) %		Import substitution %		Export effect (EE) %	Country classification (by type of real GDP growth)
1962–72	47,365	=	96.3	+	−9.2	+	12.9	DD
1972–82	87,239	=	87.1	+	−14.0	+	27.0	DD1
1982–92	223,136	=	88.1	+	−10.5	+	22.4	DD1
1992–2002	286,937	=	45.0	+	−21.9	+	76.9	EE

Source: as for Table 12.7a.

Table 12.7c GDP growth decomposition Brazil, 1962–2002

	GDP increase (constant 1995 $ millions)		Domestic demand (DD) %		Import substitution %		Export effect (EE) %	Country classification (by type of real GDP growth)
1962–72	139,625	=	99.9	+	−3.9	+	4.0	DD
1972–82	211,152	=	90.3	+	4.5	+	5.2	DD
1982–92	110,533	=	77.2	+	1.8	+	21.0	DD1
1992–2002	201,601	=	91.5	+	−12.6	+	21.2	DD1

Source: as for Table 12.7a.

Mexican case, at least, there is no obvious positive relationship between export and consumption growth (Figure 12.3). Mexico is not alone in exhibiting this kind of pattern – there is also evidence of increasing export orientation in the South Korean and, to a lesser degree, Brazilian cases. This reflects the extent to which liberalisation policies have been accepted by developing countries since the 1980s. In comparison with South Korea or Brazil, Mexico seems to be singularly dependent on demand emanating from the export sector.

Impact on the rural sector

Many critiques of the liberalisation programme have pointed to the negative impact of liberalisation on the agricultural sector. Endemic rural poverty has been a constant in the economic history of Mexico during the twentieth century. Ten years after the beginning of NAFTA, Mexico's agricultural exports (including livestock, processed food, beverages and tobacco) have nearly doubled and there has been a significant diversification of export products. Nevertheless, the Mexican agricultural sector continues to struggle and has not achieved the benefits that were expected from liberalisation (OECD, 2004: 189). From a balance of payments perspective, whereas in 1982 the agricultural and forestry sectors

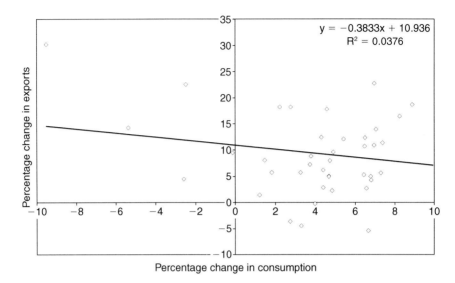

Figure 12.3 Change in consumption and exports, 1961–2001 (source: see Figure 12.1).

contributed a positive trade balance of some $182 million, by 2003 this had become a deficit of $1.53 billion. In certain products, such as rice and corn, the deficit has become a particularly sensitive issue as the increased imports are from more efficient (but subsidised) US producers (Lopez-Cordova, 2001: 24). This is a threat to some 18 million Mexicans who depend on maize for their livelihood.

On the other hand, there has been a sharp increase in exports of horticultural products, although the employment generated has not been sufficient to offset the losses in manufacturing. Mexico exports products like coffee, fresh fruits and vegetables to the US market, but only 0.09 per cent of the agricultural production units in the country actually export (Dussel Peter, 2000: 61). The model of agricultural development being pursued resembles what Carter and Barham (1996) have described as a highly-exclusionary model, with diminished peasant land access and falling sectoral employment. Whatever the fundamental cause of the job losses in agriculture, whether NAFTA or multilateral liberalisation (see above), it is clear that the export-oriented model is not providing the employment opportunities to offset the reduction of employment in the primary sector.

Towards the 'maquiliación' of the Mexican economy?

The story we have told until now has been a fairly standard story of the establishment of export-processing zones with few linkages with the rest of the economy. However, what is less recognised in the literature is the way in which this lack of linkages has spread to national firms. By inviting the entry of foreign firms into the Mexican market, national firms in many sectors have been obliged to copy the sourcing strategies of the multinational firms, importing an increasing amount of intermediate products. In the early years of the maquila programme, companies were obliged to export 100 per cent of production if they were to qualify for the corresponding tariff dispensations. However, since 1983 there has been a progressive relaxation of this requirement. From 2001, maquiladora firms were allowed to sell all their product on the domestic market. The logic of the maquila programme will, of course, eventually be undermined when, in 2010, NAFTA will have provided full duty-free access of products of Mexican origin on the US market. The maquila programme will cease to be operational.

Despite all the emphasis on export-orientation, Mexico has once again a quite substantial trade deficit (Figure 12.1). How has this come about under a policy expressly designed to improve the trade balance? The determining factor of the trade balance now is the role that imports play within the context of a process of globalisation of the Mexican economy. Under the previous import substitution model, the productive activity of multinational firms was oriented towards the domestic market: the import of capital goods was required to support the process of import substitution, but there was increasing demand for nationally produced intermediate goods. In this way, the activity of the multinationals contributed to the creation of a sector of national producers and the growth of the domestic market. However, as can be appreciated from Table 12.8, even outside the maquiladora sector, intermediate goods now represent almost two thirds of all imports while capital goods imports account for barely 20 per cent. And, as Table 12.9 reveals, approximately 60 per cent of all imports are now exclusively associated with the export sector.

Table 12.8 Imports (FOB) by type of product, 1962–2001

Year	Consumption goods		Non-maquila				Total
			Intermediate goods		Capital goods		
	US$ (m)	% of total	US$ (m)	% of total	US$ (m)	% of total	
1962–64	270.7	20.9	427.0	33.0	594.3	46.0	1,292.0
1972–74	924.0	22.0	1,613.0	38.4	1,658.7	39.5	4,195.7
1982–84	992.3	8.7	7,330.3	64.2	3,090.7	27.1	11,413.3
1992–94	8,308.7	16.0	31,709.0	61.0	11,962.7	23.0	51,980.3
1999–2001	16,211.0	15.4	66,401.0	63.2	22,385.3	21.3	104,997.3

Sources: 1970–75: Nafinsa, La Economía Mexicana en Cifras, 1982. 1976–98: Banco de México, Indicadores Económicos.

Table 12.9 Imports associated with exports, 1993–2002

	1993	1994	1995	1996	1997	1998	1999	2000	2001	2002
Intermediate products										
Associated with exports	47.0	51.4	51.2	51.7	53.8	57.7	57.5	57.7	54.8	53.5
Capital goods of exports firms	4.1	3.8	3.8	4.0	4.5	4.7	5.0	4.8	4.7	4.3
Total imports associated with exports market	51.1	55.2	55.1	55.7	58.3	62.4	62.5	62.5	59.5	57.8
Total imports associated with domestic markets	48.9	44.8	44.9	44.3	41.7	37.6	37.5	37.5	40.5	42.2
Total	100	100	100	100	100	100	100	100	100	100

Source: own estimates, derived from Bank of Mexico data.

Thus the trade deficit now has a very different cause – the export-oriented strategy has encouraged the substitution of national intermediate products by imported intermediate goods. This negatively affects the industrialisation of the country and has led to the contraction of the domestic market. The policy has not been helped by a consistent overvaluation of the Mexican currency (OECD, 2004).

> There is little doubt that both this extraordinary necessity to absorb imports as economic growth accelerates (even at a very slow rate), and the insistence of the Mexican policy makers to allow the capital account of the balance of payments to determine the exchange rate, will restrict Mexican economic growth to a stop–go cycle for many years to come. Inevitably, there is a sense of déja vu.
>
> (Palma, 2003: 32)

As a consequence, the quantity of national inputs which contribute to exports has reduced since the model of export promotion was initiated in the 1980s: whereas in 1983, over 90 per cent of the value of exports was added nationally, by 1992 the percentage had fallen to just over 40 per cent, reaching 58 per cent by 2002.

One could thus argue that the whole of the Mexican manufacturing industry is transforming itself into a kind of maquiladora, replicating the experience of the maquila zones in the north of the country. In terms of the creation of employment, it is undeniable that the maquiladora has played a positive role in the frontier states with the United States. However, in view of the weaknesses of the maquila discussed previously, this can hardly be considered as an effective model of development for this region of the country, let alone for the whole country.

Conclusion

This paper has attempted to explain the disjuncture between trade policy, performance and poverty reduction in Mexico. Our main conclusion would be that the type of export-oriented policy pursued by Mexico since the 1980s has had only a limited impact on sustainable growth of the economy, and no positive effect on poverty reduction. The Mexican story is far from unique. For example, Tanzania experienced impressive growth in the volume of exports during the 1990s, but declining commodity prices meant that export earnings fell, so trade performance offered little for poverty reduction (UNCTAD, 2004: 138). Beyond the events that we have described here, it is worth stressing the depths of the historical roots of inequality and poverty in Mexico. Whereas in the United Status in the early 1900s, 75 per cent of the household heads owned land, in Mexico that figure did not reach more than 2.5 per cent. In societies that began with extreme inequality, such as Mexico, institutions evolved in such a way as to favour the elite in terms of access to economic opportunities, and thus contributed to the persistence of extreme inequality over time (World Bank, 2004b: 184). Trade is not responsible for this situation in Mexico, but neither has it acted as a mitigating factor, as trade theory suggests.

To the extent that most of the decline in social welfare during the 1990s can be attributed to the peso crisis, it is perhaps true that the trade strategy was not the cause of increasing poverty. Chief among the culprits are the financial liberalisation of 1988–94, which provoked a massive inflow of foreign capital, the overvaluation of the exchange rate, and a concomitant collapse of domestic savings (Lustig, 2001; Palma, 2003; Polaski, 2003). Nonetheless, bearing in mind that trade liberalisation was part and parcel of the policy reform programme, it is hard to avoid the conclusion that the trade strategy was at least a contributory factor to a set of generally flawed policies. Another contributory factor has been the nature of the NAFTA agreement, which is certainly biased towards US interests (Stiglitz, 2003) and may even be harmful to the long-term interests of Mexico.

What broader conclusions can be made from our case study? The relationship between trade and poverty is complex, and depends fundamentally on the kind of trade being promoted. The same remarks apply to related areas of policy: the impact of FDI, for example, can vary enormously depending on the kind of investment and the role of the subsidiary (Mold, 2004). Another fundamental lesson is that markets based purely on external demand are vulnerable and probably unsustainable, as they have weak linkages with the local economy. Economists such as Porter (1990) have stressed that long-term export success is based on a strong domestic market, not the other way around. The de-linking of the performance of the export sector from the domestic economy, as Mexican policy over the last two decades has managed to achieve, is very prejudicial to the long-term development of the economy.

Notes

1 It is interesting to note that General Equilibrium Models of the impact of NAFTA, which were cited extensively in the early 1990s to support the case for NAFTA, were very much wide of the mark, seriously underestimating the rate of export growth between Mexico and the United States (Kehoe, 2003).
2 The irony is that the automobile sector is an activity that has not faced full international competition and for which a sectoral development policy exists. Following the Automobile Decree of 1989, assembly firms and manufacturers of auto parts were obliged to maintain a percentage of national value added from Mexican sources (Puyana and Romero, 2001: 17).
3 *The Economist*, 24 July 2003, 'The sucking sound from the East'.
4 Details available on request.
5 Empirical evidence suggests that wages paid by multinational enterprises tend to be higher than wages paid to equivalent workers in domestic firms.

6 It should be stressed that there is no contradiction between these findings and our earlier econometric findings regarding the lack of long-term relationship between economic growth and export growth. From an accounting perspective, one thing is the absolute contribution of the export sector to total growth in the economy, and quite another the impact of export growth on the dynamism of the domestic economy.

Bibliography

Abebe, K. (2002), 'Considerations for Formulating Appropriate Export Support Services: An Ethiopian Perspective', paper presented at the Eleventh Annual Conference on the Ethiopian Economy, Addis Ababa.

ADB (2002a), *Key Indicators of Developing Asian and Pacific Countries* (Manila: ADB).

ADB (2002b), *Asian Development Outlook* (Manila: ADB).

ADB (2002c), *Key Indicators 2001: Growth and Change in Asia and the Pacific* (New York: Oxford University Press).

ADB (2003), *Key Indicators 2003: Key Indicators of Developing Asia and Pacific Countries* (New York: Oxford University Press).

Afrasiabi, Kaveh (2000), Three part series on ECO: (1) The Economic Cooperation Organization aims to Bolster Regional Trade Opportunities, 14 September 2000, (2) ECO Strives to Improve Transportation and Communication Networks, 1 November 2000, (3) Economic Cooperation Organization Presses Energy Initiative, 5 December 2000 – posted at http://www.eurasianet.org.

Alfaro, L., A. Chanda, S. Kalemli-Ozcan and S. Sayek (2002), 'FDI and Economic Growth: The Role of Local Financial Markets', paper presented at Joint Conference of the IDB and World Bank on 'The FDI Race: Who Gets the Prize? Is it Worth the Effort?', Washington DC.

Andersen, L. E. and J. L. Evia (2003), 'The Effectiveness of Foreign Aid in Bolivia', working paper No. GI-E1. Grupo Integral, La Paz, September.

Andersen, L. E. and R. Faris (2002), 'Natural Gas and Income Distribution in Bolivia', working paper 02/2002. La Paz: Instituto de Investigaciones Socio-Económicas, Universidad Católica Boliviana.

Anderson, Kathryn and Richard Pomfret (2002), Relative Living Standards in New Market Economies: Evidence from Central Asian Household Surveys, *Journal of Comparative Economics*, 30(4): 683–708.

Anderson, Kathryn and Richard Pomfret (2003), *Consequences of Creating a Market Economy: Evidence from Household Surveys in Central Asia* (Cheltenham: Edward Elgar).

Antelo, E. and L. C. Jemio (2000), *Quince Años de Reformas Estructurales en Bolivia: Sus impactos sobre Inversión, Crecimiento y Equidad* (Naciones Unidas and Universidad Católica Boliviana: La Paz).

Appleton, S. 'Poverty in Uganda, 1999/2000: Preliminary Estimates for Uganda National Household Survey', University of Nottingham.

Appleton, S., A. Bigsten and D. Kulundu Manda (1999), 'Education Expansion and Economic Decline: Returns to Education in Kenya 1978–1995', working paper no. 99-6, Centre for the Study of Africa Economies, University of Oxford; Oxford.

Arbache, J. (2002), 'Comércio internacional, competitividade e políticas públicas no Brasil', IPEA Working Paper no. 903.

Arbache, J., A. Dickerson and F. Greene (2004), Trade liberalisation and wages in developing countries, *Economic Journal*, 114: 73–96.

Aredo, D. (2000), Private Investment in Ethiopia: The African Context, Regulatory Framework and Achievement, *Ethiopian Development Forum*, 1(2): 33–43.

Athukorala, Prema-chandra (1998), *Trade Policy Issues in Asian Development* (London: Routledge).

Athukorala, P. and H. S. Bambang (1996), Gains from Indonesian Export Growth: Do Linkages Matter? *Bulletin of Indonesian Economic Studies*, 33(2): 73–96.

Athukorala, P. and B. H. Santosa (1999), 'Gains from Export Growth: Do Linkages Matter?' working paper, Australian National University, Canberra.

Athukorala, P. and R. Sarath (2000), *Liberalization and Industrial Transformation* (Oxford and Delhi: Oxford University Press).

Athukorala, P. and R. Sarath (2003), Capital Flows and the Real Exchange Rate: A Comparative Study of Asia and Latin America, *World Economy*, 26(4): 613–37.

Autor, D., L. Katz and A. Krueger (1997), 'Computing Inequality: Have Computers Changed the Labour Markets?', NBER Working Paper no. 5956.

Aynekulu, A. (1996), The Emerging Monopolies of the TPLF, *Ethiopian Register* 3, 20–32 and 4, 14–22.

Barros, R. and C. Corseuil (2001), 'Apertura económica y distribución del ingreso en Brasil', in Ganuza, E., R. Barros, L. Taylor and R. Vos (eds), *Liberalización, desigualdad y pobreza: América Latina y el Caribe en los 90.* (Eudeba: PNUD – CEPAL, pp. 255–304).

Basu, K. (2003), Globalization and the Politics of International Finance: the Stiglitz Verdict, *Journal of Economic Literature*, XLI: 885–99.

Berhanu, N. (2003), The Status of the Ethiopian Leather Industry, Annex commissioned under the World Bank Diagnostic Trade Integration Study, World Addis Ababa: Bank Ethiopia (processed).

Bertrand, M., D. Miller and S. Mullainathan (2003), 'Public Policy and Extended Families: Evidence from Pensions in South Africa', *World Bank Economic Review*, 17(3): 27–50.

Bhagwati, J. (2004), *In Defense of Globalization* (New York: Oxford University Press).

Bhagwati, Jagdish and Arvind Panagariya (1996), 'Preferential Trading Areas and Multilateralism – Strangers, Friends or Foes?', in Jagdish Bhagwati and Arvind Panagariya (eds), *The Economics of Preferential Trade Agreements* (University of Maryland MD: The AEI Press and Center for International Economics, pp. 1–78).

Bhalla, S. S. (2002), *Imagine There's No Country: Poverty, Inequality, and Growth in the Era of Globalization* (Washington DC: Institute for International Economics).

Blake, A., A. McKay and O. Morrissey (2002), The Impact on Uganda of Agricultural Trade Liberalisation, *Journal of Agricultural Economics*, 53(2): 365–81.

Blanchard, Olivier (1997), *The Economics of Post-Communist Transition* (Oxford: Clarendon Press).

Bonelli, R. (2002), Labor productivity in Brazil during the 1990s, IPEA Working Paper no. 906.

Borensztein, E., J. De Gregorio and J.-W. Lee (1998), How Does Foreign Direct Investment Affect Economic Growth, *Journal of International Economics*, 45.

Bosworth, B. P. and S. M. Collins (1999), *Capital Flows to Developing Economies: Implications for Saving and Investment*. Brookings Papers on Economic Activity 1, Washington DC: Brookings Institution.

Bouzas, Roberto and Saúl Keifman (2003), 'Making Trade Liberalization Work' in Kuczynski, Pedro-Pablo and John Williamson (eds), *After the Washington Consensus: Restarting Growth and Reform in Latin America* (Washington: Institute for International Economics, pp. 157–80).

Brown, D., A. Deardorff and R. Stern (2001), 'CEG Modelling and Analysis of Multilateral and Regional Negotiating Options', University of Michigan School of Public Policy Research Seminar in International Economics, Discussion Paper No. 468. Downloaded from: www.fordschool.umich.edu/rsie/workingpapers/Papers451-475/r468.pdf.

Buitelaar, R. and R. Padilla Pérez (2000), Maquila, economic reform and corporate strategies, *World Development*, 28(9): 1627–42.

Campbell, Bruce, Andrew Jackson, Mehene Larudee and Teresa Gutierrez Haces (1999), 'Labour market effects under CUFTA/NAFTA', ILO Employment and Training Papers 29.

Carter, Michael R. and Bradford L. Barham (1996), Level Playing Fields and Laissez Faire: Postliberal Development Strategy in Inequalitarian Agrarian Economies, *World Development*, 24(7); 1133–49.

Central Statistical Authority, 'Report on Large and Medium Scale Manufacturing and Electricity' Statistical Bulletins, various issues (1997–2002), Addis Ababa.

Central Statistical Authority, 'Report on Monthly and Annual Producers' Prices of Agricultural Products in Rural Areas by Killil and Zone', various issues (1998–2001), Addis Ababa.

Central Statistical Authority, *Statistical Abstracts* (1999 and 2001), Addis Ababa.

Conlon, R. M. (1979), *Transport Cost as Barriers to Australian Trade* (Kensington (Sydney): University of New South Wales, Centre for Applied Economic Research).

Corbacho, Ana and Gerd Schwartz (2002), 'Mexico: Experiences with Pro-Poor Expenditure Policies', IMF Working Paper WP/02/12.

Corden, W. Max (1984), Booming Sector and Dutch Disease Economics; Survey and Consolidation, *Oxford Economic Papers*, 35: 359–80.

Cornia, G. A. (ed.) (2004), *Inequality, Growth and Poverty in an Era of Liberalization and Globalization* (Oxford: Oxford University Press (UNU-WIDER Studies in Development Economics)).

Cortés C., Fernnando, Daniel Hernandez, Enrique Hernández Laos, Miguel Székely, Hadid Vera Llamas (2002), 'Evolución y caracterísicas de la Pobreza en México en la Última Década del Siglo XX', SEDESOL, Serie: documentos de investigación, México, agosto.

De Melo, Jaime, Arvind Panagariya and Dani Rodrik (1993), 'The New Regionalism: A Country Perspective', in Jaime De Melo and Arvind Panagariya (eds), *New Dimensions in Regional Integration* (Centre for Economic Policy Research (CEPR): Cambridge University Press, pp. 159–93).

Deininger, K. and J. Okidi (2001), 'Rural Households: Income, Productivity and Non-farm Enterprises', in R. Reinikka and P. Collier (eds), *Uganda's Recovery, the Role of Farms, Firms and Government* (Oxford: Oxford University Press).

Deininger, K. and J. Okidi (2002), 'Growth and Poverty Reduction in Uganda, 1992–2000: Panel Data Evidence', Paper presented at the 2002 Annual Conference on Africa at the Centre for the Study of African Economies, Oxford.

Dolan, C. and K. Sutherland (2002), 'Gender and Employment in the Kenya Horticulture Value Chain', Institute of Development Studies Globalisation and Poverty, Discussion Paper No. 8.

Dollar, D. and A. Kraay (2002), 'Trade, Growth and Poverty', Discussion Paper No. 2615, The World Book.

Drabek, Z. and S. Laird (1997), 'The New Liberalism: Trade Policy in Transition and Their Integration in the Multilateral Trading System' (Processed), WTO, Geneva.

Drysdale, Peter and Ross Garnaut (1994), 'Trade Intensities and the Analysis of Bilateral Trade Flows in a Many-country World: A Survey', in Ross Garnaut and Peter Drysdale (eds) *Asia Pacific Regionalism: Readings in International Economic Relations* (Sydney: Harper Educational, pp. 20–35).

Duflo, E. (2003), Grandmothers and Granddaughters: Old Age Pension and Intrahousehold Allocation in South Africa, *World Bank Economic Review*, 17(3): 1–25.

Dussel Peter, Enrique (2000), 'El Tratado de Libre Comercio de Norteamerica y el desempeno de la Economia en Mexico', ECLAC, LC/MEXC/L.431, 14 June.

Easterly, W. (2001), *The Elusive Quest for Growth: Economist' Adventures and Misadventures in the Tropics* (Cambridge MA: MIT Press).

EBRD (1999), 'Transition Report' (various issues) (London: EBRD).

EBRD (2000), *Transition Report* (London: EBRD).

Economist Intelligence Unit (2001), *Country Report* (London: EIU).

Economist Intelligence Unit (2002a), *Myanmar (Myanmar) Country Profile*, January 2002, London.

Economist Intelligence Unit (2002b), *Ethiopia Country Profile 2002* (London: EIU).

Edwards, S. (1989), *Real Exchange Rates, Devaluation, and Adjustment: Exchange rate Policy in Developing Countries* (Cambridge MA: MIT Press).

Economist Intelligence Unit (2003), *Country Report* (London: EIU).

Elborgh-Woytek, Katrin (2003), 'Of Openness and Distance: Trade Developments in the Commonwealth of Independent States, 1993–2002', IMF Working Paper WP/03/207 (Washington DC: International Monetary Fund).

European Bank for Reconstruction and Development (EBRD) (1999), *Transition Report* (various issues) (London: EBRD).

Feenstra R. C. and G. H. Hanson (1995), 'Foreign Direct Investment and Relative Wages: Evidence from Mexico's Maquiladoras', NBER Working Paper no. 5122.

Ferreira, P. and O. Guillén (2001), O impacto da abertura comercial sobre mark up e produtividade industrial brasileira, XXIX$^{\Omega}$ Encontro Brasileiro de Economia – ANPEC, December, Salvador–Brazil.

Ferreira, P. and J. Rossi Jr (2001), New Evidence on Trade Liberalisation and Productivity Growth, *International Economic Review*, 44: 1383–407.

Fikry, T. (2003), 'Textile and Garment Subsector', study commissioned under Ethiopia Diagnostic Trade Integration Study, World Bank (processed).

Fine, Ben (2003), 'New Growth Theory', in Ha-Joon Chang (ed.), *Rethinking Development Economics* (London: Anthem Press).

Fortune (2002) (Addis Ababa), 'Interview with the British Ambassador', 2(135): 2.

Fosu, Augustin Kwasi (2000), 'The International Dimension of African Economic Growth, Center for International Development at Harvard University', CID Working Paper no. 34, January.

Fundación Milenio (2004), *Informe de Milenio sobre la Economía en el año 2003*. No. 16, April, La Paz, Bolivia.

Garcés Díaz and Daniel, G. (2003), 'La Relación a Largo Plazo del PIB Mexicano y de sus Componentes con la Actividad Económica en los Estados Unidos y con el Tipo de Cambio Real', Banco de México, Documento de Investigación Económica No. 2003 4 March.

Gelb, Alan (1988), *Oil Windfalls: Blessing or Curse?* (New York: Oxford University Press).

Gleason, G. (2003), *Markets and Politics in Central Asia Structural Reform and Political Change* (London: Routledge).

Glenday, G. and D. Ndii (1999), 'Export Platforms in Kenya', mimeo, Harvard Institute of International development.

Glenday, G. and T. C. I. Ryan (2000), 'Trade Liberalization and Growth in Kenya', mimeo, Harvard Institute of International development.

Government of Uganda (2001), *Government Interventions to Promote Production, Processing and Marketing of Selected Strategic Exports* (Kampala: MFPED and MAAIF), September.

Green, F., A. Dickerson and J. Arbache (2001), A Picture of Wage Inequality and the Allocation of Labour Through a Period of Trade Liberalisation: The Case of Brazil, *World Development*, 29: 1923–39.

Greenaway, D. and Morrissey, O. (1993), 'Structural Adjustment and Liberalisation in Developing Countries: What Lessons Have We Learned?' *Kyklos*, 46(2): 241–61.

Greenaway, D., W. Morgan and P. Wright (1998), Trade Reform, Adjustment and Growth: What Does the Evidence Tell Us?, *Economic Journal*, 108: 1547–61.

Greenaway, D., R. Hine and P. Wright (1999), A empirical assessment of impact of trade on employment in the United Kingdom, *European Journal of Political Economy*, 15: 485–500.

Greenhalg, C., M. Gregory and B. Zissimos (1998), 'The Impact of Trade, Technological Change and Final Demand on the Skills Structure of UK Employment', Discussion Paper no. 29 – Centre for Economic Performance, University of Oxford.

Hall, R. (1988), The relation between price and marginal cost in US industry, *Journal of Political Economy* 96(5): 921–47.

Hanson, Gordon H. (2003), 'What has happened to wages in Mexico since NAFTA? Implications for Hemispheric Free Trade', NBER Working Paper 9563, March.

Hanson, Gordon H. and Ann E. Harrison (1999), Trade, Technology, and Wage Inequality, *Industrial and Labor Relations Review*, 10: 271–88.

Harrison, A. (1994), Productivity, imperfect competition and trade reform, *Journal of International Economics*, 36: 53–73.

Hay, D. (2001), The post-1990 Brazilian Trade Liberalisation and the Performance of Large Manufacturing Firms: Productivity, Market Share and Profits', *Economic Journal*, 473: 620–41.

Hess, R. L. (1970), *Ethiopia: The Modernization of Autocracy* (Ithaca NY: Cornell University Press).

Heston, Alan and Robert Summers (1991), The Penn World Table (Mark 5): An Expanded Set of International Comparisons, 1950–1988, *Quarterly Journal of Economics*, May: 327–68.

Ikiara G. K. and N. S. Ndung'u (1997), *Employment and Labor Market During Adjustment: The Case of Kenya*. Mimeo (Geneva: International Labor Organization.

IMF (2000), *Kyrgyz Republic: Selected Issues and Statistical Appendix* (Washington DC: IMF).

IMF (2001), *Country Report*, Report No. 01/18 (Washington DC: IMF).

IMF (2003), *Kyrgyz Republic: Selected Issues and Statistical Appendix* (Washington DC: IMF).

IMF and World Bank (2002), *Poverty Reduction, Growth and Debt Sustainability in Low-Income CIS Countries*, Mimeo in Mexico. *Industrial and Labor Relations Review*, 52(2): 271–88.

INEGI (2001), 'Niveles de bienestar 2000', México.

INE-UDAPE (2002), available online at www.ine.gov.bo.

Institute of Southeast Asian Studies (2002), *Regional Outlook, 2002–2003* (Singapore).

Institutional Investor (1997) 'Focus on Ethiopia', Institutional Investor Supplement, February 1997.

Islamov, Bakhtior (2001), *The Central Asian States Ten Years After: How to Overcome Traps of Development, Transformation and Globalisation?* (Tokyo: Maruzen).

Jemio, L. C. and M. Wiebelt (2002), 'Orientando la Política Macroeconómica en Favor de los Pobres: Resultados de Simulaciones Seleccionados' paper presented at the IISEC-IFK-IIDEE Seminar on Poverty Impacts of Macroeconomics Reforms in Bolivia, La Paz.

Jenkins, R. O. (2004), 'Vietnam in the Global Economy: Trade, Employment and Poverty', *Journal of International Development*, 16: 13–28.

Jensen, R. T. (2004), 'Do Private Transfers "Displace" the Benefits of Public Transfers? Evidence from South Africa', *Journal of Public Economics*, 88(1–2): 89–112.

Johnson, C. J. (1995), 'Planting, Conservation and Conversion: Multiple Strategies to Sustain Myanmar's Environment', Report prepared for the United Nations Development Programme (UNDP), February, New York, unpublished.

Kalyuzhnova, Yelena (1998), *The Kazakhstani Economy: Independence and Transition* (Basingstoke: Macmillan).

Kassouf, A. L. and B. Senauer (1996), Direct and Indirect Effects of Parental Education on Malnutrition Among Children in Brazil: A Full Income Approach, *Economic Development and Cultural Change*, 44(4): 817–38.

Kaufmann, Kraay, and P. Zoido-Lobaton (2002), *Governance Matters II: Updated Governance Indicators for 2000–01*. World Bank Institute quoted in Gleason (2003).

Kehoe, Timothy J. (2003), 'An Evaluation of the Performance of Applied General Equilibrium Models of the Impact of NAFTA', Staff Report 320, Federal Reserve Bank of Minneapolis.

Khin Maung Kyi, R. Findlay and R. M. Sundrum (eds) (2000), *Economic Development in Myanmar: a Vision and a Strategy* (Stockholm and Singapore: Olaf Palme International Center and Singapore University Press).

Klasen, S. (2000), Measuring Poverty and Deprivation in South Africa, *Review of Income and Wealth*, 46(1): 33–58.

Klasen, S. and R. Thiele. (2004), 'Operationalizing Pro-Poor Growth. Country Case Study Bolivia.' Draft, World Bank.

Kose, M. Ayhan, Guy M. Meredith and Christoper M. Towe (2004), 'How has NAFTA Affected the Mexican Economy? Review and Evidence', International Monetary Fund Working Paper WP/04/59.

Krause, L. B. (1988), *U.S Economic Policy Towards the Association of southeast Asian nations: meeting the Japanese Challenge* (Washington DC: The Brookings Institution).

Krueger, Anne O. (1999), Are Preferential Trading Arrangements Trade-Liberalizing or Protectionist?, *Journal of Economic Perspectives* 13: 105–24.

Krugman, Paul (1993), 'Regionalism Versus Multilateralism: Analytical Notes', in Jaime De Melo and Arvind Panagariya (eds), *New Dimensions in Regional Integration* (Centre for Economic Policy Research (CEPR): Cambridge University Press, pp. 58–79).

Kume, H., G. Piani and F. de Souza (2003). 'A Política Brasileira de Importação no Período 1987/1998: Descrição e Avaliação', in Corseuil, C. and H. Kume (eds), *A abertura comercial brasileira nos anos 1990: impactos sobre emprego e salário.* MTE – IPEA, pp. 9–37.

Kyrgyz Republic Official Website, http://stat-gvc.bishkek.su.

Larkin, S. and San Thein (1999), 'Myanmar Research: Agriculture Sector', paper prepared for Irrawaddy Advisors Ltd, February, Yangon, unpublished.

Larson, D. and K. Deininger (2001), 'Crop Markets and Household Participation', in Reinikka, R. and P. Collier (eds), *Uganda's Recovery: The Role of Farms, Firms and Government* (Kampala: Fountain Publishers).

Lawrence, R, (1996a), *Single World, Divided Nations?* (Paris: OECD).

Lawrence, Robert Z. (1996b), *Regionalism, Multilateralism and Deeper Integration* (Washington DC: The Brookings Institution).

Little, I. M. D. (1981), 'The Experience and Causes of Rapid Labour-Intensive Development in Korea, Taiwan Province, Hong Kong, and Singapore, and Possibilities for Emulation', in Edy Lee (ed.), *Export-led Industrialization and Development* (Geneva: ILO) (Reproduced in I. M. D. Little (1999) *Collection and Recollections: Economic Annexes and their Provenance* (Oxford: Clarendon Press, pp. 213–40)).

Little, I. M. D., R. Cooper, W. M. Corden R. and Sarath, R (1993), *Boom, Crisis, and Adjustment: The Macroeconomic Experience of Developing Countries* (New York: Oxford University Press).

Lopez-Cordova, J. Ernesto (2001), 'NAFTA and the Mexican Economy: Analytical Issues and Lessons for the FTAA', Occasional paper 9 (Washington DC: Inter-American Development Bank) July.

Lopez-Cordova, Ernesto and Mauricio Mesquita Moreira (2003), 'Regional Integration and Productivity: The Experiences of Brazil and Mexico', IDB Working Paper 14 July.

Lora, E. (2001), 'Structural Reforms in Latin America: What Has Been Reformed and How to Measure It?' Research Department Working Paper 466 (Washington DC: Inter-American Development Bank, Research Department).

Lustig, Nora (2001), Life is not Easy: Mexico's Quest for Stability and Growth, *Journal of Economic Perspectives*, 15(1); 86–106.

McCulloch, N. and M. Ota (2002), 'Export Horticulture and Poverty in Kenya', IDS Working Paper 174, University of Sussex, Institute for Development Studies.

McGillivray, M. and Morrissey, O. (eds) (1999), *Evaluating Economic Liberalisation* (London: Macmillan).

Madini, Dorsati (2000), 'A Review of the Role and Impact of Export Processing Zones', World Bank, Working Paper.

Maia, K. (2003), O impacto do comércio internacional, da mudança tecnológica e da demanda final na estrutura do emprego por nível de qualificação no Brasil – 1985/95, *Economia Aplicada*, 7(2): 327–57.

Maitra, P. (2002), 'The Effect of Household Characteristics on Poverty and Living Standards in South Africa', *Journal of Economic Development*, 27(1): 75–96.

Maitra, P. and R. Ray (2003), 'The effect of transfers on household expenditure patterns and poverty in South Africa', *Journal of Development Economics*, 71: 23–49.

Maitra, P. and R. Ray (2004a), 'The Impact of Resource Inflows on Child Health: Evidence from Kwazulu-Natal, South Africa, 1993–98', *Journal of Development Studies*, 40(4): 79–115.

Maitra, P. and R. Ray (2004b), 'Household Resources, Expenditure Patterns and Resource Pooling: Evidence from South Africa', mimeo, Monash University, Clayton Campus, Australia (revised, May 2004).

Maluccio, J. (2000), 'Attrition in the Kwazulu-Natal Income Dynamics Study, 1993–1998', International Food Policy Research Institute, Food Consumption and Nutrition Division Discussion Paper No. 95.

Maluccio, J. L. Haddad and J. May (2000), 'Social Capital and Household Welfare in South Africa, 1993–98', *Journal of Development Studies*, 36(6): 54–81.

Maluccio, J., D. Thomas and L. Haddad (2003), 'Household Structure and Child Well-Being: Evidence from Kwazulu-Natal', in A. Quisumbing (ed.), *Household Decisions, Gender and Development; A Synthesis of Recent Research* (Baltimore MD: Johns Hopkins University Press, pp. 121–30).

Manda, D. K. and K. Sen (2004), 'The Labor Market Effects of Globalization in Kenya', *Journal of International Development*, 16: 29–43.

Markwald, R. (2001), O impacto da abertura comercial sobre a indústria brasileira: balanço de uma década, *Revista Brasileira de Comércio Exterior*, 13(3): 4–25.

May, J., M. R. Carter, L. Haddad and J. Maluccio (2000), 'Kwazulu-Natal Income Dynamics Study (KIDS), 1993–1998: A Longitudinal Household Database for South African Policy Analysis', Centre for Social and Development Studies Working Paper No. 21, University of Natal, Durban.

Mbabazi, J., C. Milner and O. Morrissey (2003), 'The Fragility of Empirical Links between Inequality, Trade Liberalisation, Growth and Poverty', in van der Hoeven and Shorrocks (eds), Chapter 4, pp. 113–43.

MECOVI 2001 (Bolivia).

Medina-Smith, Emilio J. (2001), 'Is the Export-Led Hypothesis Valid for Developing Countries? A Case Study of Cost Rica', UNCTAD Policy Issues in International Trade and Commodities Study Series No. 7.

Menezes Filho, N. and M. Rodrigues Jr (2001), Abertura, tecnologia e qualificação: evidências para a manufatura brasileira, paper presented in the 'Seminar on Trade Liberalisation and Labour Markets in Brazil', Departamento de Economia – UNB e Instituto de Pesquisa Econômica Aplicada – IPEA, Brasília–Brazil.

MFPED (1999), *Background to Budget 1999/2000* (Kampala: Ministry of Finance, Planning and Economic Development).

MFPED (2000), *Background to Budget 2000/2001* (Kampala: Ministry of Finance, Planning and Economic Development).

MFPED (2001), *Fighting Poverty in Uganda: The Poverty Action Fund* (Kampala: Ministry of Finance, Planning and Economic Development (February)).

MFPED (2002), *Background to the Budget 2002/2003* (Kampala: Ministry of Finance, Planning and Economic Development).

Michalopoulos, C. (1998), 'WTO Accession for Countries in Transition', available at http://bank.org/html/publications/workingpapers/wps1900 series/wps/1934/ wps1934.Pdf.

Milanovic, Branko (1998), *Income, Inequality, and Poverty during the Transition from Planned to Market Economy* (Washington DC: World Bank).

Mold, Andrew (2004 – forthcoming), 'FDI and Poverty Reduction: An Appraisal of the Evidence', Region et Developpment (in press).

Moon, Bruce E. (2000), *Dilemmas of International Trade*, 2nd Edn (Boulder CO: Westview Press).

Morales, J. A. and J. D. Sachs. (1990), 'Bolivia's Economic Crisis' in J. D. Sachs (ed.) *Developing Country Debt and Economic Performance*, Vol. 2 (Chicago: University of Chicago Press).

Moreira, M. and S. Najberg (1997), Abertura comercial: criando ou exportando empregos, *Pesquisa e Planejamento Econômico*, 28(2): 371–98.

Muendler, M. (2001), Trade, technology and productivity: a study of Brazilian manufactures – 1986/98, University of California – Berkeley and Pontifícia Universidade Católica – Rio de Janeiro, mimeo.

Mya Than (2000), 'Recent Developments in Myanmar: Impacts and Implications of ASEAN Membership and Asian Crisis', in Pedersen, M. B., E. Rudland and R. J. May (eds), *Myanmar/Myanmar: Strong Regime, Weak State?* (Adelaide: Crawford House Publishing, pp. 138–63).

National Institute of Statistics of Bolivia, official files.

Nayyar, D. (2002), 'Towards Global Governance', in D. Nayyar (ed.), *Governing Globalization: Issues and Institutions* (Oxford: Oxford University Press, Chapter 1, pp. 3–18).

Nazarbayev, Nursultan (1996), *Five Years of Independence* (Kazakhstan: Almaty).

Neri, M. and C. Considera (1996), 'Crescimento, desigualdade e pobreza: o impacto da estabilização', in Levy, P. (ed.), *A economia brasileira em perpectiva – 1996*, Ed. IPEA, pp. 49–82.

Nina, O. and F. Rojas (2001), 'Atractivo de Bolivia a los Inversionistas Extranjeros', Working Paper 06/2001. La Paz: Instituto de Investigaciones Socio-Económicas-Universidad Católica Boliviana.

O'Brien, F. S. and T. C. I. Ryan (2000), 'Kenya' in Devarajan, S., D. Dollar and T. Holmgren (eds), *Aid and Reform in Africa* (Washington DC: The World Bank).

OECD (2002), *Foreign Direct Investment for Development: Maximising Benefits, Minimising Costs* (Paris, OECD).

OECD (2004), *OECD Economic Surveys 2002–2003 Mexico* (Paris, OECD).

Olcott, Martha Brill (2002), *Kazakhstan: Unfulfilled Promise* (Washington DC: Carnegie Endowment for International Peace).

Palazuelos Manso, Enrique (2001), Desequilibrio Externo Y Crecimiento Economico En Mexico. Una Perspectiva De Largo Plazo, Boletin del ICE, November–December, No. 795.

Palma, Gabriel (2003), 'Trade Liberalisation in Mexico: Its Impact on Growth, Employment and Wages', ILO Employment Paper 2003/55.

Panagariya, Arvind (2004), Opponents Comments on 'Subsidies and Trade Barriers' by Kym Anderson, Copenhagen Consensus 2004.

Pavcnik, N., A. Blom, P. Goldberg and N. Schady (2002), 'Trade liberalization and labor market adjustment in Brazil', World Bank Policy Research Working Paper no. 2982.

PMAU (2002a), *Ugandan Poverty Status Report 2001* (Kampala: PMAU, MFPED).

PMAU (2002b), 'Uganda's Poverty Line', mimeo (Kampala: PMAU, MFPED).

Polaski, Sandra (2003), 'Jobs, Wages and Household Income', in 'NAFTA Ten Years After', Chapter 1 (Washington: Carnegie Endowment for International Peace).

Pomfret, Richard (1995), *The Economies of Central Asia* (Princeton NJ: Princeton University Press).

Pomfret, Richard (1997), *The Economics of Regional Trading Arrangements* (Oxford: Clarendon Press; paperback edition with new Preface, Oxford University Press, Oxford, 2001).

Pomfret, Richard (1999), *Central Asia Turns South? Trade Relations in Transition* (London: The Royal Institute of International Affairs and Washington DC: The Brookings Institution).

Pomfret, Richard (2000a), 'Trade Initiatives in Central Asia: The Economic Cooperation Organization and the Central Asian Economic Community', in Renata Dwan and Oleksandr Pavliuk (eds), *Building Security in the New States of Eurasia: Subregional Cooperation in the Former Soviet Space* (Armonk NY: M.E. Sharpe, Armonk, pp. 11–32).

Pomfret, Richard (2000b), 'Central Asian Regional Integration and New Trade Patterns', in Yelena Kalyuzhnova, Dov Lynch and Nicholas Tucker (eds), *The Euro-Asian World: A Period of Transition* (Basingstoke: Macmillan and New York: St. Martin's Press, pp. 188–206).

Pomfret, Richard (2002), *Constructing a Market Economy: Diverse Paths from Central Planning in Asia and Europe* (Cheltenham: Edward Elgar).

Pomfret, Richard (2003a), Trade and Exchange Rate Policies in Formerly Centrally Planned Economies, *The World Economy*, 26(4), 585–612.

Pomfret, Richard (2003b), 'Economic Performance in Central Asia since 1991: Macro and Micro Evidence', *Comparative Economic Studies*, 45(4): 442–65.

Pomfret, Richard (2003c), *Central Asia since 1991: The Experience of the New Independent States* (Paris: OECD Development Centre Technical Papers, Organisation for Economic Co-operation and Development).

Porter, Michael E. 'Dónde radica la ventaja competitiva de las naciones?', Harvard-Deusto Business Review, 4° trimestre 1990, pp. 3–26.

Puyana, Alicia and José Romero (2001), 'The Mexican Economy After Two Decades Of Trade Liberalization', mimeo.

Ravallian, M. (2004), 'Growth, Inequality and Poverty: Looking Beyond the Averages', in Shorrocks and van der Hoeven (eds), Chapter 3, pp. 62–80.

Ray, R. (2000), 'Poverty and expenditure pattern of households in Pakistan and South Africa: a comparative study', *Journal of International Development*, 12(2): 241–56.

Reimer, J. (2002), 'Estimating the Poverty Impacts of Trade Liberalisation', World Bank Working Paper Series no. 2790.

Reinnika, R. (1996), 'The credibility program in trade liberalization: empirical evidence from Kenya', *Journal of African Economies*, 5(3): pp. 444–68.

Revenga, Anna L. (1997), Employment and Wage Effects of Trade Liberalization: The Case of Mexican Manufacturing, *Journal of Labor Economics*, 15(3): S20–43.

Ribeiro, F. and H. Pourchet (2002), Coeficientes de orientação externa da indústria brasileira: novas estimativas, *Revista Brasileira de Comércio Exterior*, 74: 14–27.

Riedel, J. (1974), Factor Proportions, Linkages and the Open Developing Economy, *Review of Economics and Statistics*, 75(4): 487–94.

Riedel, J. (1976), A Balanced-growth Version of the Linkage Hypothesis: A Comment, *Quarterly Journal of Economics*, 90(3): 319–22.

Rodrik, D. (1997), *Has Globalization Gone Too Far?* (Washington DC: Institute for International Economics).

Rodrik, D. (1998), Trade Policy and Economic Performance in Sub-Saharan Africa. *Working Annex 6562*, National Bureau of Economic Research (Cambridge MA: NBER).

Rodrik, D. (1999), *The New Global Economy and Developing Countries: Making Openness Work*, ODC Policy Essay No. 24 (Washington DC: Overseas Development Council).

Rodrik, D. (2000), *Comments on 'Trade Reforms, Growth and Poverty' by Dollar and Kray.* mimeo. available on online at www.ksghome.harvard.edu/~drodrik.academic.ksg/Rodrik%20on%20Dollar-Kraay.PDF.

Rodrik, Dani (2001), 'Trading in Illusions', *Foreign Policy*, 123 March/April: 54–62.

Rosenberg, Tina (2002), 'The Free-Trade Fix', *New York Times,* www.nytimes.com.

Rozo, Carlos A. and Cuauhtémoc Pérez Llanas (2003), 'Flujos de Inversión extranjera directa a México y el TLCAN', in Carlos A. Rozo (ed.), *Capital Global e Integración Monetaria* (México: UAM-Editorial Porrua, pp. 177–215).

Rudaheranwa N., F. Matovu and W. Musinguzi (2003), 'Enhancing Uganda's Access to International Markets: A Focus on Quality', in J. Wilson and V. Abiola (eds), *Standards & Global Trade: A Voice for Africa* (Washington DC: World Bank).

Rumer, Boris and Stanislav Zhukov (eds) (1998), *Central Asia: The Challenges of Independence* (Armonk NY: M.E. Sharpe).

Sachs, Jeffrey and Andrew Warner (1995), 'Natural Resource Abundance and Economic Growth', Harvard Institute of Economic Research Discussion Paper 517 (Cambridge MA).

Sadni-Jallab, Mustapha and Enrique Blanco de Armas (2004), 'A Review of the Role and Impact of Export Processing Zones in World Trade: The Case of Mexico', in Leo Michelis and Mark Lovewell (eds), *Exchange Rates, Economic Integration and the International Economy* (Toronto: APF Press).

Sahn, D. and D. Stifel (2003), 'Urban–Rural Inequality in Living Standards in Africa', *Journal of African Economies*, 12: 564–97.

Sakwa, Richard and Mark Webber (1999), The Commonwealth of Independent States, 1991–1998: Stagnation and Survival, *Europe–Asia Studies*, 51: 379–415.

Sala-i-Martin, X. (2002), 'The World Distribution of Income Estimated from Individual Country Distribution', NBER Working Paper no. 8933 (Cambridge MA: National Bureau of Economic Research).

Sala-i-Martin, Xavier and Arvind Subramanian (2003), Addressing the Natural Resource Curse: An Illustration from Nigeria, IMF Working Paper WP/03/139 (Washington DC: International Monetary Fund, Washington DC, July).

Shaffer, P. (1999), 'Studies in social deprivation in Myanmar', Report prepared for the United Nations Development Programme (UNDP) and the United Nations Department for Economic and Social Affairs (UNDESA), MYA/98/004, April, New York.

Sharma, K. (ed.) (2003), *Trade, Growth and Poverty in Asian Developing Countries* (London: Routledge).

Sharma, K. (2004), 'Development Challenges of a Newly Independent State: Lessons from Tajikistan', in C. Tisdell (ed.), *Politics of Globalisation* (New Delhi).

Shorrocks, A. and R. van der Hoeven (eds) (2004), *Growth, Inequality and Poverty:*

Prospects for Pro-Poor Economic Development (Oxford: Oxford University Press (UNU-WIDER Studies in Development Economics)).

Siegelbaum, P. L., K. Sherif, M. Borish and G. Clarke (2002), 'Structural Adjustment in the Transition: Case Studies from Albania, Azerbaijan, Kyrgyz Republic and Moldova', World Bank Discussion Paper No. 429 (Washington DC: World Bank).

Soares, S., L. Servo and J. Arbache (2001), O que (não) sabemos sobre a relação entre abertura comercial e mercado de trabalho no Brasil, XXIX$^{\underline{O}}$ Encontro Nacional de Economia – ANPEC, December, Salvador–Brazil.

Srinivasan, T. N. (2001), Growth and Poverty Alleviation: Lessons from Development Experience', ADBI Institute Working Paper 17 (Tokyo: ADB Institute).

Srinivasan, T. N. and J. N. Bhagwati (1999), 'Outward-orientation and Development: Are Revisionists Right?', Economic Growth Centre Discussion Paper No. 806 (New Haven CT: Yale University).

Stiglitz, J. (2002), *Globalization and Its Discontents* (New York: W. W. Norton & Company).

Stiglitz, Joseph (2003), *The Roaring Nineties – Why We're Paying the Price for the Greediest Decade in History* (London: Penguin Books).

Summers, Lawrence (1991), 'Regionalism and the World Trading System', Federal Reserve Bank of Kansas City.

Tarr, David (1994), How Moving to World Prices Affects the Terms of Trade of 15 countries of the Former Soviet Union, *Journal of Comparative Economics*, 18(1): 1–24.

The Economist (2003), 24 July.

Thiele, R. and D. Piazolo (2002), A Social Accounting Matrix for Bolivia Featuring Formal and Informal Activities, *Latin American Journal of Economics. Instituto de Economia PUC.* Santiago, Chile 40: 1–34.

Thirlwall, A. P. (2003), *Trade, the Balance of Payments and Exchange Rate Policy in Developing Countries* (Cheltenham: Edward Elgar).

Todd, Emmauel (2002), *Apres l'empire: Essai sur la decomposition du systeme américain*, Editions Gallimard.

Tomiuc, Eugen (2002), Central Asia: Eurasian Economic Community Members discuss Customs Union, WTO Membership, *Radio Free Europe/Radio Liberty (REFE/RL)*, http://www.rferl.org/nca/features/2002/05/13052002083624.asp – posted 13 May 2002.

Tornell, Aaron and Philip Lane (1999), The Voracity Effect, *American Economic Review*, 89(1): 22–46.

Tornell, Aaron, Frank Westermann and Lorenza Martinez (2003), 'NAFTA and Mexico's Less-Than-Stellar Performance', NBER Working Paper 10289, February.

Transparency International (2004), *Global Corruption Report 2004* (Berlin: Transparency International).

UBOS (1999), *Statistical Abstract 1999* (Entebbe: Uganda Bureau of Statistics).

UBOS (2000), *Statistical Abstract 2000* (Entebbe: Uganda Bureau of Statistics).

UNCTAD (2000) 'Investment and Innovation Policy of Ethiopia' (Geneva).

UNCTAD (2002), 'World Investment Report 2002 – Transnational Corporations and Export Competitiveness' (Geneva and New York).

UNCTAD (United Nations Conference on Trade and Development) (2002) *Investment and Innovation Policy Review: Ethiopia* (New York and Geneva: United Nations).

UNCTAD (2004), 'The Least Developed Countries Report 2004 – Linking International Trade with Poverty Reduction' (Geneva and New York).

United Nations (2002), UNCOMTRADE database, Geneva.

van der Hoeven, R. and A. Shorrocks (eds) (2003), *Perspectives on Growth and Poverty* (New York: United Nations University Press).

Vedia, J. L. (2002), Análisis de los Cambios y Determinantes en la Concentración del Ingreso Urbano en Bolivia, *Estadísticas & Análisis*, 1: 149–250.

Velde, D. W. te. (2002), 'Foreign Direct Investment and Income Inequality in Latin America', paper presented at the IISEC-ODI Seminar on Foreign Direct Investment and Development, La Paz.

Vestal, Theodore M. (1999), *Ethiopia: A Post-Cold War African State* (Westport CT: Praeger).

Vidaurre, G. (2002), 'Inversión Extranjera en la Industria Boliviana', Paper presented at the IISEC-ODI Seminar on Foreign Direct Investment and Development, La Paz.

Viner, J. (1950), *The Customs Union Issue* (New York: Carnegie Endowment for International Peace).

Warr, Peter (2002), 'The Failure of Myanmar's Agricultural Policies', *Southeast Asian Affairs 2000*, Institute of Southeast Asian Studies, Singapore, 2000, pp. 219–38.

Webber, Mark (1997), *CIS Integration Trends: Russia and the Former Soviet South* (London: The Royal Institute of International Affairs and Washington DC: The Brookings Institution).

White, H. (1980), A Heteroscedasticity Consistent Covariance Matrix Estimator and a Direct Test for Heteroscedasticity, *Econometrica*, 48: 817–38.

Wonnacott, Paul and Mark Lutz (1989), 'Is There a Case for Free Trade Areas?', in Jeffery J. Schott (ed.), *Free Trade Areas and US Trade Policy* (Washington DC: Institute for International Economics, pp. 59–84).

Wood, A. (1994), *North–South Trade, Employment and Inequality: Changing Fortunes in a Skill-Driven World* (Oxford: Clarendon Press).

World Bank (1987), *Kenya: Industrial Sector Policies for Investment and Export Growth* (Washington DC).

World Bank (1993), *World Development Report* (Washington DC: World Bank).

World Bank (1998), *World Development Indicators* (CD-ROM) (Washington DC: World Bank).

World Bank (2000), *Trade Blocs* (Washington DC: World Bank).

World Bank (2001), 'World Development Report 2000/2001' (Washington DC: World Bank).

World Bank (2002a), World Development Report (Washington DC: World Bank).

World Bank (2002b), *The Federal Democratic Republic of Ethiopia: Developing Exports to Promote Growth* (Washington DC: World Bank).

World Bank (2002c), *World Development Indicators* (CD-ROM) (Washington DC: World Bank).

World Bank (2003), *Country Assistance Strategy for the Republic of Tajikistan* (Washington DC: World Bank).

World Bank (2003), *World Development Report 2003: Sustainable Development in a Dynamic World* (New York: Oxford University Press for the World Bank).

World Bank (2004a), 'La Pobreza en México: Una Evaluación de las Condiciones, las Tendencias y la Estrategia del Gobierno' (Mexico: World Bank (June)).

World Bank (2004b), 'Inequality in Latin America and the Caribbean: Breaking with History'

World Bank (2004c), 'NAFTA: Positive for Mexico, but not enough', http://web. worldbank.org/WBSITE/EXTERNAL/NEWS.

World Trade Organization (WTD) (2001) Trade Policy. Review of Uganda. Available online at www.wto.org/english/tratop_e/tp182_e.htm.

Yeats, A. (1981), *Shipping and Development Policy: An Integrated Assessment* (New York: Prager).

Yudaeva, Ksenia (2003), 'Globalization and inequality in CIS Countries: Role of Institutions', Centre for Economic and Financial Research (CEFIR – Moscow) Academic Paper 25, available online at www.cefir.org/papers_academic.html.

Zhalimbetova, Roza and Gregory Gleason (2001), 'Bridges and Fences: The Eurasian Economic Community and Policy Harmonization in Eurasia', unpublished paper, University of New Mexico – shorter version 'Eurasian Economic Community comes into being', *Central Asia – Caucasus Analyst*, 20 June 2001, posted at http://www.cacianalyst.org.

Index

south essex college

FURTHER & HIGHER EDUCATION
SOUTHEND CAMPUS

Lightning Source UK Ltd.
Milton Keynes UK
27 January 2011

166508UK00002B/22/P